CONSUMER SOCIAL VALUES

Social values are central to people's lives, guiding behaviors, and judgments, and define who we are. This book advances understanding of consumer social values and their roles in the global marketplace by refining and directing existing knowledge of consumer behaviors.

With a diverse set of contributors from different parts of the world, this engaging collection provides a unique examination of social values through cross-cultural research. It incorporates input from researchers with varying academic backgrounds from marketing to psychology and philosophy, and also focuses on a range of methodological approaches including surveys, ethnography, interviews, semantic analysis, and neuroscience. The book introduces innovative concepts and provides comprehensive coverage of several specialized areas, to offer an important contribution to values research and discussion. Key topics include values and choice; means-end chains; relations among goals; motives; religion and personality; value measurement and values related to specific services and industries.

Consumer Social Values is an essential resource for scholars, students, and practitioners of consumer psychology and marketing communications.

Eda Gurel-Atay (PhD, University of Oregon) is an independent scholar conducting academic research on consumer values, materialism, sustainability, consumer well-being, and celebrity endorsements.

Lynn R. Kahle is a Professor at Pace University in New York and a Professor Emeritus of Business at the University of Oregon. He serves on American Psychological Association Council of Representatives.

Marketing and Consumer Psychology Series

Curtis P. Haugtvedt, Ohio State University
Series Editor

For a complete list of all books in this series, please visit the series page at: https://www.routledge.com/Marketing-and-Consumer-Psychology-Series/book-series/LEAMCPS

CONSUMER SOCIAL VALUES

Edited by Eda Gurel-Atay and Lynn R. Kahle

Routledge
Taylor & Francis Group

NEW YORK AND LONDON

First published 2019
by Routledge
52 Vanderbilt Avenue, New York, NY 10017

and by Routledge
2 Park Square, Milton Park, Abingdon, Oxon, OX14 4RN

Routledge is an imprint of the Taylor & Francis Group, an informa business

© 2019 Taylor & Francis

Library of Congress Cataloging-in-Publication Data
A catalog record for this title has been requested

ISBN: 978-1-138-24042-1 (hbk)
ISBN: 978-1-138-24043-8 (pbk)
ISBN: 978-1-315-28373-9 (ebk)

Typeset in Bembo
by codeMantra

CONTENTS

SECTION I

Key Issues in Social and Cultural Values

Values are described as the most important construct by many researchers in social science. They are central to people's lives and serve several functions for people. They define who we are and help us to differentiate ourselves from others. In a way, they convey what is important to us in our lives. Accordingly, the chapters in this section attempt to discuss some key issues regarding social and cultural values.

Gurel-Atay and Kahle discuss how the word "value" means different things in the academic discipline of economics and the academic discipline of psychology, both of which can be considered as parents of the academic discipline of marketing. Economists, for instance, mean something logical and look at the monetary worth of objects. Psychologists, on the other hand, mean something less than rational and focus on cognitive structures about the social worth of activity. Kahle and Gurel-Atay also discuss the importance of values from a psychology perspective for marketing researchers and practitioners.

Reynolds states that in order to be more profitable and successful in a business environment, companies need to have a superior strategy and superior execution. And the key to superior strategy and execution is understanding customer decision-making as a basis to develop and optimize strategy because customer decision-making is exactly what companies want their strategy to effect. Reynolds suggests that the means-end theory and the laddering methodology can be used to systematically gain insight into relevant decision-making of key customers. This theory and method are used to understand the four levels of meaning (i.e. product attributes, functional consequences, psychosocial consequences, and personal values), which then yield the basis for a decision-based segmentation and provide the necessary structure required to develop strategic options for discussion and evaluation.

1

INTRODUCTION: ADVANCES IN SOCIAL AND CULTURAL VALUES

Implications for Communications and Consumer Researchers

Eda Gurel-Atay and Lynn R. Kahle

The academic discipline of marketing has two parents, the academic discipline of economics and the academic discipline of psychology. It's a mixed marriage because neoclassic economists assume people are rational and most psychologists assume that much behavior is irrational. Both disciplines talk about "value," but the meanings differ widely. Economists look at the monetary worth of objects, and psychologists focus on cognitive structures about the social worth of activity. Economists mean something logical, and psychologists mean something psychological, something less than purely rational.

Interestingly, in economics, the irrational nature of understanding the world has recently received more attention. The recent Nobel Prize in Economics went to Richard Thayer, who helped develop "Prospect Theory," which originally was known as "Value Theory." The theory recognizes that the human brain sometimes processes information in ways that deviate from purely rational. Behavioral economists now recognize that sometimes thought processes of consumers appear to gravitate toward processes that are irrational (Thayer, 2016).

This book is firmly rooted in the psychological tradition. It assumes that we develop social values as abstractions about how to adapt to life, given our culture and history (Kahle, 1983). Our individual talents and experiences teach us abstractions about how to respond to what we encounter, and those values help us cope, however imperfectly, with what we find in the world. When consumers choose brands, they look to their values and their attitudes derived from those values (Homer and Kahle, 1988).

The continued growth of social values as an area of study dates back to the pioneering work of Rokeach (1973), although certainly others had previously recognized the importance of values. Rokeach identified psychological values as the most important construct in social science. In the decades since then, a steady stream of research has continued to explore the utility of this highly heuristic construct (Kahle, 1996; Kahle and Chiagouris, 1997; Kahle and Valette-Florence, 2012; Kahle and Xie, 2008; Suh and Kahle, 2018).

Values can illuminate numerous issues of interest to consumer researchers. For example, consumer motives drive desires and choices consumers seek in products and services (Kahle, Homer, O'Brien, and Boush, 1997). People who want a lifestyle centered around a central value of "fun" may seek different product attributes in a home entertainment system, or almost any other product or service, than people who want a lifestyle centered around "sense of accomplishment" or "sense of fulfillment."

This motivation difference can dictate a different segmentation approach (Kahle, 1986; Madrigal and Kahle, 1994). People seeking a culturally enriching vacation will display different values than people who strive for a sensation-seeking vacation. All of the aspects of segmentation will differ because the underlying values differ. Places can also differ according to segmentable values (Kahle, 1986; Kau, Jung, Tambyah, and Tan, 2004).

Likewise, the marketing communication that targets consumers with different values will use different message content to reach people (Kennedy, Best, and Kahle, 1988; Lee and Kahle, 2016). For example, Nike positions itself as the sports apparel brand of the successful, performing athlete and thus tweets more often than other sports apparel brands about the value of "accomplishment." Adidas positions itself as the sports apparel brand of enjoyment and thus tweets more often than other sports apparel brands about the value of "fun."

Possibly the most interesting application of social value research is as a monitor of how people are changing (cf. Gurel-Atay, Xie, Chen, and Kahle, 2010; Kau, Jung, Tambyah, and Tan, 2004). We can precisely estimate how the world or its parts are transforming before our very eyes by asking the same questions over time.

This book includes chapters that develop a number of innovative and new approaches to understanding social values. It continues to improve our understanding of this important construct.

The Chapters of the Book

The chapters of this book make significant contributions to the understanding of social and cultural values in a global age by bringing researchers from different disciplines and different countries together. The book is divided into four sections with individual sections focusing on various aspects of values. The first section provides an overview of the conceptual and theoretical approaches in the values research. In the second section, the authors introduce various applications of values research and theory. Spiritual aspects of values are discussed in the third section. Finally, the last section focuses on different methodological approaches to study values.

Section 1: Key Issues in Social and Cultural Values

Chapter 2: Strategic Marketing Imperatives and Insights: Common Pitfalls and Solutions

"Why are some companies more profitable than others?" In Chapter 2, Reynolds asks this question and provides an answer: superior strategy and superior execution. And the key to superior strategy and execution is understanding customer decision-making as a basis to develop and optimize strategy because customer decision-making is exactly what companies want their strategy to effect. After discussing five common and fatal flaws that lead to suboptimal marketing strategies, Reynolds suggested using the means-end theory (Gutman, 1982) and the laddering methodology (Reynolds and Gutman, 1988) to systematically gain insight into relevant decision-making of key customers. This theory and method are used to understand the four levels of meaning (i.e. product attributes, functional consequences, psychosocial consequences, and personal values), which then yield the basis for a decision-based segmentation and provide the necessary structure required to develop strategic options for discussion and evaluation.

Section 2: Specific Applications of Values Research and Theory

Chapter 3: Self-Sufficiency and Materialism: Scale Development and Its Implications

Based on the prior literature on mindful consumption and self-sufficient economy philosophy (UNDP, 2007), Patara and Tanskul introduce the concept of self-sufficiency and suggest that self-sufficiency values may dilute the negative effect of materialism on happiness. The authors first develop a scale of self-sufficiency values based on a "middle path" that is embedded in Buddhist teaching with its three core elements: moderation, reasonableness, and self-immunity. Then, through experiments, Patara and Tanskul look at the relations among materialism, social support, self-sufficiency, and happiness. Their findings show that those consumers who are self-sufficient are happier with their lives, regardless of their exposure to materialistic values. The authors suggest that self-sufficiency can also guard against other negative effects of materialism.

Chapter 4: "I" Value Contrast, but "We" Appreciate Harmony: Self-construal Reflects Cultural Differences in Response to Visual Design

The literature on self-construal, described as the extent to which the self is defined as an autonomous and unique individual or is seen as embedded within a larger social group, suggests that self-construal may have an important impact on various consumer behaviors (Trafimow, Triandis, and Goto, 1991). In this chapter, Haberstroh and Orth examine how self-construal influences consumer response to marketing visuals. More specifically, the authors suggest that visual harmony is more attractive to people with an interdependent, compared to independent, self-construal. Because visual harmony is perceived as a congruent pattern or arrangement of parts that combines symmetry, balance, and proportion (Henderson and Cote, 1998), it is more consistent with a collective self, viewing oneself in agreeable relationships with others. By using an experimental design, the authors collected data from seven countries (Australia, Brazil, China, France, Italy, Germany, and the U.S.) and tested their predictions. The results show that interdependent self-construal indeed enhances the positive effect of design harmony on consumer evaluation of attractiveness. This finding will help marketing managers and product designers to employ visual design across cultures that have different social and cultural values.

Chapter 5: Subcultural Ethos: The Dynamic Reconfiguration of Mainstream Consumer Values

Most studies on consumer values tend to focus more on the mainstream culture and less on subcultures (Kahle, 1996). In this chapter, Ulusoy and Barretta examine the value systems and their influences on the process of fragmentation in the culture and the development of the subcultural ethos. Based on a theoretical model, the authors discuss how subcultural ethos emerges. Specifically, they argue that the problems (social, cultural, and environmental) associated with the mainstream culture lead to discontentment with and resistance to the mainstream culture. As a result, people start the quest for social and cultural transformation as well as the quest for the alternative identities and self-expression. This quest eventually leads to the fragmentation of the mainstream culture through subcultures. As an example, Ulusoy and Barretta discuss how some of the values from the List of Values (Kahle, 1996) may mean different things to the members of subcultures.

Chapter 6: Handmade: How Indie Girl Culture Is Changing the Market

In Chapter 6, Larsen and Kahle examine the success of the Independent DIY (Do It Yourself) Lifestyle Blogging Business model through the Indie Girl Culture (IGC), a subculture of young women that has developed around this model. More specifically, the authors analyzed how three historical movements (i.e. the Handmade movement, the Arts and Crafts movement, and the punk subculture) combined with progressive marketing theories (i.e. Permission Marketing and Relationship Marketing), and made possible with the new opportunities created through the Internet (i.e. blogs and social media), helped to develop the Independent DIY Lifestyle Blogging Business model. The authors concluded that the growth and success within IGC highlight innovative approaches that are influencing the marketing industry and prove the Independent DIY Lifestyle Blogging Business model to be an effective, sustainable form of small business marketing.

Chapter 7: Understanding the Voter Decision Trade-off Analysis as a Foundation for Developing More Predictive Polling Methodologies

"Why did Donald Trump win the election?" Many explanations have been offered to answer this question since the 2016 presidential elections, but probably the main question to ask was the following: "Why did traditional political polling not predict the victory of Donald Trump over Hillary Clinton?" In this chapter, Reynolds outlines a detailed explanation of how political strategy is developed and uses this explanation as a framework for developing more predictive polling methods. He suggests that, similar to creating effective advertising strategies to create purchase intent, the new polling methodology should be based on voter decision segmentation (the core principle of strategy development) and a decision model grounded by personal values.

Chapter 8: Money Attitudes and Social Values: A Research Program and Agenda

Money generates personal, complex, and subjective attitudes, and it is related to symbolic values. In Chapter 8, Rose, Merchant, Rose, Bakir, and Gentina outline a series of studies exploring attitudes toward money. By using a four-dimensional scale (i.e. achievement, status, worry, and security) to measure symbolic money attitudes and a variety of qualitative and quantitative techniques (e.g. focus groups, depth interviews, and surveys) to collect data, the authors explore the meanings of and attitudes toward money in different cultural settings (e.g. Hindu families in India). Accordingly, their research has produced a rich and diverse set of cross-cultural findings that compliment and supplement the findings of research on personal values.

Chapter 9: Social Media and Values

Social media have been very influential in almost every aspect of life, including, but not limited to, politics, sports, marketing, health, and interpersonal relationships. Moreover, social media can be perceived as an effective tool to convey social and personal values. In spite of the enormous growth of social media and the importance of values, studies that examine social media and values together are limited. In this chapter, Lee and Kahle reviewed studies that looked at how values and social media usage are related. In one study, Lee and Kahle (2016) analyzed over 20,000 tweets across four Major League Baseball teams and four sports apparel companies and found significant differences in the communication of values (e.g. The Yankees and Red Sox emphasized the values of self-respect, The Dodgers emphasized fulfillment, and The Giants emphasized fun and enjoyment in life). In another study, the authors found that people who endorse certain values (e.g. a sense of belonging, fun, and enjoyment in life) are more likely to spend time on social media. Lee and Kahle concluded that social media offer a lens into the communication of values and thus should be examined more in the future.

Section 3: Spiritual Aspects of Values

Chapter 10: Meditation and Consumption

Previous research shows that although people may adopt materialistic values to feel happier or to gain status, the end result of materialism is usually unsatisfaction with life (Richins and Dawson, 1992). In Chapter 10, Tanskul and Patara suggest that meditation can be used to divert consumers' focus away from materialistic aspirations, which then improves consumer well-being. Based on an ethnographic study and personal interviews, the authors explore how meditation affects consumer values, well-being, and happiness. Specifically, their research suggests that meditation focuses people's attention on the awareness of self, leads to higher self-acceptance, and decreases the importance of social comparison of success and wealth.

Chapter 11: Religion: The New Individual Difference Variable and Its Relationship to Core Values

Although religion has not been one of the main variables used to understand consumer behavior, some studies show that religion does affect different aspects of consumer behavior (Bailey and Sood, 1993; Essoo and Dibb, 2004). In Chapter 14, Minton and Kahle suggest that religion may serve as a determinant of core values for many people. More specifically, they propose that religion provides additional insight as an individual difference variable above and beyond other individual difference variables (e.g. need for cognition). Accordingly, this chapter suggests that examining this religious individual difference variable will provide a more comprehensive understanding of value differences among consumers.

Section 4: Methodological Approaches

Chapter 12: Mapping Human Values: Enhancing Social Marketing through Obituary Data Mining

Alfano, Higgins, and Levernier believe that obituaries include only the features that the author(s) find most salient for both themselves as relatives/friends of the deceased and to signal to others in the community the socially recognized aspects of the deceased's character. Accordingly, by linking two concepts from the field of marketing (*means-end theory* and *laddering*) with one from the philosophical field (*virtue theory*) in four studies, the authors of Chapter 12 try to understand, or "map," virtue and value through obituaries. The first study included the analyses of obituaries from four local newspapers from four different cities, whereas the second study focused on obituaries from *The New York Times*. Both studies were conducted through manual reading, coding, and analyzing over 1,000 obituaries. Study 3 introduced a semiautomated data mining process and tested this new method test on several thousand obituaries. Study 4 aimed to test if the values described in obituaries are shared with the living obituary writers and their intended readers in the community. In addition to introducing a novel approach to study values, Alfano, Higgins, and Levernier also found that geography, gender, and elite status influence the virtues and values associated with the deceased.

Chapter 13: Apple's Religious Value: A Consumer Neuroscience Perspective

Consumers' loyalty to and perceptions of Apple have been compared to devotees' loyalty to and perceptions of a religion (Belk and Tumbat, 2005). In Chapter 13, Wu, by using the "Seven Dimensions of Religion" as a theoretical framework, examines the religion-brand relationship. A two-part study, an online survey and an electroencephalography (EEG) experiment, revealed that Apple devotees did not have transcendent feelings. More specifically, the results of EEG showed that when exposed to the Catholic visual stimuli, Catholic devotees triggered higher Alpha waves than their Apple counterparts did; however, when exposed to the Apple visual stimuli, Apple devotees did not trigger high Alpha waves than their Catholic counterparts did. Still, averaged Alpha waves found with the EEG study suggest that Apple taps into some of the same dimensions as religion, especially in the Material, Ritual, and Emotional aspects.

Chapter 14: Country-to-Animal-to-Brand-to-Consequences Unaided Evocations: Uncovering Consumer-Brand DNA Using Zoomorphic Metaphor Elicitation

Country images, which may also include cultural values, are usually measured through direct questioning methods. Martin, Palakshappa, and Woodside, on the other hand, claim that this kind of complex relationship requires an indirect and unstructured method. Accordingly, in this chapter, these authors introduce a novel method called zoomorphic forced metaphor-elicitation technique (FMET) to map Consumer DNA (C-DNA). In this research method, research participants identify an animal for a specific country and explain how the animal's attributes fit the specific country and the country's products or brands. For example, Indian consumers identified the sheep and kiwi bird metaphors to describe New Zealand as timid, docile, not aggressive, and innocent. By combining research participant's FMET data from multiple countries, Martin, Palakshappa, and Woodside create that person's C-DNA. These authors suggest that these C-DNA maps can help researchers and marketing practitioners to understand how country and brand images compare and contrast from the consumer's perspective.

Chapter 15: A Comparing and Contrasting of the List of Values and the Schwartz Value Scale

The List of Values (LOV), developed by Kahle (1983, 1996) based on the Social Adaptation Theory, and the Schwartz Value Scale (SVS), developed by Schwartz (1992) based on the Theory of Basic Human Values, are among the most dominant value scales used in psychology, marketing, communication, and other relevant disciplines. In this chapter, by using data from a cross-cultural online study, Gurel-Atay, Kahle, Lengler, and Kim provide a comparison and contrast of these two value scales. Their results show that LOV and SVS values are correlated with each other in a meaningful way. Based on these results, the authors discuss several advantages of using the LOV over using the SVS in consumer research.

References

Bailey, J., and J. Sood (1993). The effects of religious affiliation on consumer behavior: A preliminary investigation. *Journal of Managerial Issues*, 5 (3), 328–352.

Belk, R. W., and G. Tumbat (2005). The cult of Macintosh. *Consumption, Markets and Culture*, 8 (3), 205–217.

Essoo, N., and S. Dibb (2004). Religious influences on shopping behaviour: An exploratory study. *Journal of Marketing Management*, 20 (7), 683–712.

Gurel-Atay, E., G. X. Xie, J. Chen, and L. R. Kahle (2010). Changes in social values in the United States, 1976–2007: 'Self-Respect' is on the upswing as 'Sense of Belonging' becomes less important. *Journal of Advertising Research*, 50 (1), 57–67.

Gutman, J. (1982). A means-end chain model based on consumer categorization processes. *Journal of Marketing*, 46 (2), 60–72.

Henderson, P. W., and J. A. Cote (1998). Guidelines for selecting or modifying logos. *Journal of Marketing*, 62 (4), 14–30.

Homer, P. M., and L. R. Kahle (1988). A structural equation test of the value-attitude-behavior hierarchy. *Journal of Personality and Social Psychology*, 54 (April), 638–646.

Kahle, L. R., Ed. (1983). *Social Values and Social Change: Adaptation to Life in America*. New York, NY: Praeger.

Kahle, L. R. (1986). The nine nations of North America and the value basis of geographic segmentation. *Journal of Marketing*, 50 (April), 37–47.

Kahle, L. R. (1996). Social values and consumer behavior: Research from the list of values. In C. Seligman, J. M. Olson, and M. P. Zanna, Eds. *The Psychology of Values: The Ontario Symposium, Vol. 8*. Mahwah, NJ: Lawrence Erlbaum Associates, 135–151.

Kahle, L. R., and L. Chiagouris, Eds. (1997). *Values, Lifestyles, and Psychogra* Mahwah, NJ: Lawrence Erlbaum Associates.

Kahle, L. R., P. M. Homer, R. M. O'Brien, and D. M. Boush (1997). Maslow's hierarchy and social adaptation as alternative accounts of value structures. In L. R. Kahle and L. Chiagouris, Eds. *Values, Lifestyles, and Psychographics.* Mahwah, NJ: Lawrence Erlbaum Associates, 111–137.

Kahle, L. R., and P. Valette-Florence (2012). *Marketplace Lifestyles in an Age of Social Media: Theory and Method.* Armonk, NY: M. E. Sharpe.

Kahle, L. R., and G.-X. Xie (2008). Social values in consumer psychology. In C. P. Haugvedt, P. M. Herr, and F. R. Kardes, Eds. *Handbook of Consumer Psychology.* Mahwah, NJ: Lawrence Erlbaum, 275–285.

Kau, A. K, K. Jung, S. K. Tambyah, and S. J. Tan (2004). *Understanding Singaporeans: Values, Lifestyles, Aspirations, and Consumption Behaviors.* Singapore: World Scientific.

Kennedy, P., R. J. Best, and L. R. Kahle (1988). An alternative method for measuring value-based segmentation and advertisement positioning. *Current Issues and Research in Advertising,* 11, 139–155.

Lee, C., and L. Kahle (2016). The linguistics of social media: Communication of emotions and values in sport. *Sport Marketing Quarterly,* Morgantown, 25 (4), 201–211.

Madrigal, R., and L. R. Kahle (1994). Predicting vacation activity preferences on the basis of value-system segmentation. *Journal of Travel Research,* 32 (Winter), 22–28.

Reynolds, T. J., and J. Gutman (1988). Laddering theory, method, analysis and interpretation. *Journal of Advertising Research,* 28, 11–31.

Richins, M. L., and S. Dawson (1992). A consumer values orientation for materialism and its measurement: Scale development and validation. *Journal of Consumer Research,* 19 (3), 303–316.

Rokeach, M. (1973). *The Nature of Human Values.* New York, NY: Free Press.

Schwartz, S. H. (1992). Universals in the content and structure of values: Theory and empirical tests in 20 countries. In M. Zanna, Ed. *Advances in Experimental and Social Psychology,* Vol. 25. New York, NY: Academic Press, 1–65.

Suh, W. S., and L. R. Kahle (2018). Social values in consumer psychology: Key determinants of human behavior. In M. R. Solomon and T. M. Lowrey, Eds. *The Routledge Companion to Consumer Behavior.* New York, NY: Routledge, 165–174.

Thayer, R. H. (2016). *Misbehaving: The Making of Behavior Economics.* New York, NY: Norton.

Trafimow, D., H. C. Triandis, and S. G. Goto (1991). Some tests of the distinction between the private self and the collective self. *Journal of Personality and Social Psychology,* 60 (5), 649–655.

United Nations Development Programme (2007). *Sufficiency Economy and Human Development.* Thailand Human Development Report. Bangkok: UNDP.

ЗІС MARKETING
ГIVES AND INSIGHTS

Common Pitfalls and Solutions

Thomas J. Reynolds

Introduction

The overriding management question is: "*Why are some companies more profitable than others?*" There are two mutually dependent answers; namely, superior strategy and superior execution.

The strategic management component can also be defined as that set of managerial goal setting and decisions and actions to achieve those goals that determine the long-term performance of a business enterprise. It involves formulating and implementing strategies that will help in aligning the organization to achieve organizational goals.

The role of marketing strategy is the process construct that allows a company to focus limited resources on the best marketplace opportunities to achieve sustainable competitive advantage and thus increase sales. The operational word here is sustainable.

The most common mistake is not having a strategy at all. Many executives think that they have a strategy when they really don't, at least not a strategy that meets any kind of rigorous, detailed specification as to exactly *why* it will work, including the underlying relevant assumptions.

What are the biggest obstacles to good strategy?

There are many barriers that distract, deter, and divert managers from making clear strategic choices, ranging from faulty research data to poor competitive analysis. From my experience over four decades in developing corporate and brand strategy, some of the most significant barriers come from the many hidden biases embedded in internal systems, organizational structures, and the very process of management decision-making. Managers all too often have latent, unstated assumptions which they base their strategy evaluation processes upon that are incorrect. Unfortunately, it is inherent to a vast majority of man-agement DNA: we pervasively overlook the assumptions that provide the basis of how we frame and analyze problems. Managers cannot resist the belief that their self-confirmatory strategic insights will lead to more growth and more profit. Unfortunately, false assumptions result in poor strategies, so in reality, most strategies fail from within.

The fundamental realization to be asserted and agreed upon is that the only reality in the marketplace is in the minds of customers. If we assume we know that, we better have a concrete, detailed understanding as a verifiable basis, more specifically, as managers, we need to understand the basis of customer decision-making. There are a myriad of external inputs, such as industry ex-perts, market analysts, and high-tech CRM conceptual frameworks, which divert us from this simple truth. The questions worth noting are: why do customers buy our brands (and those of our competitors), and why are some customers loyal to our brand (and to competitive brands)? Said another way, what are the relevant strategic decision-based equities and disequities that un-derlie the choice trade-offs relative to the competitive environment of the mar-ketplace? These answers lie in the minds of customers.

Having a superior strategy in the first place is difficult. Successfully exe-cuting the strategy is also difficult. Simultaneously maintaining an executing strategy is even harder. This combination represents the answer to the "why some companies are more profitable" question.

Returning to the prior point, the fact is that many companies do not even have a clearly specified, marketplace-driven, customer-based strategy at all. That is, senior management frequently "thinks" that they have a strategic plan when, indeed, they do not. This misconception typically stems from labeling operational or financial plans as strategies. The strategic centerpiece, again, is understanding customer decision-making as a basis to develop and optimize strategy. Why? Because customer (existing and potential) decision-making is exactly what we want our strategy to affect.

So, what do these "non-strategy" companies mistake for strategy? Typi-cally, they think that coming up with ideas and testing a variety of tactics can lead to success. Of course, the shortcoming here is that this all-to-common situation can result in a variety of dangers including missed opportunities and inadvertently giving the competition a competitive advantage. The bottom line is that this hit-and-miss approach tends to both waste time and company resources.

To illustrate, consider a direct selling company that is on a downward slide that embraces a weekly sales strategy of discounting some array of products to their sales force to stimulate their sales effort, primarily to generate needed cash flow. The result? They train the sales force to wait until products go on sale before they consider buying for resale. The pejorative problem is that over 90% of the sales force is in a "buying club," meaning that they effectively only buy for themselves, which simply results in passing through very low-margin goods and damaging what brand equity that existed prior. Having weekly sales is not a strategy. In fact, it is a strategic equity minimizing tactic for the direct sales space.

Given the nature of the strategic problem briefly outlined, the next issue of interest is the role of senior management. The fact is that designing effective strategies should be "Job 1" for senior executives. Whose responsibility is marketing strategy? The answer is the direct involvement of the CEO. That's why David Packard of Hewlett Packard fame was once quoted as saying, "Marketing is too important to be left to the marketing people." Yes, the Chief Marketing Officer can bring his or her ideas, but the final decision, and responsibility, is that of the CEO.

Who is a good example of CEO responsibility for marketing strategy? Consider Steve Jobs, who is beyond a doubt the most successful marketing CEO. He intimately had his hand in product design, branding decisions, distribution strategy, and advertising strategy and execution. He took full responsibility for all facets of marketing. Is this too much to ask? I don't think so.

Fatal Marketing Flaws and Solutions

There are five common, sometimes near-fatal flaws that lead to suboptimal marketing strategy.

1 Failure to specify and test assumptions that serve as the underpinning of the strategy development process. Specifically, the failure is not dimensionalizing customer decision-making in the marketplace (for your brand as well as for your competitors), which serves as the basis to frame the marketing problem and identify strategic equities and disequities underlying brand choice. It is this understanding of choice that allows one to optimize strategy under the general canon of: leverage decision equities and supplant decision disequities.

2 Basing strategy on false assumptions typically results in mis-framing the marketing problem. Perhaps an analogy that will best illustrate this is determining where to drill for oil. Geophysical experts analyze a series of measurements and then tell you the location of where is the highest probability of finding oil. They frame the analytical problem utilizing multiple measurements with known reliability and validity. Similarly, marketing strategists frame a problem which determines the optimal solution space. If one of the framing assumptions is wrong (e.g. not reliable or not valid), the solution space is suboptimal, essentially in the framing context one is solving the wrong problem, which is oftentimes referred to as Type III

error. Put simply, the framing process is what determines the problem definition and thus possible solution space (read as: where to drill with the highest probability of finding oil).

There are four framing questions that serve as the basis of problem definition, which sets up the specification of which decision structures will provide the most valuable input to solving your marketing problem. It is highly recommended that this is an exercise that the senior marketing groups undertake individually, and then are asked to present their respective points of view. My experience is that this exercise leads to significantly different answers which serve as a basis for very fruitful discussions. These questions (Olson & Reynolds, 2001) will be detailed with examples in a later section; however to stimulate thinking, they will be outlined here.

A   Who are the key customers?
B   What are the competitive choice alternatives?
C   What is the relevant decision context?
D   What are the relevant decision behaviors?

Can you answer these fundamental questions that define the problem—solution space from which your strategy will be forthcoming? How much consistency of responses do you think would be generated by your marketing group? The fact is, if you focused your discussions on these inconsistencies, you would then have the opportunity to get at the latent assumptions management have, which defines the problem space. Again, this framing process is invaluable.

3   Failure to know the definitions and rationales underlying fundamental marketing terms and acronyms, such as market segmentation, positioning strategy, brand equity (and types thereof), brand loyalty, and retention rate. Over the years when terms are used in meetings, I simply ask for the definition, which all too often results in either a blank look or a "you know" response. Marketing strives to become a science, which requires a common, clearly defined, and understood lexicon.

4   Failure to specify brand positioning strategy in customer-ese. Given customer perceptions and decision-making is precisely what you are trying to affect, to write strategy in marketing-ese very frequently leads to miscommunication and ineffectual evaluation research, due to back-and-forth translations.

Brand positioning must be defined in customer terminology, namely, what specific perceptions that underlie decision-making are the strategic goal. Remember, the only reality is in the minds of customers in the marketplace. Their language is the only one of import.

Failure to recognize the fact that marketing campaigns are tactical in nature and are not strategic. Strategy, again, is about how you will affect customer decision-making. How to efficiently affect this end provides the motivating basis of creating a marketing plan, which typically involves the executional coordination of some combination of marketing mix elements.

5   Failure to realize the basis of strategic equity is loyal customers (Reynolds & Phillips 2005). Thus, by definition, this requires different metrics to assess a brand's health in the marketplace. How do you define loyal customers? Do you know what percentage of your sales can be attributed to loyal customers? How has this measure, reflective of the health of your brand franchise, varied over time? Can you attribute marketing actions (yours or that of your competition) to these longitudinal changes? This assessment is much like a physician giving a stress test and monitoring the patient's EKG. Loyal customers are in fact the heart of the strategic equity of the brand franchise.

In brief, strategic equity, defined as the value current or potential that exists in a firm because of its *ownership of brand equity*, *distribution channels*, and *limited resources* (Reynolds & Westberg 2001), comprises these three global constructs, all with multiple subcomponents. It is worth mentioning that formally specifying these equities and using this framework as a checklist to assess strategic decisions has also proven to be very worthwhile exercise. The management question of issue is: to what degree, positively or negatively, does this decision affect the designated equities of your brand?

A simple, five-step hierarchy presented in Figure 2.1 reflects the relationship of strategic equity as the foundation to tactical marketing plans.

Management Goal: Maximizing Strategic Equity

FIGURE 2.1   Component Parts of the Strategy Process Hierarchy.

Beware: Market Research is NOT Decision Research

As has been repeatedly emphasized, optimizing marketing strategy requires understanding customer decision-making; unfortunately, traditional marketing research is NOT decision research. Not recognizing this simple fact is all too often fatal.

To say market research has fundamental limitations is to truly understate reality. The fact is that very frequently market research "findings" can be misleading. Believing that the interpretations of data leading to the underlying rationales as to what people think and the basis of their (likely) decision-making are seriously flawed. Yes, research is a valuable tool, but when interpretations are accepted as facts, one is clearly at risk of mis-framing the marketing reality.

Another popular fallacy is the assumption that customers know precisely and can perfectly assess the differences between and among brands on dimensions whose meanings are consistently interpreted by all. And that these differences can be quantified (yes, the erroneous belief is that research numbers can't lie). One would think with so much time and energy focusing on marketing strategy determination, one might think that these types of obvious flaws would have been eliminated. Not so. To illustrate this point, consider the following examples.

Basing strategy on traditional marketing research is tenuous as best. Why? Because marketing research is inherently fraught with the assumptions noted earlier which are questionable at best, and at worst not valid. These problems frequently result as to how the research was designed or how it is executed. Errors often occur with customer surveys as a result of including questions not being asked correctly, the use of flawed scales, and the samples from which data are gathered (e.g. noncustomers completing the survey). The bottom line is that marketing research is valuable for keeping score, but not necessarily valuable for gaining insight into customer decision-making. It is this latter input that is the fundamental building block of the strategy development process. Yes, the primary marketing research output of nice charts with clever language remains highly suspect in terms of revealing new insights that you need. Researchers try to tell a story with an ending in mind. It is this interpretative ending to their story that can be the source of misperceptions.

A tried-and-true way to garner strategic insight is to go out into the marketplace. Observe and ask questions of your customers and those of your competitors. You will honestly be amazed as to what and how much you will learn. I recently asked senior executives from a large home improvement company conducting strategic research what they had learned from their most recent trips into their and their competition's stores. Their response was that they didn't have time, and that they had researched to tell them what was important. Hogwash. Do you want to trust frequently flawed questions and interpretations without taking time to develop your own insights?

The primary issue, then, is how to systematically gain insight into relevant decision-making of key customers.

Means-End Theory and the Laddering Methodology

Means-end theory (Gutman, 1982) posits that there are psychological levels of abstraction in which personal meanings are associated with concrete product descriptors (Gutman & Reynolds, 1978). There are typically four levels of meaning: product attributes, functional consequences (of consumption or use)—both of which are product extrinsics—psychosocial consequences (of consumption or use) and personal values—both of which are personal intrinsics.

The levels of associated meanings represent what can be thought of as a neural network that underlies perception which ultimately serves as the platform for decision-making. The definitions of the connected levels between the Product and the Self are detailed below. The question is how best to uncover these common networks of meaning that underlie customer decision-making. The methodology to accomplish this is laddering (Reynolds & Gutman, 1988), whose goal is to identify the associative network of meaning across levels, defined as follows:

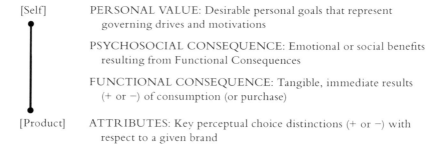

[Self]   PERSONAL VALUE: Desirable personal goals that represent
               governing drives and motivations

               PSYCHOSOCIAL CONSEQUENCE: Emotional or social benefits
               resulting from Functional Consequences

               FUNCTIONAL CONSEQUENCE: Tangible, immediate results
               (+ or −) of consumption (or purchase)

[Product]   ATTRIBUTES: Key perceptual choice distinctions (+ or −) with
               respect to a given brand

The noteworthy distinction seen in Figure 2.2 between theory and method is that Means-end theory is top-down: the importance of a given attribute is because it satisfies a higher-level functional consequence, and that is important because it satisfies yet another higher-level psychosocial consequence. Importance of a given attribute ultimately is determined by the highest-level value construct that it satisfies. And, the laddering methodology is typically bottom-up. For example, if a respondent is asked in a one-on-one interview: which brand do you prefer, and why? (thereby eliciting a choice distinction, which is usually an attribute). Having obtained the choice distinction, the respondent is then asked, "why is (that choice distinction) important to you"? which results in a higher-level reason. This probing continues until all four levels of the means-end chain (MEC) are identified.

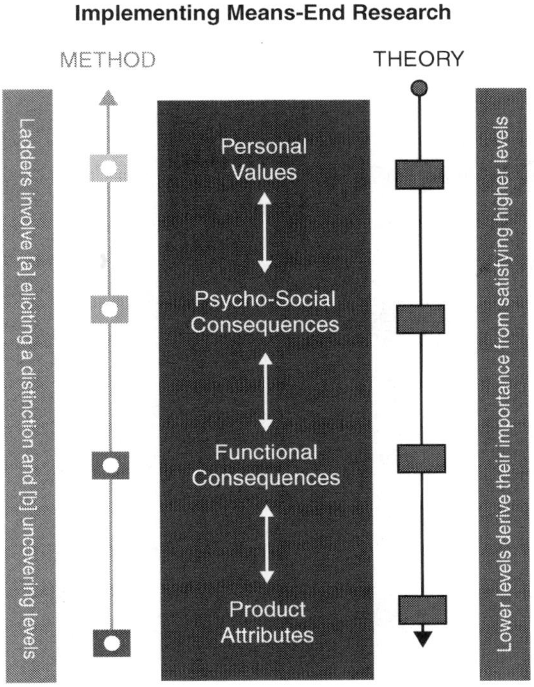

Implementing Means-End Research

FIGURE 2.2   Means–End Theory vs. the Laddering Methodology.

The resulting ladders (MECs) are then coded by level, quantified, and sum-marized (usually based upon the magnitude of pairwise connections between codes) in the form of a hierarchical Customer Decision Map. It is this decision map that represents the basis for strategy development, essentially a strategic "game board." One such game board illustrating this output seen in Figure 2.3 is from the Reagan–Bush '84 campaign (Norton, 2008) (note: the blue rect-angles are owned by Mondale and the red ovals are owned by Reagan). Note-worthy of this example voter decision representation are several facts, namely, the equity data were collected from polling noncommitted voters (Undecideds and Leaners) and the structural relationships across the levels were constructed from laddering data.

The following list summarizes the basic rules for utilizing the game board in the political arena, which directly correspond to *brand politics*, as follows:

1   Own as much "decision space" (as many nodes) as you can.
2   Control the higher levels.
3   Develop strategies that connect from bottom to top (and one can develop new connections).

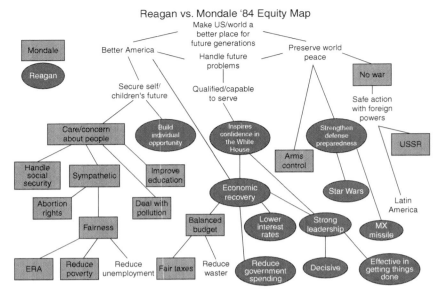

FIGURE 2.3   Reagan-Bush '84 Voter Decision Summary Map.

Bearing in mind the basic rules, then, construct an optimal strategy by:

4   Reinforcing you "base" equities (the reasons your "loyals" are loyal).
5   Appealing to "swing vote" (non-loyal customers, in this case Undecided/ Leaner voters).
6   Neutralizing (blocking) your opponent's largest equities by:

   a   Leveraging your own largest equity as a basis for strategy.
   b   Developing a new "reason for being/believing."

Given these rules, if you were Mondale, what would your strategy be? If you were Reagan, what would you do? How and why did you decide upon that strategy? (Hint: assume your opposition had the same perfect information that you do. Develop the opposition's optimal strategy first, and then using that as input, determine yours. Why do you think this two-step process has merit? I have yet to see this simple process worked through in the marketing realm, without first explaining why this way of strategic thinking is relevant. Marketing is a game of war. Should you not consider where you are most vulnerable to attack before you develop your army's strategy?)

   Recent developments to efficiently conduct laddering interviews via the Internet using a voice-over-Internet protocol have yielded significantly superior decision-based data, in part due to the graphical interface implemented within the software (Reynolds & Phillips, 2010). Additionally, these online methods bridge to efficient computer systems to streamline the tedious coding of laddering verbatims (Reynolds, 2010).

Laddering Research Design: Distinction Types

There are three ways to gain meaningful distinctions from which to base ladders and to base strategic insights upon.

- Latent, valenced Top-of-Mind associations. This is accomplished by asking the respondent:
  - What is the first thing that comes to mind when I say (Brand…)?
  - Is that a positive or negative to you?
  - Why is that a (positive or negative)? Ladder this response.

    This distinction reveals potential equities that can be leveraged. Consider, for example, a prestigious brand of cookies, like Pepperidge Farm. What would be its latent equities?

- Preference contrast distinctions.
  1 What is the brand you purchase most often (#1) (in this occasion)?
  2 What is the brand you purchase second most often (#2) (in this occasion)?
  3 What is the primary reason you purchase #1 over #2. Ladder the response.

  Why do respondents prefer your brand, and why is that personally relevant to them? And, what are the preference-based ladders when competitors are the #1 brand? Contrasting the decision-based equities and disequities (the competitor's equities) provides a framework to assess key groups (e.g. How are loyals different from competitive loyals? How are loyal heavy users different from loyal light users? What do former loyals who switched believe?)
- Common unmet needs (two options: on-the-margin (+ and −) and gold standard).

  1 How would you rate the (#1 brand) in terms of overall satisfaction on a numerical scale (anchored by "Perfect")?
  2 + equity: What one thing caused you to rate it at this level and not one point lower?
  3 − equity: What one thing if changed would cause you to rate it one point higher?

  and,

  4 What one thing would cause you to rate your #1 product "Perfect" on the satisfaction scale?

The decision as to which combination of distinction types to be laddered in the research design is dependent upon the "where the oil is most likely to be found." For a brand with a long-standing, positive tradition, latent equities frequently provide potentially leverageable ideas.

The reasons for preference, thereby determining both your decision equities and disequities, especially when you contrast different groups as noted earlier, are always important to understand. And, understanding potential unmet needs very frequently offers valuable strategic positioning concepts. These questioning strategies obviously equally are applicable to any informal discussions one may have with customers in their space.

The two challenges are to determine which distinctions are most relevant to ladder, and how to represent in the same Customer Decision Map this strategic research output. Recently, developments in decision segmentation methodologies (Reynolds, 2006) have provided the basis to solve the identification and quantification of key decision structures, thereby simplifying the integration of laddering results into one composite decision "game board" (Phillips & Reynolds, 2009). The underlying strategy-determining logic is: if you know how somebody makes a decision, you are more likely to be able to sell them your product offering.

Decision Segmentation is Key to Optimizing Positioning Strategy

Segmentation is a powerful tool for facilitating the strategy development process. Unfortunately, segmentation is much like kissing: everyone thinks they are good at it. One can apply powerful statistical algorithms to generate segments and represent the output into beautiful PowerPoint slides with catchy labels. However, one must first bear in mind that the objective of research is to focus your company on the best opportunities and provide insight as to how to design a positioning that would be appealing to your target market. Why? Because the latent assumption is that the identification of segments defines groups that will behave in a predictable manner with the change of a given marketing variable. Given this objective, traditional segmentation methods are really only surrogates for identifying homogeneous decision-making groups. This monumental leap of faith reflects the primary shortcoming of segmentation.[1]

In addition, there are three common pitfalls for consideration for building an optimal segmentation model.

- *Segment names are not intuitive.* Be as accurate as possible, rather than creative. A female high-end shopper for clothes is better described as "image conscious" rather than a "fashionista." Everyone should have a common definition in mind when they think about a given segment. Of course, knowing how they evaluate and make a purchase decision would be optimal.
- *Too many segments and subsegments create more of a problem.* Consolidate the number of segments into only those with at least some reasonable threshold value (e.g. 10%) in the target marketplace. Too many segments, though interesting to chart and explain, tend to muddle the strategy development process.

- Segment definitions that do not combine both attribute descriptors and the reason they are important to the customer can be misinterpreted. This is exactly what decision segmentation yields. Consider, for example, two men who graduated from high school together, married their high school sweethearts, and both have a boy and a girl, who work in the same mill with the same job title and income, and happen to live next door to one another. One primarily votes for Democratic and the other primarily for Republican. Understanding the decision segments based upon differences in political choice clearly offers the potential for more interesting insights as opposed to either demographics or simple attitudinal statements. Why? Because decisions are what marketers are trying to affect, and this understanding is the closest thing to reality in the marketplace.

To illustrate, consider the decision segments in Figure 2.4 (taken from Reynolds & Rochon, 2001). The segment names are clear. The number of segments presented in this study was six, which was very manageable. And the segment definitions with the corresponding decision MECs cannot be misinterpreted. A closer look at the decision structures selected to be highlighted here reveals that the bases of Environmentalist and Parent are identical; however, the higher levels, the personal reasons why these lower level differentiators are important, are different for these individuals. By understanding the entire decision network as a basis of segmentation provides much richer insight as to what marketing activity would be more likely to affect behavioral actions. Interestingly, in this applied research

Decision Segmentation Examples

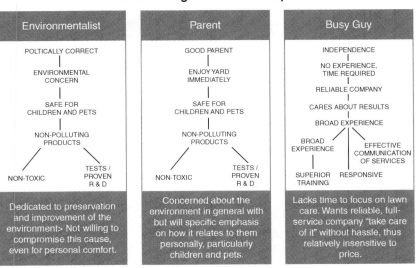

FIGURE 2.4 Lawn Care Decision Segments (Reynolds & Rochon, 2001).

study which was conducted for the purpose or company acquisition, specific marketing tactics were developed for each segment.

A recent study in the pet food category contrasted *a priori* segments determined from attitudinal questions to decision-based segmentation. Both methods were evaluated with respect to predicting brand preference. Not surprisingly, the decision segmentation was twice as discriminating with respect to brand choice. The lesson is: one should always evaluate their segmentation approach with respect to how well it predicts brand preference as well as consumption. If the segmentation approach is not predictive, it is likely not worth much. Interestingly, this analysis was done without the client's knowledge. When the results were submitted to the research group, the decision was made to not share these results with senior management due to political reasons. Apparently, the attitudinal segmentation as a basis of strategy development is still being used.

A critical issue, however, is the need to link decision segments to media selection. This is addressed by first determining the segments from decision-based laddering, and then using the segments as the basis for larger scale quantitative research (see Reynolds & Rochon, 2001). The challenge here is to convert the decision structure in the diagram into a form that can be assessed directly in the segment-determining research.

Framing Questions

The Mary Kay Example

The best way to overview the framing process is to work through a simple example that leads to defining the marketing problem to be solved, then once the steps are understood, revisit each of the concepts adding some background color, meaning things to consider when evaluating possible framing answers. The easiest example is Mary Kay Cosmetics circa the late '80s (extracted from Reynolds, Rochon & Westberg, 2001).

Background. Mary Kay, a direct seller of cosmetics and skincare products, has experienced steady sales growth for 20 years, and is confronted with significant sales declines for the last 12 months, greatly reducing its market value (reduction in stock price of 80%). Because the perception of growth and financial opportunity is critical to maintaining and recruiting new sales associates, the decline in stock price causes the company to begin the "death spiral" to financial ruin.

Market research reports that the Company's beauty products and packaging have an older, out-of-date look that is not appealing to either their existing or potential end users. Management must make an immediate decision as to which strategic issues to address, before the company loses critical mass necessary to fund the overhead cost of operations and fund its debt load (note: the more pressing fact is that Mary Kay has just decided to go private, which required extensive leveraging, even with the sales of virtually all company assets).

Who are the key customers?

Management is divided in their points of view: marketing believes that it is the end users who buy the product who are the key customers. This group uses market research data that say the product line is old-fashioned and must be updated. The Sales faction believes that it is the sales associates who sell to the end users that are the key customers. This group presents an analysis demonstrating that sales are nearly perfectly correlated (.97) with the number of sales associates.

The much-debated answer is…the Independent Sales Consultants.

What are the competitive choice alternatives?

Given recruiting is the life blood of direct selling (about half of sales are from first time, new recruit purchases), competition is primarily alternative income options.

The answer is…other direct-selling companies, 9–5 secretarial work and retail sales.

What is the relevant decision context?

Decision context refers to environmental or lifestyle factors underling decision-making.

The answer is…new career opportunity with no limits on income, need money from a part-time job, and flexible hours is a positive because I can have more time to spend with my children.

What are the relevant decision behaviors?

The decisions to be understood are straightforward.

The answer is…Why do they join" Why do they continue? and Why do they leave?

A summary of the framing questions appears in Figure 2.5. The marketing problem can be summarized as:

How to develop a marketing strategy that assures long-term growth… by focusing on the relevant life experiences that the Company can provide to the sales force vs. alternative job or career options, that will motivate the recruitment of new sales people and, at the same time, maximize their expected time with the Company.

As mentioned earlier, this management exercise is invaluable. Without framing the problem specifically (and correctly), one is very unlikely to find an optimal solution. The outcome of this work was initially increasing recruiting by 42%, which resulted in less than ten years of a 500% sales increase.

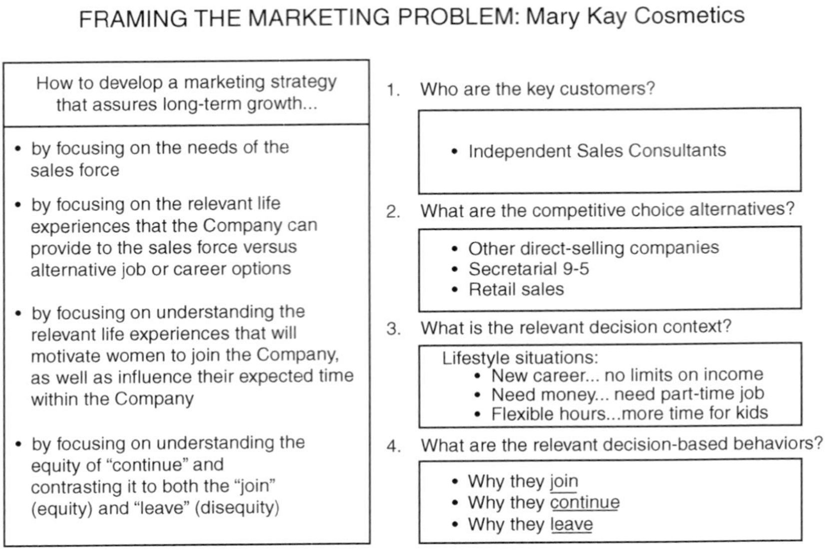

FRAMING THE MARKETING PROBLEM: Mary Kay Cosmetics

How to develop a marketing strategy that assures long-term growth...	
• by focusing on the needs of the sales force	**1.** Who are the key customers? • Independent Sales Consultants
• by focusing on the relevant life experiences that the Company can provide to the sales force versus alternative job or career options	**2.** What are the competitive choice alternatives? • Other direct-selling companies • Secretarial 9-5 • Retail sales
• by focusing on understanding the relevant life experiences that will motivate women to join the Company, as well as influence their expected time within the Company	**3.** What is the relevant decision context? Lifestyle situations: • New career... no limits on income • Need money... need part-time job • Flexible hours...more time for kids
• by focusing on understanding the equity of "continue" and contrasting it to both the "join" (equity) and "leave" (disequity)	**4.** What are the relevant decision-based behaviors? • Why they join • Why they continue • Why they leave

FIGURE 2.5   Mary Kay Framing Answers and Corresponding Rationales.

Framing Questions: Pitfalls, Issues, and Ideas

Experience with the development of the responses to the framing questions suggests that this process provides the needed focus to define virtually any positioning issue. And, it provides the basis to uncover the latent assumptions underlying how management thinks about the marketplace. As is likely obvious, it is to be expected during the framing process that these answers are all interconnected, meaning the responses are very much mutually dependent.

What follows are some perspectives that may help to facilitate the process, including some dead ends to avoid.

Who are the key customers?

Companies frequently want to be all things to all people. They fear they will be missing an opportunity is they don't include some group. The fact is that successful marketers realize by narrowing their target audience that they can increase the specificity and therefore intensity of their positioning message, as well as be more specific in media selection.

Some time ago, a seven-page brand narrative existed for a major soft drink brand which was detailed enough to be summarized as "the brand would be all things to all people." The point here is that ubiquity is not a strategy. Be specific as to the target audience and what decision–based associations you want to implant in their brains.

Purchase (choice) behavior is typically the best criterion, specifically including a measure of brand loyalty or participation. For example, consider the value of understanding the decision-making of your companies' loyal customers vs. your primary competitors' brand loyals. Or, consider contrasting your "heavy" loyals vs. your "light" loyals (the answer to be understood in this case is what do my "heavy" loyals believe that my "lights" do not?).

One interesting marketing problem encountered was to gain an understanding of why a leader in the light beer category was losing share directly to one of its competitors. In this case, the key customer was defined as the "previously loyal to brand X, who recently switched to Brand Y." Of course, the primary decision behavior of interest for this sample group was the reason for switching.

What are the competitive choice alternatives?

Most marketers when asked to name their competitors can readily provide a prioritized list. This output demonstrates knowledge of the marketplace; however frequently, what is also important is who is not on the list. Brands not viewed as competitors are potentially some of the biggest threats to a company. To illustrate, there are both in-kind and functional competitors. What does functional competition mean? Consider products outside of the manufacture-determined product class. The soft drink research database in France, for example, permitted the contrasting of diet drink beliefs between the two major competitors. However, when consumers were asked about their consumption of nonalcoholic beverages to determine a share-of-stomach, the primary competitor was neither of the in-kind, branded competitors; rather, it was water. The point here is that the mis-definition of the problem space will in all likelihood not result in an optimal solution.

Another misunderstanding with regard to competitive choice involves different levels of decision-making. Consider, for example, you are interested in designing a market research segment tracking program for an automobile company. You can either assume the manufacturer supplied product class definitions, or you can try to understand (a) the basis of the clusters of competition in the consideration set and then (b) the basis of car choice within these segments. The fact is that the first hurdle is to get into the consideration set, and this has noticeably different criteria than the basis of car choice. Thus, assuming product-based, manufacturer-determined product classes oftentimes derails the problem framing.

What is the relevant decision context(s)?

Other than the environmental or lifestyle classifications noted earlier, there are at least two other major delineations to consider, namely, need states and/or specific occasions of consumption.

Need states activate different preference structures (yes, this means preference is a multidimensional construct (Perkins & Reynolds, 1995)) which, in turn, generates different competitive sets. Consider for cookies the need states of Entertaining at Home, Others in the Household Like, Great Indulgence for Taking a Break in the Day. Understanding need states serves to both frame the most relevant competition and provide insight as to where your brand is not competitive.

Occasions are frequently defined as a tripartite combination of time, place, and relevant others. To conceptually illustrate both the multidimensional notion of preference and the relevant competition by occasion, consider the framing for canned soup: time (lunch—main meal *or* dinner—first course); place (at home *or* away), others (self *or* with others). Different preference structures exist, which translates into different brand equities and disequities relative to the competition (which is both in-kind and functional). In this example, knowing the potential size of these respective occasions would provide the key input to answer this problem framing question.

What are the relevant decision behaviors?

The auto-example suggests understanding the basis of how a car, especially one that is in the manufacturer's predefined product class, gets into or does not get into the consideration set.

The obvious example is, of course, by direct #1 vs. #2 preference contrast. However, another interesting decision can be illustrated with a seven-point bipolar political scale anchored on the two poles by definitely voting for candidate A and candidate B, with the midpoint being Undecided. The decision of particular interest with regard to likely voting behavior is understanding what the barriers are for movement on the scale, essentially utilizing the on-the-margin idea. The application of this approach also works well when trying to understand the percentage of consumption differences between #1 and #2 brands. As is apparent, this methodology yields different insights than simply a "brand of candidate" preference distinction.

In sum, the framing process is the key to defining the strategic problem which understanding the basis of customer decision-making can solve. A final suggestion is to assign this task before the strategy meeting in which these issues will be addressed. Clear thinking is required, and it is highly beneficial to undertake this on one's own. By doing this, one learns how to evaluate the nuance of trade-offs between the alternative definitions, and not just relying on "group think," which is often guided by political considerations.

Brand Strategy Specification and Communication Optimization

Positioning Specification

Branding is a common marketing term, which essentially means to create an identifiable brand persona that makes a promise of value. Value is a function of quality and price, where quality can be defined as more than performance. Quality means recognizing and satisfying the reason why and how the product fits into my life. This is the fundamental basis of brand choice.

Marketing traditionally has rested on the branding construct of a unique selling proposition (USP), which is communicated in all of the marketing materials. The USP is typically one single statement that defines your brand in the minds of customers. Can you think of a superior method than to define the USP in terms of how you want customers to think, and ultimately make the decision to buy and continue to buy your brand?

There are many practical dos and don'ts about branding, but at the heart of the issue is the formal definition and then specification of the USP positioning strategy. Consider the following: *The unique selling proposition of a brand is the positioning specification of the manner by which the brand will be meaningfully differentiated with respect to motivating desired choice behavior by the target consumer.* At the core of this definition is orienting the USP toward *motivating desired choice behavior,* which is explicitly grounded in understanding decision-making within the competitive marketplace.

The first step is to define a brand positioning platform that is isomorphic to the decision-making process. Consider the MECCAS (an acronym for Means-End Conceptualization of the Components of Advertising Strategy) model (Reynolds & Craddock, 1988; Reynolds & Gutman, 1984) seen in Figure 2.6. All that is required is to be decided upon by management; then, it is what the optimal decision structure(s) are that define both the USPs which also serve as the basis of the communication strategy specification (see Phillips, Reynolds & Reynolds, 2010 for an example using decision segmentation). Importantly, communication strategies can differ in two distinct ways, namely, different decision elements and a different level of emphasis by component level within the MECCAS framework. Imagine, for example, that the level of emphasis is

Means-End Conceptualization of the Components of Advertising Strategy

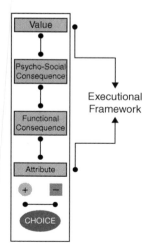

DRIVING FORCE represents the motivating value orientation of the strategy, the end-level focus of the message. Values may be explicitly communicated, or implied.

LEVERAGE POINT is the manner, usually a Psycho-Social consequence by which the message activates or "taps into" the individual's personal value system.

EXECUTIONAL FRAMEWORK is the "delivery vehicle" for the four fundamental strategic components. It is the tone, the action scenario, the Gestalt of the plot of the commercial.

CONSUMER BENEFITS are the direct functional consequences, usually performance outcomes, which result from the product's attributes.

MESSAGE ELEMENTS are the differentiating physical attributes of the product explicitly communicated, either verbally or visually, in a commercial

FIGURE 2.6 Decision-based Framework for Positioning Strategy Specification.

scored in terms of allocating 100 points. One could have, from bottom-up, 40–30–20–10, or with the same strategic elements, 10–20–30–40. These are different strategies, one of which, given the competitive communication environment, is demonstrably better than the other.

The management decisions as to determining both the differentiating decision-based orientations and the relative weighting assume an understanding of the existing, competitive strategies in the marketplace. This suggests that management has documented in this customer-decision format the competitive communication strategies over time. To be overly optimistic, this process of strategic assessment of advertising is present in less than 5% of companies. This assessment obviously has a considerable impact on the determination of the optimal brand strategy specification.

What is more than curious is the fact that when asked, marketing professionals give significantly different assessments of the same ads. A recent exercise across a group of managers in the process of conducting strategic research to optimize brand strategy is that the range of their subjective assessments of the relative strength of the respective levels varied, on average, by over 30%, with some more than 50%. Put as delicately as possible, how can strategy be optimized if there is a lack of common understanding of even how ads, including their own, actually do communicate a given strategy? Thus, it is highly recommended that this strategic grounding skill be incorporated into the marketing function. To not do so is tantamount to endorsing the point of view that management knows what is best and why, and doesn't need to be confused by any systematic assessment of the historical, competitive media environment. Unfortunately, this is the common status quo.

Strategic Assessment and Implications for Advertising Development

To provide norms for advertising assessment so as to provide a basis for learning, a strategic assessment or ads based upon the principles of neural networks works well (Reynolds & Rochon, 1991). The quantitative portion of this conceptual framework provides the following: (a) for each code element by level of abstraction in the MECCAS model, a percentage of respondents which believed that ideas were clearly communicated, (b) the strength of the connection or association between the decision elements/codes at the adjacent levels of abstraction, and (c)] measures of brand affect (motivates purchase) and ad affect (entertainment value).

Figure 2.7 illustrates how a given *a priori* positioning strategy for cookies in a MECCAS format can be translated to statement codes at the respective levels. Again, the percentages reflect the number of respondents who thought that concept was clearly communicated in this ad. The association or linkage scores range from 0–9 based upon a combination of the pair of code scores and the degree of association directly rated by the respondent. The affect scores

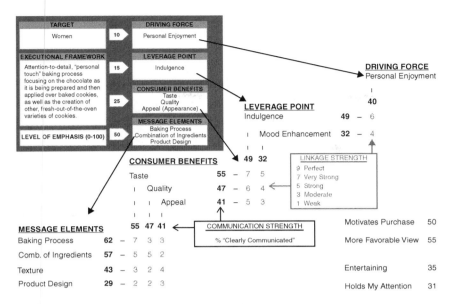

FIGURE 2.7 Strata Ad Assessment Framework.

also represent measures of the percentage of respondents which indicated that this code phrase was clearly true. For example, in the "Chocolate" ad summarized here, 50% of the respondents believed that this ad "Motivates Purchase."

The interpretation of this neural analysis framework is primarily based on two criteria, namely, to what degree does the ad correspond to the *a priori* strategy and how strongly the strategic elements are connected, building one complete network from Message Elements (attributes) to Driving Force (personal values). In this example, the largest complete network is 7+7+6 or 20 or a possible 27. This is excellent, which corresponds to the very high rating of Motivating Purchase at 50%. This research-based diagnostic methodology provides the basis for both understanding how ads communicate and providing a basis for training.

Preliminary findings of meta-analysis of 240 ads, across seven countries, four distinct product spaces (with varying ranges of involvement), and two levels of executional type (finished vs. animatics), using the strata framework, yielded the following findings in terms of the relationship between the sum of the complete network of connections:

There is no difference between finished and animatic ads (they about equally predict Motivates Purchase at a very high level of R-square of .60 (see Reynolds & Gengler, 1991). Importantly, this finding offers a strong reason to subject animatics to strategic assessment, because this methodology can accurately assess the potential success of an ad idea, therefore impacting the management decision whether to go to finish production, or, in virtually all cases, providing specific input as to how to improve the ad.

Contrasting the predictive ability of the Strategic model (sum of highest connections by one common ladder) and Entertainment level to Motivates Purchase suggests that different models (central and peripheral) exist based on the level of involvement, meaning that advertising works differently for different level-of-involvement categories (see Petty, Cacioppo & Shuman, 1983). Knowing what the relative importance of the strategy vs. entertainment provides insight as to creative focus. In general, for consumer goods and services, the neural-based strategy model (central) accounts for Motivating Purchase five times more than does Entertainment (peripheral).

Overall, the learning by management provides them significant insight into assessing all of their communications, as well as those of the competition, which reinforces the skills needed to conduct and manage an ongoing historical file.

In sum, the conclusion is that means-end is a special case of neural networks that corresponds to the basis of decision-making. This finding gives validity to the entire research and strategy optimization process.

Also noteworthy are the prior research findings using the strata model (Reynolds, Gengler & Howard, 1995) which indicate that advertising works differently depending on a customer's brand loyalty. The key finding here is that it is critical for ads to be effective for the target audience of competitive brand loyals to build connections or linkages between the decision elements. Why? Because new associations that underlie decision-making have to be constructed, this finding simply may be explained as learning.

Given the importance of connections with respect to their predictive relationship to Motivating Purchase, a key takeaway with regard to the advertising development process is to focus creatives on this critical task. Creative should be asked to specify what in the ad will cause the connected associations between the designated key strategic elements (Gengler & Reynolds, 1995). If they cannot clearly specify how these key strategic associations will be made in the mind of the customer, the creative ad concept is in question. Some general ideas for the implementation of means-end-based strategy to advertising creative are provided by Reynolds and Whitlark (1995).

Summary

The centerpiece of this article is that the key to optimizing marketing strategy is to gain an understanding of customer decision-making, in particular, the basis of brand loyalty for one's own brand as well as for the competition. The contrasting of these findings defines the marketing battle field. The guiding strategic principle is that optimal strategy leverages decision equities and supplants the corresponding disequities relative to the competition. The pathway to solve marketing problems involves the management process of formally answering four fundamental questions, which then can be answered through formal decision-making research methodologies that yield as the basis for a

decision-based segmentation. It is this output that provides the necessa
ture required to develop strategic options for discussion and evaluatio

The primary rationale underling this strategy development proce
marketing management is not typically on the same page, due to the
form of bias exists as a result of managers defining the marketing prob
both explicit and implicit assumptions. These latent assumptions, which managers are not typically aware of, create the bias guiding the strategy development
and implementation process. The marketing problem framing process, which is
suggested to be individually developed prior to strategy development discussion,
provides the basis to both understand and resolve this problem. This critical
management outcome results from contrasting, exploring, and questioning the
different responses to the framing questions. The perspective offered is that the
CEO is ultimately responsible for the management of this brand strategy development process, and that the framing exercise suggested here gives a management
blueprint to both focus and thus improve the long-term marketing management
contributions to maximizing the strategic equity of the brand franchise.

Once the marketing problem is framed, the answer lies in understanding
customer decision-making. The distinction highlighted is that marketing research is not decision research, and should not be assumed to provide these
critical, strategy-determining insights. The best way to summarize strategy
process is a graphical depiction (see Figure 2.8), where the darken icons reflect
management's direct responsibilities.

Management and Research Component Functions

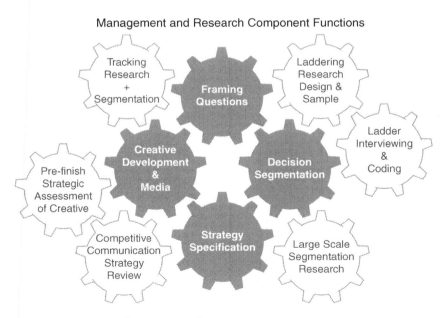

FIGURE 2.8 Strategy Optimization Process.

Note this process summary the light-colored, interconnected "gears" of laddering research[2] provide the decision segments, which can then be used as a basis for larger scale quantification. This marketing research function is a hybrid, in that its primary focus is to uncover the relationships of these decision segments in a traditional marketing research framework.

The decision segmentation combined with the additional marketing research input, then, affords the strategists the necessary insight into optimizing brand positioning strategy. Importantly, an additional input of value is a communication strategy audit of the entire competitive marketplace over time.

With the strategy in place, the handoff to the creative process is discussed with a point of view, based upon recent research findings regarding the centerpiece of successful positioning advertising. This centerpiece is simply making as tight as connections as possible between the adjacent levels of the decision-making network.

Suggested as part of the creative development process is to assess the degree to which rough copy, traditionally in the form of animatics, creates these success-determining connections in the minds of customers (current and potential). The obvious value of this research step is providing additional insight with respect to how to improve the strength of the connections, or in some cases, to make the decision to not go ahead with the finished production.

The last "gear" in Figure 2.8 was not discussed, but is worth brief mention. Completing the strategic research function is tracking, with decision segmentation as a foundation. This marketplace monitor should also include (a) demographics, (b) current consumption or use, and brand consumption trends, (c) brand equity assessment, (d) promotional involvement, e advertising recognition, and (f) media profiles. This format should provide the necessary feedback to revisit, identify, and reframe marketing problems.

Notes

1 Prototypical consumer goods and services segmentation utilizes a combination of demographic and attitudinal variables to develop homogeneous clusters or groups. As part of this statistical analysis, variable weighting systems are put into place for future segment classification. These methodologies rarely, if ever, report how well the segments discriminate combinations of brand preference, brand loyalty, and/or consumption amount. Without evaluative statistics of this type (simple indexing does not count), relying on these methods as the pillar of strategy development is suboptimal.

2 Reynolds and Phillips (2010) found that a majority of companies that sell laddering research do not follow the stated methodology (Reynolds & Gutman, 1988) which requires formal coding and the development of decision maps based upon quantitative analysis. Rather, these nonconforming companies treat laddering as simply a qualitative technique, and base the output maps on subjective judgment. (Note: Be sure to check the laddering data, coding, and quantitative counts underlying map construction.)

References

Gengler, C. & Reynolds, T. J. (1995). Consumer Understanding and Advertising Strategy, Analysis, and Strategic Translation of Laddering Data. *Journal of Advertising Research*, 35, 19–33.

Gutman, J. (1982). A Means-end Chain Model based on Consumer Categorization Processes. *Journal of Marketing*, 46, 60–72.

Gutman, J. & Reynolds, T. J. (1979). An Investigation at the Levels of Cognitive Abstraction Utilized by Consumers in Product Differentiation. In *Attitude Research Under the Sun*. (ed.) J. Eighmey, Chicago: American Marketing Association.

Norton, J. Reagan-Bush '84 (2008). Darden Case No. UVA-M-0340. SSRN: http://ssn.com/abstract=909944.

Olson, J. C. & Reynolds, T. J. (2001). The Means-End Approach to Understanding Consumer Decision Making. In *Understanding Consumer Decision-Making: The Means-End Approach to Marketing and Advertising Strategy*. (eds.) T.J. Reynolds, and J.C. Olson, Mahwah, NJ: Lawrence Erlbaum Associates.

Perkins, W. S. & Reynolds, T. J. (1995). Interpreting Multidimensional Data with Cognitive Differentiation Analysis. *Psychology & Marketing*, 12, 481–499.

Petty, R. E., Cacioppo, J. T. & Schumann, D. (1983). Central and Peripheral Routes to Advertising Effectiveness: The Moderating Role of Involvement. *Journal of Consumer Research*, 10, 532–543.

Phillips, J. & Reynolds, T. J. (2009). On the Hierarchical Structure of Means-end Theory: A Hard Look at Hard Laddering. *Qualitative Marketing Research – An International Journal*, 12, 83–99.

Phillips, J. & Reynolds, T. J. & Reynolds, K. (2010). Decision-based Voter Segmentation: An Application for Campaign Message Development. *European Journal of Marketing*, 44, 310–330.

Reynolds, T. J. (2006). Methodological and Strategy Development Implications of Decision Segmentation. *Journal of Advertising Research*, 46, 445–461.

Reynolds, T. J. (2010). Determining Strategies for Increasing Loyalty of a Population to an Entity." United States Patent Nos. 7,769,626 and 8,301,482 (Decision Research Methodology and Decision Analysis Program and Algorithms, respectively).

Reynolds, T. J. & Craddock, A. (1988). The Application of the MECCAS Model to the Development and Assessment of Advertising Strategy: A Case Study. *Journal of Advertising Research*, 28, 43–54.

Reynolds, T. J. & Gengler, C. (1991). The Strategic Assessment of Advertising: The Animatic Versus Finished Issue. *Journal of Advertising Research*, 31, 61–71.

Reynolds, T. J., Gengler, C. & Howard, D. (1995). A Means-End Analysis of Brand Persuasion through Advertising. *International Journal of Research in Marketing*, 12, 257–266.

Reynolds, T. J. & Gutman, J. (1984). Advertising is Image Management. *Journal of Advertising Research*, 24, 27–36.

Reynolds, T. J. & Gutman, J. (1988). Laddering Theory, Method, Analysis and Interpretation. *Journal of Advertising Research*, 28, 11–31.

Reynolds, T. J. & Phillips, C.B. (2005). In Search of True Brand Equity Metrics: All Market Share Ain't Created Equal. *Journal of Advertising Research*, 45, 171–186.

Reynolds, T.J. & Phillips, J. (2009. A Review and Comparative Analysis of Laddering Research Methods: Recommendations for Quality Metrics. In *Review of Marketing Research*. (ed.) N. Malhotra. Bingley: Emerald Group Publishing Limited.

Reynolds, T. J. & Rochon, J. (1991). Strategy-Based Advertising Research: Copy Testing is Not Strategy Assessment. *Journal of Business Research*, 22, 131–142.

Reynolds, T. J. & Rochon, J. (2001). Consumer Segmentation Based on Cognitive Orientations: The ChemLawn Case. In *Understanding Consumer Decision-Making: The Means-End Approach to Marketing and Advertising Strategy.* (eds.) T. J. Reynolds, and J. C. Olson. Mahwah, NJ: Lawrence Erlbaum Associates.

Reynolds, T. J., Rochon, J. & Westberg, S. (2001). A Means-End Chain Approach to Motivating the Sales Force: The Mary Kay Strategy. In *Understanding Consumer Decision-Making: The Means-End Approach to Marketing and Advertising Strategy.* (eds.) T. J. Reynolds and J. C. Olson. Mahwah, NJ: Lawrence Erlbaum Associates.

Reynolds, T. J. & Westberg, S. J. (2001). Beyond Financial Engineering: A Taxonomy if Strategic Equity." In *Understanding Consumer Decision-Making: The Means-End Approach to Marketing and Advertising Strategy.* (eds.) T. J. Reynolds, and J. C. Olson. Lawrence Erlbaum Associates.

Reynolds, T. J. & Whitlark, D. B. (1995). Applying Laddering Data to Communication Strategy and Advertising Practice. *Journal of Advertising Research*, 35, 9–17.

SECTION II

Specific Applications of Values Research and Theory

Values guide behaviors and judgments across specific situations, including consumer behaviors, politics, and lifestyles. Accordingly, this section introduces examples of values research and values theory applications.

Patara and Tanskul introduce the concept of self-sufficiency and suggest that self-sufficiency values (SSV) may dilute the negative influence of materialism on happiness. After developing a scale of SSV based on a "middle path" that is embedded in Buddhist teaching, Patara and Tanskul look at the relations among materialism, social support, self-sufficiency, and happiness. Their findings show that those consumers who are self-sufficient are happier with their lives, regardless of their exposure to materialistic values. The authors suggest that self-sufficiency can also guard against other negative effects of materialism.

Haberstroh and Orth examine how self-construal influences consumer response to marketing visuals. More specifically, the authors suggest that visual harmony is more attractive to people with an interdependent, compared to independent, self-construal. Because visual harmony is perceived as a congruent pattern or arrangement of parts that combines symmetry, balance, and proportion, it is more consistent with a collective self, viewing oneself in agreeable relationships with others. Based on experimental data from seven countries, the authors found that interdependent self-construal indeed enhances the positive effect of design harmony on consumer evaluation of attractiveness. This finding will help marketing managers and product designers to employ visual design across cultures that have different social and cultural values.

Ulusoy and Barretta examine the value systems and their effects on the process of fragmentation in the culture and the development of the subcultural ethos. Specifically, the authors argue that the problems (social, cultural, and environmental) associated with the mainstream culture lead to discontentment with and resistance to the mainstream culture. As a result, people start the quest for social and cultural transformation as well as the quest for the alternative identities and self-expression. This quest eventually leads to the fragmentation of the mainstream culture through subcultures. As an example, Ulusoy and Barretta discuss how some of the values from the List of Values (Kahle, 1996) may mean different things to the members of subcultures.

Larsen and Kahle examine the success of the Independent DIY (Do It Yourself) Lifestyle Blogging Business model through the Indie Girl Culture (IGC). More specifically, the authors analyzed how three historical movements (i.e. the Handmade movement, the Arts and Crafts movement, and the punk subculture) combined with progressive marketing theories (i.e. Permission Marketing and Relationship Marketing), and made possible with the new opportunities created through the Internet (i.e. blogs and social media), helped to develop the Independent DIY Lifestyle Blogging Business model.

Reynolds outlines a detailed explanation of how political strategy is developed and uses this explanation as a framework for developing more predictive polling methods. He suggests that, similar to creating effective advertising strategies to create purchase intent, the new polling methodology should be based on voter decision segmentation (the core principle of strategy development) and a decision model grounded by personal values.

Rose, Merchant, Rose, Bakir, and Gentina outline a series of studies exploring attitudes toward money. By using a four-dimensional scale (i.e. achievement, status, worry, and security) to measure symbolic money attitudes and a variety of qualitative and quantitative techniques (e.g. focus groups, depth interviews, and surveys) to collect data, the authors explore the meanings of, and attitudes toward, money in different cultural settings. Accordingly, their research has produced a rich and diverse set of cross-cultural findings that compliment and supplement the findings of research on personal values.

Lee and Kahle reviewed studies that looked at how values and social media usage are related. In one study, Lee and Kahle (2016) analyzed over 20,000 tweets across four Major League Baseball teams and four sports apparel companies and found significant differences in the communication of values. In another study, the authors found that people who endorse certain values (e.g. a sense of belonging, fun, and enjoyment in life) are more likely to spend time on social media. Lee and Kahle concluded that social media offer a lens into the communication of values and thus should be examined more in the future.

3

SELF-SUFFICIENCY AND MATERIALISM

Scale Development and Its Implications

Yupin Patarapongsant * *and Nicha Tanskul*

The rise of materialism has shifted our values toward having and owning to display social status or to have material possessions to substitute for relationships. Somehow, these material possessions eventually have been perceived as our Holy Grail of personal happiness. While a constant feed of material consumption and possession may provide a viable short-term solution for momentary happiness, it also deteriorates our long-term happiness and subjective well-being. We propose that there is another viable approach, which could lead to more sustainable long-term happiness through the adoption of SSV. SSV conceptualized as the quality of feeling secure and content with one's ability. The measurement developed in our study was derived from the concept of sufficiency in the literature from psychology, consumer behavior, economics, and economic development.

Background

Back in 1932, Bernreuter pioneered in defining self-sufficiency trait as one's ability to live independently from others regarding the ordinary affairs of life. His self-sufficiency measurement was developed and tested against student subjects and demonstrated that students living away from home scored higher in self-sufficiency than those who lived at home, and male students scored higher than female students did. Follow-up research has defined self-sufficiency as one

* Corresponding author: Dr. Yupin Patarapongsant, E mail: yupin.patara@sasin.edu. Yupin Patarapongsant currently works at the Behavioral Research and Informatics in Social Sciences Research Unit, SASIN School of Business, Chulalongkorn University, Bangkok, Thailand. This research has been supported by National Research University Project, Office of Higher Education Commission, Thailand, awarded to principle investigator, Dr. Yupin Patarapongsant.

of the traits in the Narcissistic Personality Inventory (NPI) (Foster & Campbell, 2007; Raskin & Terry, 1988). In the subscale of the NPI, self-sufficiency captures awareness of one's own actions, ability to achieve something without help from others, and certainty in one's ability (Raskin & Terry, 1988). Recent research has defined someone who is self-sufficient as the one who has the ability toward personal goals or emphasis on behaviors of his or her own choosing accomplished without active involvement from others. Thus, being in a self-sufficient state would mean being hesitant to allow others to involve themselves in one's activities (Vohs, Meed, & Goode, 2006, 2008).

From an economic perspective, John Maynard Keynes (1933) introduced the concept of national self-sufficiency, which refers to the way that countries rely on their own economy rather than international trade. Recently, the United Nations Development Program [UNDP] (2007) also suggested the concept of sufficiency economy, which involves the concepts of moderation, reasonableness, and self-immunity (knowledge and integrity). The aim is to take the middle path, or middle way, from Buddhist principles as guidance in making economic decisions. Specifically, the middle path, the balance, or moderation between the otherwise polarized extremes (Kumar, 2002; Marlatt, 2003) is a guideline for developing the economy to keep up with globalization. There are three levels of sufficiency economy according to this principle. The fundamental sufficiency economy philosophy refers to the lifestyle of individuals, a group, or a small community, which places emphasis on self-reliance and work according to one's lifestyle without greed and taking advantage of others. The progressive sufficiency economy refers to mutual benefits of exchanges and cooperation among those in the community to attain community development and societal advancement. Finally, the network sufficiency economy refers to the extension of the sufficiency economy concept to macroeconomic policy.

In addition, we also investigate the concept of mindful consumption (Sheth, Sethia, & Srinivas, 2011), which overlaps with the concept of sufficiency economy in terms of the mindful mind-set in making consumption decisions.

Scale Construction

Item Generation and Initial Refinement

A Likert scale of SSV was developed based on the three conceptual thoughts, namely self-sufficiency (Foster & Campbell, 2007; Raskin & Terry, 1988; Vohs et al., 2006, 2008), the concept of mindful consumption (Sheth et al., 2011), and sufficiency economy according to United Nations Development Program (UNDP, 2007). As mentioned earlier, someone who is self-sufficient has been defined as the one who has the ability toward personal goals (Vohs et al., 2006, 2008). According to the concept of consumption stated by Sheth et al.

(2011), consumption actually is composed of tangible and intangible aspects. The tangible aspect is consumption behavior, while the intangible aspect is consumption mind-set. The consumption mind-set is the attitude, values, and expectations surrounding consumption behavior. The consumption mind-set is important because it affects consumption choice as well as how consumption has been interpreted. Mindful consumption in this case refers to the consciousness in thought and behavior regarding the consequences of consumption. The mindful mind-set refers to consumers' conscious caring toward self, community, and nature, while mindful behavior refers to a restraint from acquisitive consumption (consumption that exceeds one's needs or one's capacity to consume), repeated consumption (consumption that involves the circle of buying, discarding, and buying again), and aspirational consumption (consumption that is linked to an upward shift in consumer aspirations). Hence, consumers are more likely to make comparisons with others whose incomes are three to five times their own. In the case of sufficiency economy, as suggested by the UNDP (2007), the conceptualization of this construct contains three components: moderation, reasonableness or insights, and self-immunity system. First, the concept of moderation is focused on the idea of the middle path between basic needs and extravagance. Thus, moderation is intertwined with both the acquisitive consumption concept and the aspirational consumption concept under the big umbrella of mindful consumption. Second, the concept of reasonableness is based on the idea of evaluating the reasons for any action and understanding its consequences toward self, society, and environment. Thus, reasonableness is intertwined with the overarching approach of mindful consumption, which focuses on consumers' conscious caring toward self, community, and nature. Finally, the self-immunity concept is focused on consumers' ability to cope with unpredictable or uncontrollable events and circumstances. Besides these three components, sufficiency economy according to UNDP also requires two additional components, which are knowledge and integrity. With these combined concepts of self-sufficiency, mindful consumption, and sufficiency economy, the 50 Likert-type statements with a seven-point response scale were developed, ranging from 1 (strongly disagree) to 7 (strongly agree).

The initial list was given to panels of experts composed of two marketing professors and two industry experts. These experts were given the definition of the construct and asked to rate each item as a very good, good, fair, or poor representation of its content. According to responses from the experts, 16 items were retained. The 16 items were rated very good by at least three of the judges and poor by none of the judges. Thus, based on experts' judgment on the meaning of these items, we proceeded with a preliminary 16-item scale of SSV.

The items were arranged in a randomized order. The scale was identified as a measure of values toward self-sufficiency and administered to 430 nationally representative samples in Thailand. The survey is approximately 15 minutes in length and was administered through a telephone interview.

Items Reduction

Initial analyses involved items-to-remaining total correlation and principal components exploratory factor analysis. Three out of the 16 items were dropped due to item-to-remaining total correlations of less than .50. The remaining items were factor-analyzed. The resulting factor loadings and scree plot indicated four dominant factors with 11 items. A subsequent factor analysis on these 11 items resulted in four factor solutions that explained 63% of the total variance. Items of the resulting scale (hereinafter, SSV), respective factor loadings, and item-to-remaining total correlations are shown in Table 3.1.

Reliability and Dimensionality

Table 3.1 also contains indicators of reliability and dimensionality discussed subsequently. As for indicators of the scale's internal consistency, we calculated Cronbach's coefficient α (.893). Factor structure was examined with a confirmatory factor analysis using a principal components analysis. For a four-factor model, χ^2 (36) = 88.83, p <.01. The Comparative Fit Index (CFI) = .97. Each item's indicator t-value was significant at p <.01.

TABLE 3.1 Self-Sufficiency Values Scale Items: Dimensionality and Internal Consistency Results

Items	Second Administration Thailand	
	Factor Loading	Item-Total Correlation
I am conscious in any action I take.	.71	.65
I have right mindfulness.	.61	.64
I am living with integrity despite the hardships in life.	.56	.77
I am honest despite the hardships in life.	.50	.68
Difficult situations can be overcome.	.52	.72
I feel secure in my abilities to meet life's challenges.	.59	.63
I can perform high-quality work with little support from others.	.65	.59
I am happy with what I have.	.78	.67
I am content with what I have.	.81	.66
There are reasons for any action.	.57	.71
I believe in causes and consequences of things.	.74	.55
$\chi^2(df)$	88.83 (36)	
Significance	p <.01	
CFI	.973	
Explained variance	62.715	
Cronbach's coefficient (α)	.906	

Scale Validation

Content Validity

We assessed the construct validity throughout a different kind of validity test. We assessed the content validity through the experts to evaluate whether test items assess defined content and more rigorous statistical tests than does the assessment of face validity.

Predictive Validity

To test for predictive validity, we conducted two experimental studies in Thailand. Our hypothesis was that consumers who have high self-sufficiency would be happier despite the fact that they have faced circumstances that would lead them to become more materialistic, which generally leads to less happiness.

Data Collection: Thai Consumers Study

Design

In the study 1A, we set up a 3 × 2 quasi-experimental design with the three social supports (lack vs. control vs. high) × two SSV (high vs. low). The social support had been manipulated and SSV had been measured utilizing our self-sufficiency scales. The manipulation of social support has been proven to enhance or lessen materialistic value. Thus, those who have high social support will be less materialistic than those who are low in social support. Previous literature also demonstrated that those who are materialistic are less happy than those who are less materialistic. Hence, in this case, we have predicted that those who are high in SSV would be happier than those who are low in SSV despite the fact that they have been faced with circumstances that enhance materialistic value (lack of social support) or lessen materialistic value (strong social support). The data were collected by administering the survey to college students at a major university in Bangkok, Thailand in 2014, with the total sample size of 90.

Procedure

First, research participants were asked to rate themselves on the SSV scale. Then, participants were assigned to one of the three conditions, namely lack of social support, control social support, or high social support. We manipulated these three conditions using the manipulation adopted from Wang, Zhu, and Shiv (2012) and Pieters (2013), where in the lack of social support condition, research participants read the following statement: "I

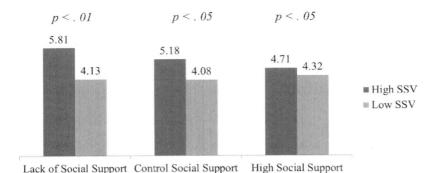

FIGURE 3.1 The Effect of Self-Sufficiency Values on Social Support and Happiness Is Significant ($F_{1,89}$ = 42.353, p = .01).

miss company. I feel I do not have real contact with people. I feel socially excluded and feel that I have no one to fall back on. I feel lonely," while in the control condition, participants read the following statement: "I have a normal relationship with others. I can have contact if I want to, but I do not always want this. I am not particularly excluded from or included in groups," and in the high social support condition, participants read the following statement: "I easily find company. I feel that I have real contact with people. I feel socially included, and I feel that I can rely on others." After reading their assigned manipulation, participants were asked to rate their happiness through the satisfaction-with-life scale (SWLS; Diener, Emmons, Larsen, & Griffin, 1985). Then, they were asked to rate their materialism using the materialism value scale by Richins (2004) as well as their perceived social support as our manipulation check before answering the general demographic questions.

Result

The result (Figure 3.1) demonstrates the significant main effect ($F_{1,89}$ = 24.353, $p < .01$) that the SSV have an impact on happiness, as we expected. Hence, those who score high in SSV are happier than those who score low in SSV regardless of whether they have faced the circumstances that enhance or lessen their materialistic values. Hence, in this case, regarding the mean score of life satisfaction composite index in the lack of social support condition (high materialistic values), the happiness scores of those who were high in SSV were significantly higher than those who were low in SSV ($M_{\text{High SSV}}$ = 5.31 vs. $M_{\text{Low SSV}}$ = 4.13, $t = 4.012$, $p < .01$). For those who were in the control social support condition (control materialistic value), the happiness scores of those who were high in SSV were marginally significantly higher than those who were low in SSV ($M_{\text{High SSV}}$ = 5.18 vs. $M_{\text{Low SSV}}$ = 4.08, $t = 2.733$, $p < .05$).

For those who were in the high social support condition (low materialistic value), the happiness scores of those who were high in SSV were marginally significantly higher than those who were low in SSV ($M_{\text{High SSV}}$ = 4.71 vs. $M_{\text{Low SSV}}$ = 4.32, t = 1.835, $p < .10$).

Discussion

The results have shown that those who report a higher SSV score are less influenced by the negativity of materialism despite the fact that they have been placed in a situation that perpetuates the rise of materialism (low social support). In this case, consumers who hold stronger SSV would be happier than consumers who rely less on SSV. Furthermore, in the case when consumers are in the control situation, when there is no situation that perpetuates the rise of materialism (control group), consumers are also able to gain benefits from holding a strong SSV. Nevertheless, in the case of those consumers already in a situation or environment that is detrimental to the rise of materialism, SSV may or may not help improve their subjective well-being significantly, as they already have other mechanisms in place to compensate for the needs of material consumption and possession, which in this case is perceived social support.

Nomological Validity

To test for nomological validity, we actually measured the related constructs, which in this case comprise Belief in Karma, New General Self-Efficacy, Long-Term Orientation, and Meaning in Life. We found that our self-sufficiency scales, which are based on moderation, reasonableness, self-immunity, knowledge, and integrity, are significantly correlated with Belief in Karma (Kopalled, Lehmann, & Farley, 2010), in which good actions or bad actions in the present also have an impact on our future ($r = .384$, $p <. 01$). The Belief in Karma construct is related to the reasonableness component of our self-sufficiency scale, in which consumers evaluate reasons for any action and understand the consequences of it. Our self-sufficiency scale also significantly correlated with New General Self-Efficacy Scale (Chen, Gully, & Eden, 2001), in which self-efficacy is defined as belief in one's capabilities to mobilize the motivation, cognitive resources, and action needed to meet given situational demand ($r = .461$, $p < .01$). The self-efficacy construct is related to the self-immunity component of our self-sufficiency scale, in which consumers built in their internal resilience to withstand the shock and external change and their ability to cope with unpredictable or uncontrollable events. Our self-sufficiency scale also significantly related to Long-Term Orientation (Bearden, Money, & Nevins, 2006), which refers to willingness to sacrifice present benefits for long-term benefits ($r = .439$, $p < .01$). The Long-Term Orientation construct is related to the moderation and integrity components of our self-sufficiency scale, in which consumers are living in moderation as well as taking virtue as their guiding principal in living life.

Hence, they do not overindulge themselves in spending in order to ensure they have saved for the future while also seriously taking integrity as their guiding principle, so their behavioral decisions must benefit or not harm the larger society. Our self-sufficiency scale also significantly related to Meaning in Life Presence (Steger, Freizer, Oishi, & Kaler, 2006). Meaning in Life Presence refers to the situation where one feels he or she understands the purpose of his or her existence ($r = .442$, $p < .01$). Hence, when Meaning in Life is present, consumers understand what their life purpose is and what they should set priority on. Therefore, they become mindful when consuming. Our self-sufficiency scale also significantly related to Meaning in Life Search (Steger et al., 2006). Meaning in Life Search refers to the situation where consumers are aware that they are looking for their life meaning and try to find their life meaning ($r = .392$, $p < .01$). Hence, during their journey to find their life meaning, they will look for what really is important to them. Thus, this will make them look at consumption in a deeper way than before, and they will not be overly focused on just acquiring, which results in mindfulness.

Discriminant Validity

Additionally, we tested the discriminant validity of our SSV scale against the materialism scale. We found that the SSV scale does not relate to the materialism value scale. The correlation between the SSV scale and the materialism value scale by Richins (2004) was not significant. In addition, we also tested the correlation between our SSV scale and the materialism subscales, namely success, centrality, and happiness. However, the correlations between the SSV scale and the materialism value subscale were not significant. Hence, we can conclude that our SSV scale is distinct from the materialism value scale, and it is not the negative measures or reverse measures of the materialism value scale. In short, the SSV can guard against the negative effect of materialism. It is a distinct construct from materialism value, which encapsulates not only the perception toward consumption but also the guiding principle of how consumers would live their lives (Table 3.2).

Conclusion and Future Research

We hope this initial attempt on the scale development of SSV construct may generate interest to academics. We examine the SSV and demonstrate how the adoption of this value can help guard against the negative effects that arise from globalization and the rise of materialism. In this initial development scale, we have identified that our scale is able to withstand the tests of content validity, predictive validity, nomological validity, and discriminant validity. We also

TABLE 3.2 Correlation between Self-Sufficiency Values Scale and Other Scales

	Means	SD	Correlations									
			1	2	3	4	5	6	7	8	9	10
1 Belief in Karma Composite Index (1–7 scale)	6.22	1.17	1									
2 New General Self-Efficacy Composite Index (1–7 scale)	6.46	.88	.203	1								
3 Long-Term Orientation Composite Index (1–7 scale)	6.56	.95	.187	.547	1							
4 Materialism Value Short Form Composite Index (Richins) (1–7 scale)	3.66	1.37	.009	.049	.041	1						
5 Materialism Value Success Composite Index (1–7 scale)	3.96	1.89	.104	.067	.082	.734	1					
6 Materialism Value Centrality Composite Index (1–7 scale)	3.39	1.44	-.013	.037	-.020	.703	.261	1				
7 Materialism Value Happy Composite Index (1–7 scale)	3.63	2.06	-.068	.010	.021	.833	.368	.466	1			
8 Meaning in Life Present Composite Index (1–7 scale)	5.97	.95	.167	.351	.292	-.049	.019	-.023	-.099	1		
9 Meaning in Life Search Composite Index (1–7 scale)	5.95	1.26	.225	.291	.286	.161	.166	.091	.105	.439	1	
10 Self-Sufficiency Composite Index (1–7 scale)	6.55	.73	.384	.461	.439	.005	.084	-.019	-.053	.442	.392	1

Note: n = 431; all values >.15 or < –.15 are significant ($p < .05$, two–tailed) and shown in bold.

48 Yupin Patarapongsant and Nicha Tanskul

revealed that when consumers are placed in a situation where there will be the rise of materialistic value, those who have high SSV would be able to neutralize its negative impact and sustain their level of subjective well-being.

Further research can focus on whether the scale can be used in other countries with different cultural backgrounds. It would be worthwhile to study whether those who adopt a high SSV will have a higher level of happiness when faced with situations that perpetuate the rise of materialism than those who do not adopt a high SSV.

It is interesting to explore whether the SSV scale is able to withstand the validity issues with data in other countries. How does SSV mitigate the negative impact of materialism on subjective well-being? Would the value be able to reduce other negative consumption behaviors such as impulsive consumption (Baumeister, 2002) or conspicuous consumption (Belk, 1988; Berger & Ward, 2010; Douglas & Isherwood, 1978; Holt, 1995, 1998; Veblen, 1899) and enhance other positive consumption behaviors such as mindful consumption (Sheth et al., 2011).

References

Baumeister, R. F. (2002). "Yielding to temptation: Self-control failure, impulsive purchasing, and consumer behavior." *Journal of Consumer Research* **28**(4): 670–676.
Bearden, W. O., R. B. Money, and J. L. Nevins (2006). "A measure of long-term orientation: Development and validation." *Journal of the Academy of Marketing Science* **34**(3): 456–467.
Belk, R. W. (1988). "Possessions and the extended self." *Journal of Consumer Research* **15**: 139–167.
Berger, J., and M. Ward (2010). "Subtle signals of inconspicuous consumption." *Journal of Consumer Research* **37**(4): 555–569.
Bernreuter, R. G. (1932). "The measurement of self-sufficiency." *The Journal of Abnormal and Social Psychology* **28**(3): 291.
Chen, G., S. M. Gully, and D. Eden (2001). "Validation of a new general self-efficacy scale." *Organizational Research Methods* **4**(1): 62–83.
Diener, E., R. Emmons, R. Larsen, and S. Griffin (1985). "The satisfaction with life scale." *Journal of Personality Assessment* **49**(1): 71–75.
Douglas, M., and B. Isherwood (1978). *The World of Goods: Towards an Anthropology of Consumption.* New York, NY: Norton.
Foster, J. D., and W. K. Campbell (2007). "Are there such things as "narcissists" in social psychology? A taxometric analysis of the Narcissistic Personality Inventory." *Personality and Individual Differences* **43**(6): 1321–1332.
Holt, D. B. (1995). "How consumers consume: A typology of consumption practices." *Journal of Consumer Research* **22**(1): 1–16.
Holt, D. B. (1998). "Does cultural capital structure American consumption?" *Journal of Consumer Research* **25**(1): 1–25.
Keynes, J. M. (1933). "National self-sufficiency." *Studies: An Irish Quarterly Review* **22**(86): 177–193.

Kopalle, P. K., D. R. Lehmann, and J. U. Farley (2010). "Consumer expectations and culture: The effect of belief in karma in India." *Journal of Consumer Research* **37**(2): 251–263.

Kumar, S. M. (2002). "An introduction to Buddhism for the cognitive-behavioral therapist." *Cognitive and Behavioral Practice* **9**(1): 40–43.

Marlatt, G. A. (2003). "Buddhist philosophy and the treatment of addictive behavior." *Cognitive and Behavioral Practice* **9**(1): 44–50.

Pieters, R. (2013). "Bidirectional dynamics of materialism and loneliness: Not just a vicious cycle." *Journal of Consumer Research* **40**(4): 615–631.

Raskin, R., and H. Terry (1988). "A principal-components analysis of the Narcissistic Personality Inventory and further evidence of its construct validity." *Journal of Personality and Social Psychology* **54**(5): 890.

Richins, M. L. (2004). "The material values scale: Measurement properties and development of a short form." *Journal of Consumer Research* **31**(1): 209–219.

Sheth, J. N., N. K. Sethia, and S. Srinivas (2011). "Mindful consumption: A customer-centric approach to sustainability." *Journal of the Academy of Marketing Science* **39**(1): 21–39.

Steger, M. F., P. Freizer, S. Oishi, and M. Kaler (2006). "The meaning in life questionnaire: Assessing the presence of and search for meaning in life." *Journal of Counseling Psychology* **53**(1): 80.

Veblen, T. (1899). *The Theory of the Leisure Class.* New York, NY: Penguin.

Vohs, K. D., N. L. Mead, and M. R. Goode (2006). "The psychological consequences of money." *Science* **314**(5802): 1154–1156.

Vohs, K. D., N. L. Mead, and M. R. Goode (2008). "Merely activating the concept of money changes personal and interpersonal behavior." *Current Directions in Psychological Science* **17**(3): 208–212.

Wang, J., R. J. Zhu, and B. Shiv (2012). "The lonely consumer: Loner or conformer?" *Journal of Consumer Research* **38**(6): 1116–1128.

4

"I" VALUE CONTRAST, BUT "WE" APPRECIATE HARMONY

Self-Construal Reflects Cultural Differences in Response to Visual Design

Kristina Haberstroh and Ulrich R. Orth

Introduction

Firms and businesses are operating in an increasingly multinational and multi-cultural environment. Here, they encounter customers and consumers varying in cultural values and concepts of self. Because values and self-concepts guide consumer behavior (Kim et al., 2002; Limon, Kahle, & Orth, 2009), better tailoring marketing stimuli, especially visuals, to target audiences requires a more in-depth understanding of the specific processes involved in individual and cultural differences.

Effects of visual design on consumer response have been established with a number of marketing stimuli including products (Bloch, 1995; Cho & Schwarz, 2010), packages (Orth & Crouch, 2014), logos (Henderson, Giese, & Cote, 2004; Zhang, Feick, & Price, 2006), and typefaces (Giese et al., 2014). In the marketplace, visual design distinguishes offers and aids in the formation of consumer relationships (Hollins & Pugh, 1990), driving first impressions and judgments, which, in turn, affect consumption decisions (Bloch, 1995).

In line with Gestalt theory (Wertheimer, 1925; Koffka, 1935), the visual appearance of a stimulus (i.e. its design) traces back to a few generic design factors (such as harmony) and ultimately to specific elements which conspire to impact individual perception, processing, and response (Henderson & Cote, 1998). A few studies have examined cultural similarities and differences in viewer response to marketing visuals. The findings include effects of individual values on the impressions consumers infer from brand packages (Limon, Kahle, & Orth, 2009), effects on the evaluation of company logos (Van der Lans et al., 2009), and proportion as a design element influencing aesthetic perception (Pittard, Ewing, & Jevons, 2007). Outside the realm of marketing visuals, cross-cultural research has concentrated on people's individualism-collectivism as a key concept reflecting individual and cultural differences in *self-construal*. In individualistic cultures (e.g. the United States and Australia), people view themselves as independent, emphasizing self-reliance, autonomy, and competition (Markus & Kitayama, 1991). Contrasting this perspective, people in collectivistic cultures (e.g. China) view themselves as interdependent, emphasizing in-group harmony and sociability (Markus & Kitayama, 1991).

While anecdotal evidence exists linking cultural values with visual harmony (e.g. the Chinese Feng Shui principle which requires objects to be positioned in a specific order so as to achieve harmony), little is known on how self-construal relates to harmony across cultures. Addressing this gap, this chapter aims to shed light on this issue, particularly on how an interdependent versus independent self-construal relates to consumer perception of harmony in marketing visuals. Understanding these relations should enable readers to more successfully employ design harmony across cultures and types of marketing visuals.

Summarizing and refining what is known about marketing and consumer psychology research in relation to visual design and cross-cultural issues, the chapter is structured as follows: the first section introduces literature on the visual design of products, the generic design factor harmony, and consumer response to visual harmony, including a comprehensive overview and empirical studies. Then, a detailed review of effects of self-construal on consumer behavior follows, with a particular emphasis on the role of self-construal in the evaluation of visual design. This section also introduces empirical results of a large international study detailing the moderating effect of self-construal on the design harmony—attractiveness relationship. Finally, the chapter closes with a discussion of implications for research and practice, elaborating guidelines for optimizing products, packages, logos, and typefaces.

Visual Design and Harmony in Design

Visual Design

While human response to design is informed by the full range of input received through all senses (vision, touch, taste, smell, and hearing), this chapter focuses solely on visual design because the sense of vision is the primary one (Hollins & Pugh, 1990).

Visual design is an important phenomenon in our lives and a key consideration in creating commercial offers (Bloch, 1995). Marketing visuals in a stricter sense include logos, typefaces, packages, and the design of products, and in a broader sense include interiors of retail environment, cars, or servicescapes (Orth & Crouch, 2014). Bloch (1995) conceptualizes consumer reactions to the visual design of products. According to his framework, designers create the visual appearance of a product by combining basic elements such as shape, materials, and colors, with the aim of forming a unified whole. When viewing a visual, design elements are then aggregated into more complex higher-level factors of design. Initially, Henderson and Cote (1998) identified *naturalness, harmony,* and *elaborateness* as generic design factors for logos and typefaces. Orth and Malkewitz (2008) later corroborated these three design factors with more complex objects such as packages of fast-moving consumer goods. The factors also apply across national samples and can thus be considered universal (Van der Lans et al., 2009). Taken together, extant research suggests that consumer response to design should be studied from a perspective of higher-order design factors rather than single design elements.

Viewer response to visual design includes cognition and affect. Cognitive response refers to the judgments consumers consciously form about a stimulus. These judgments include aesthetic impression (e.g. judgment of attractiveness), semantic interpretation (e.g. ease of use, functional benefits, and quality), and symbolic association (Crilly, Moultrie, & Clarkson, 2004). For example, the symbolic associations elicited by a product or brand may transmit the kind of person someone is or wants to be because consumers use possessions to create and define their self-concept (Creusen & Schoormans, 2005). Affective response includes feelings such as pleasure, and extends to liking (Reber, Schwarz, & Winkielman, 2004). Ultimately, design-evoked cognition and affect influence consumer behavior toward the stimulus, often conceptualized as approach-avoidance (Bloch, 1995).

A number of individual and situational factors can impact how visual design relates to consumer response. Prominent among those factors are individual differences in visual perception (e.g. CVPA: Bloch, Brunel, & Arnold, 2003; field dependence: Orth & Crouch, 2014), but also enduring traits and personality characteristics such as personal values (Limon, Kahle, & Orth, 2009) and concepts of self (Zhang, Feick, & Price, 2006). Initial findings suggest that individual response to visual design could be a reflection of the values and self-concept a person holds (Bloch, 1995; Crilly, Moultrie, & Clarkson, 2004).

A key consideration in visually designing commercial stimuli is to increase their attractiveness (Dion, Berscheid, & Walster, 1972; Orth & Malkewitz, 2008). Attractive designs catch viewer attention (Pieters, Wedel, & Batra, 2010), enhance liking (Bloch, 1995), add value (Orth, Campana, & Malkewitz, 2010), distinguish offers (Orth & Malkewitz, 2012), and build equity (Henderson et al., 2003). Capturing the hedonic value of an offer, attractiveness also contributes to the formation of consumer-brand relationships (Chitturi, Raghunathan, &

Mahajan, 2008), preferences (Stoll, Baecke, & Kenning, 2008), intentions (Chitturi, Raghunathan, & Mahajan, 2008), and behavior (Vieira, 2010). Although consumer behavior may be influenced by a score of other factors, a stimulus' attractiveness plays a pivotal role as it shapes the first encounter.

Harmony: A Generic Design Factor

Design research has made great strides with the advent of Gestalt psychology. Conceived in the 1920s by German psychologists Wertheimer, Koffka, and Köhler (Koffka, 1935), the Gestalt principle posits that viewers group concrete elements of a visual scene together such that they form a greater whole. Designers are particularly interested in the Gestalt principle because it provides them with a widely acknowledged and commonly applicable conceptual model for explaining the human tendency to group objects. According to Gestalt theory, the whole is not merely the sum of its parts or elements, but rather a holistic (higher-level) configuration (or interpretation) which appears unified (Graham, 2008) and more attractive (Eysenck, 1942; Reber, Schwarz, & Winkielman, 2004).

Aesthetics and thus attractiveness of a stimulus follow Gestalt principles with commonly acknowledged drivers of attractiveness including balance, proportion, *harmony,* and variety (Kim, 2006; Kumar & Garg, 2010). Harmony is also one of the design factors found to drive attractiveness evaluations for logos, typefaces, and packages across countries (Henderson & Cote, 1998; Orth & Malkewitz, 2008).

The Oxford English Dictionary (2014) defines harmony as the combination or adaptation of parts, elements, or related things, so as to form a consistent and orderly whole. Synonyms of harmony are agreement, accord, and congruity. Design researchers more narrowly view harmony as "a congruent pattern or arrangement of parts that combines symmetry and balance and captures good design from Gestalt perspective" (Henderson & Cote, 1998, p. 16). According to Henderson and Cote's research, for example, a logo that uses elements symmetric around multiple axes would be perceived as more harmonious than the one that does not. For typefaces, harmony includes balance, smoothness, symmetry, and uniformity (Henderson, Giese, & Cote, 2004).

Kumar and Garg (2010) emphasize unity as a constitutive element of design harmony. Here, harmony is defined as the degree to which the visual resources of a composition's design form a coherent, unified pattern. This is why harmony and unity are often used interchangeably (Lin, 2013). Unity hereby refers to a "congruity among the elements of a design such that they look as though they belong together or as though there is some visual connection [...]" (Veryzer, 1993, p. 226).

In summary, key characteristics of a harmonious design include symmetry, proportion, and balance. These elements are employed to make a design well-ordered and, therefore, favorable to look at. Symmetry affects the visual perception of form and is detected holistically during the first glance (Locher & Nodine, 1989). Symmetry can be achieved with relative ease by reflecting objects about one or more axes (Hekkert & Leder, 2008). Proportion can be defined as the relationship between the horizontal and vertical dimensions (Wong, 1993) and some proportions—especially the one labeled "divine" (a ratio of 1.618:1)—are more aesthetically pleasing than others (Plug, 1980). Balance in design represents an equilibrium between two weights or components of the design (Henderson & Cote, 1998).

Another consideration in creating harmonious designs is the interplay of colors (Wei et al., 2014). Low contrast between colors that appear close to each other, matching color combinations, and little variety in colors make for more harmonious designs (Orth & Malkewitz, 2008; Lin, 2013). As such, color harmony is defined as an interaction between saturation harmony and hue and lightness harmony (Pieters, 1979).

Finally, design harmony traces back to smoothness, roundness, and visual connectedness (Henderson, Giese, & Cote, 2004). Angular (unharmonious) designs tend to induce associations with conflict and masculinity, whereas roundness is associated with friendliness and softness (Pittard, Ewing, & Jevons, 2007). Roundness has been suggested to be a major driver for cultural differences in response to design harmony.

In sum, a number of design characteristics and elements contribute toward visual harmony, leading Lin (2013, p. 1114) to conclude that harmony is "the extent to which the arrangement of design elements makes the relationship between the elements aesthetically pleasing."

Consumer Response to Visual Harmony

Research has found design elements individually (e.g. color, symmetry, and proportion) as well as jointly (as the holistic factor harmony) to influence consumer response. Generally, consumers prefer harmony to disharmony because humans have an innate tendency to see things that are close together or that look, sound, or feel as though as they belong together (Wertheimer, 1925). In other words, consumers prefer designs that follow Gestalt laws of harmony and unity over designs that violate those laws (Veryzer, 1993).

Among the drivers of preference is positive affect. For example, harmonious logo design can elicit positive feelings with viewers (Henderson & Cote, 1998). With Chinese consumers, angular stimuli evoke feelings of power but also of conflict, bad luck, and friction (Schmitt & Simonson, 1997). Japanese respondents perceive abstract figures with rounded elements as good, beautiful, strong, and powerful (Tzeng, Trung, & Rieber, 1990). The results of an experiment by Veryzer and Hutchinson (1998) provide proof of positive effects of unity on aesthetic emotions across nine different product categories (e.g. bathroom scales, clocks, and telephones).

Regarding cognitive responses, the visual harmony of packaged consumer goods strongly relates to brand personality (Orth & Malkewitz, 2008). Symmetry in abstract patterns is a strong predictor in attractiveness judgments (Jacobsen & Höfel, 2003; Tinio & Leder, 2009). Similar results are found in context of facial attractiveness research where symmetrical faces are preferred over nonsymmetrical ones (Grammer & Thornhill, 1994). Harmony also directly and positively impacts the perceived ease of use of websites (Lin, 2013), the price consumers expect to pay for a bottle of wine, and quality judgments (Orth, Campana, & Malkewitz, 2010). Taken together, across a range of categories, there is substantial evidence for the impact harmony has on viewer response to visual stimuli including logos (Henderson & Cote, 1998), packages (Orth, Campana, & Malkewitz, 2010), and products (Veryzer & Hutchinson, 1998) but also for websites (Lin, 2013).

The reasons for people's overall positive response to visual harmony, however, are not fully understood (Hekkert & Leder, 2008), in part because people lack the ability to articulate the relationship between harmony and their response (Veryzer, 1993). This gap in knowledge is magnified by a number of individual differences that possibly impact the visual design–response relationship. Often classified as personal characteristics, cultural influences, innate design preferences, and situational factors, these individual differences moderate (i.e. enhance or mute) cognitive, affective, and behavioral responses to visual design (Bloch, 1995; Crilly, Moultrie, & Clarkson, 2004). Evaluation of a design's attractiveness thus not only depends on properties of the stimulus (e.g. the harmony factor) but additionally on characteristics of the viewer. For example, a person's centrality of visual product aesthetics (Bloch, Brunel, & Arnold, 2003), motivation (Chitturi, Raghunathan, & Mahajan, 2008), and cultural context (Bloch, 1995) have all been related to divergent outcomes in individuals' evaluation of design attractiveness. In particular, a person's culture has been suggested to be a major factor in how attractive people find marketing stimuli (Bloch, 1995; Crilly, Moultrie, & Clarkson, 2004). Cross-cultural marketing studies, in fact, demonstrate that significant differences exist in how consumers respond to visual harmony overall (Henderson et al., 2003; Van der Lans et al., 2009) and specific elements such as angularity (Zhang, Feick, & Price, 2006). An overview of studies examining consumer response to visual harmony is summarized in Table 4.1. In summary, not all people respond in the same way to the configural aspects captured in the design factor harmony, and a significant portion of those differences may trace back to cultural factors, reflecting different concepts of self.

TABLE 4.1 Summary of Findings of Consumer Response to Visual Harmony

Study	Stimuli	Harmony Variable	Dependent Variable	Moderator	Key Findings
Grammer and Thornhill (1994)	Faces	Symmetry	Attractiveness	Sex	Facial symmetry has a positive influence on facial attractiveness ratings
Jacobsen and Höfel (2003)	Graphic pattern	Symmetry	Aesthetic judgment	None	Symmetry shows a strong positive correlation with beautiful judgments
Tinio and Leder (2009)	Visual pattern	Symmetry (and complexity)	Aesthetic judgment	None	Symmetry is a strong predictor of beauty judgment
Veryzer and Hutchinson (1998)	Nine product categories (e.g. lamps, telephones)	Unity (and prototypicality)	Aesthetic response	None	The results provide strong evidence for positive effects of unity on aesthetic response
Lin (2013)	Websites	Design factor harmony	Perceived aesthetic, perceived ease of use	None	Harmony has direct effects on perceived aesthetics and perceived ease of use
Orth and Malkewitz (2008)	Wine packages	Design factor harmony	Consumer brand impressions	None	Generic holistic designs are associated with brand impressions responses (e.g. excitement)
Orth, Campana, and Malkewitz, (2010)	Wine packages	Design factor harmony	Price expectation	CVPA	Design harmony exerts a direct effect on price expectations and indirect effect through quality judgments
Henderson and Cote (1998)	Logos	Design factor harmony	Impressions created by logos	None	Harmony has positive influence on correct recognition and affect (U.S. consumer)

Study	Object	Design factor	Dependent variable	Moderator	Findings
Henderson et al. (2003)	Logos	Design factor harmony	Impressions created by logos	None	Harmony has positive influence on clear meaning and feng shui (Asian consumer)[a]
Van der Lans et al., 2009	Logos	Design factor harmony	Impressions created by logos	Culture	Harmony universally increases positive affect and subjective familiarity. The effect on subjective familiarity differs between the West and Asia
Tzeng, Trung, and Rieber (1990)	Icons & graphics	Roundness	Evaluation, Potency, Activity, Distinctiveness	Country	Japanese perceive rounded graphics as more beautiful and powerful than as Mexicans and Columbians
Zhang, Feick, and Price (2006)	Logos	Roundness	Attractiveness	Self-construal, consumption situation	People with independent self-construals perceive rounded shapes as less attractive than those with interdependent self-construals. The effect was more pronounced for public than for private consumption
Henderson, Giese, and Cote (2004)	Typefaces	Design factor harmony	Impressions created by typefaces	None	Harmony creates pleasantness, less engaging fonts, more reassuring fonts, and less prominent designs

a The positive influence of harmony on meaning and feng shui in Asia and not in the United States is consistent with the values placed on balance and curved elements in Asia (Henderson et al., 2003).

Self-Construal and Consumer Behavior

Over the last decades, consumer, marketing, and psychology scholars have expressed an increased interest in the concept of self. Prevalent in consumer research is Belk's (1988) use of the terms "self," "sense of self," and "identity" as synonyms for how a person subjectively perceives who she or he is. According to his theorizing, individuals possess a core self that is expanded to include items (e.g. possessions such as products and brands) that then become part of the extended self. The self also includes various groups and levels of group affiliation that extend from the core self as they become larger and more impersonal (Gaertner et al., 2012).

The groups' facet of the self is central to Social Identity Theory (Tajfel & Turner, 1979) which posits that people define their self-concepts by their connections with social groups. Researchers in marketing adopted this theory (Muniz & O'Guinn, 2001; Algesheimer, Dholakia, & Herrmann, 2005) to explain how people use brands, products, symbols, and other artifacts to construct and maintain identity (O'Donohoe, 1994). In line with symbolic interactionism theory (Levy, 1959; Solomon, 1983), consumers reflexively refer to their self-concept when encountering marketing stimuli, utilizing them as symbols (Lam et al., 2013), continuously monitoring and adjusting their behavior and consumption practices (Elliott & Wattanasuwan, 1998; Ahuvia, 2005; Escalas & Bettman, 2005), and generally behaving in agreement with their most salient self (Oyserman, 2009). We adopt this perspective and extend it to discuss how the perceived harmony in marketing visuals relates to consumer response contingent upon a person's self-construal. The following sections detail the role of self-construal in consumer behavior, including the connection between self-concept and consumer values, cultural differences in self-construal, and, in particular, the impact of self-construal on people's response to visual harmony.

Self-Concept and Values

Value theory (Kahle, Beatty, & Homer, 1986; Schwartz, 1992) aims at developing approaches to understand how, why, and to what degree people value objects; these objects could be persons, ideas, items, or anything else. Consumer values are frequently categorized according to three dimensions: internal, external, and fun and enjoyment (Kahle, Beatty, & Homer, 1986; Homer & Kahle, 1988; Kahle & Kennedy, 1988; Batra, Homer, & Kahle, 2001). Internal values include self-fulfillment, sense of accomplishment, and self-respect, whereas external values encompass sense of belonging, being well respected, security, and warm relationships with others. The last dimension, fun and enjoyment, includes excitement, fun, and enjoyment.

A number of studies have empirically demonstrated the influence of values on consumer behavior (Kamakura & Novak, 1992; Rose et al., 1994;

Kim et al., 2002). According to Homer and Kahle's (1988) cognitive hierarchy model, values exert their influence on behavior indirectly through changes in attitudes. According to this perspective, attitudes play a mediating role in the value—behavior relationship. A key factor in Kahle's List of Values (LOV) as well as in other models (Rokeach, 1973; Schwartz, 1992) is the distinction between internal versus external beliefs people hold about specific modes of conduct and as guiding principles in their life.

The literature on self-concept (Trafimow, Triandis, & Goto, 1991) suggests that differences in internal (e.g. self-fulfillment) and external (e.g. sense of belonging, warm relationships with others) values are further reflected in how people answer the question "Who am I" by focusing on the extent to which they see themselves as an autonomous and unique individual (private self) or as inextricably and fundamentally embedded within a larger social group (collective self).

Figure 4.1 illustrates the distinction between an independent and an interdependent self-construal with the larger circles representing the self, and the smaller circles representing others. For people holding independent selves (left side), the circle around the individual does not overlap with any of the "others" circles. In addition, the bold "X's," reflecting especially important, self-defining aspects of identity, tend to lie within the individual circle. The line representing the individual's self is solid to indicate that the person's self is bounded and its experiences are therefore rather stable. These features contrast with those in the right-hand side figure depicting an interdependent view of self. Here, the border surrounding the interdependent self overlaps with the other circles. Additionally, the bold "X's" rest at the intersection between the individual and his or her close relationships (i.e. with mother, brother, and friends). This shows that people holding an interdependent self are importantly connected with others and grounded in their diverse relationships.

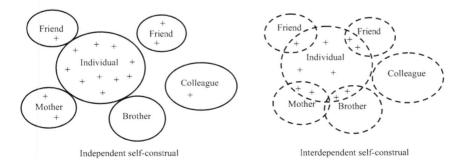

FIGURE 4.1 Representation of the Self.
Source: Adapted from Markus and Kitayama (1991), p. 226.

What people believe about the relationship between the self and others has been conceptualized as independent–interdependent *self-construal*. Self-construal captures the degree to which people see themselves as separate from others or as connected with others (Singelis, 1994). As such, self-construal refers to how an individual thinks, feels, and acts about his or her self in relationship to others. People who have an independent self-construal hold a view of self that emphasizes their separateness, autonomy, and uniqueness, whereas an interdependent self-construal is associated with a more relationship-driven, interdependent self-view, which stresses connectedness, social context, and relationships (Ahluwalia, 2008). Linking self-construal with personal values, people with an independent self-construal tend to hold more internal values such as self-fulfillment, and fun and enjoyment. People with an interdependent self-construal, in contrast, hold more external values such as sense of belonging and warm relationships with others.

Cultural Differences in Self-Construal

Culture relates to several key aspects of the self-concept, and a substantial body of research has examined cultural differences in self-construal. Extant studies converge on finding a strong and close relationship between a person's self-construal and the classification of cultures along the individualism–collectivism dimension identified by Hofstede (1980). Hofstede's work involved mapping the world in terms of individualism–collectivism by estimating individualism scores for more than 40 countries based on individual-level characteristics of IBM employees. According to his data, the most individualistic country is the United States, closely followed by other English-speaking countries and Western nations. On the other end of the continuum, countries scoring high on collectivism were found in Latin America and Asia (Hofstede, 1980, 1983).

Hofstede's conceptualization dovetails closely with a parallel stream of research (Triandis, 1989; Markus & Kitayama, 1991) showing that people from Western cultures hold more independent self-concepts, whereas people from collectivist cultures hold more interdependent self-concepts. For example, individuals in China hold family welfare more important than the well-being of the individual. If necessary, Chinese individuals would sacrifice their own well-being for the benefit of the group (Lowe & Corkindale, 1998). Kim and Markus' (1999) work corroborates cultural differences reflected in value systems as East Asian cultures emphasize harmony and individual responsibility to groups. Conformity with group standards and norms elicits positive connotations of connectedness and harmony. Western cultural values, in contrast, emphasize freedom and individual rights; uniqueness triggers positive connotations of freedom and independence (Kim & Markus, 1999). The relation between people's self-concept and culture, however, appears to be two-sided: on the one hand, self-concepts are shaped by the cultural practices that direct what individuals attend to, value, believe, and are able to attain; on the other hand, cultural practices are impacted by the self-concepts members of a culture hold (Heine, 2008).

Using dimensions of cultural variability (e.g. individualism–collectivism) to explain individual-level outcomes, however, is problematic (Gudykunst et al., 1996). First, people cannot be categorized unanimously into categories (individualistic versus collectivist) as a person can simultaneously hold both individualistic and collectivist aspects of self (Trafimow, Triandis, & Goto, 1991). Second, cultures are highly heterogeneous and contain a great variety of people as self-construal is influenced by the culture in which individuals are raised, but varies in explaining an individual's perception, evaluation, and behavior (Markus & Kitayama, 1991). Studies focusing on the influence of individual-level factors should thus investigate culturally diverse settings to increase variance and external validity.

The Impact of Self-Construal on Consumer Behavior

A number of studies have shown that people's self-concept influences their perception, evaluation, and behavior in general (Triandis, 1989; Markus & Kitayama, 1991). While some studies report a direct influence, for example, by impacting consumer decision-making styles (Hahn & Kean, 2009), others suggest an indirect effect where self-construal impacts price-quality judgments via holistic thinking (Lalwani & Shavitt, 2013). Self-construal itself can also function as a mediator, transmitting the influence of cultural individualism–collectivism on communication behavior (Gudykunst et al., 1996). Specifically, independent self-construal and individualistic values mediate the influence of cultural individualism–collectivism on the use of low-context communication (explicit and direct messages), and interdependent self-construal and collectivistic values mediate the influence of cultural individualism–collectivism on the use of high-context communication (implicit and indirect messages).

Consumer psychology research has focused on the moderating role of self-construal. For example, Ahluwalia (2008) suggests that people with an interdependent self-construal have a relational processing advantage, or a superior ability to uncover relationships, connections, or similarities between a brand and its extension. Escalas and Bettman (2005) show that—compared with consumers holding an interdependent self-construal—independent consumers respond more negatively to brands projecting images that are consistent with an out-group. One reason for these findings may be that consumers holding an independent self-construal need to emphasize uniqueness by differentiation from the out-group. More support for the moderating effect of self-construal on a variety of consumer behavioral outcomes comes from Sung, Choi, and Tinkham's (2012) report that interdependent (rather than independent) consumers evaluate a brand more favorably when situational cues in a social context are congruent with brand personality.

The main goal of individuals holding interdependent self-concepts is to belong to and fit in for the sake of relational harmony, whereas people holding an independent self-concept emphasize their separateness and uniqueness (Kanagawa, Cross, & Markus, 2001). It appears that this motivation is reflected across a range of consumer behaviors as (independent versus interdependent) consumers are strongly motivated to maintain and protect their self (Baumeister, 1986). Motivational consequences may also extend to marketing visuals as consumers prefer those that are congruent with salient aspects of their self (Wheeler, Petty, & Bizer, 2005; Sung & Choi, 2012).

The Role of Self-Construal in Consumer Evaluation of Visual Design

Consumers use marketing stimuli to construct, define, and enhance their self and to project a desired image toward themselves and others (Escalas & Bettman, 2005). As such, the visual appearance of marketing stimuli conveys a symbolic value (Creusen & Schoormans, 2005); the symbolic associations elicited by the stimulus carry information and meaning about their owner or user (Crilly, Moultrie, & Clarkson, 2004).

Among the factors influencing how visual characteristics impact consumer response, cultural values have been suggested to be one of the most influential moderators (Crilly, Moultrie, & Clarkson, 2004). Culture is an important determinant of the interpretations consumers infer and the associations they have with specific elements or factors of a visual's appearance (Creusen & Schoormans, 2005). For example, examining the visual design of food packages, Limon, Kahle, and Orth (2009) report that consumers in Turkey and Germany infer divergent brand values and develop differential purchase intentions based on those values. Highlighting the moderating role of personal values, consumers scoring high on internal values inferred greater internal brand values from packages, whereas consumers scoring high on external values inferred greater external brand values.

Cultural differences have been studied in many aspects of design evaluation (Bloch, 1995; Crilly, Moultrie, & Clarkson, 2004), but only a few studies have examined the effect of culture, values, or self-concept on design harmony, including the relationship with attractiveness. Prominent among those studies is Henderson et al.'s (2003) investigation of *cultural* differences in self-reported affective response to the design of logos in the U.S.A., China, and Singapore. Asian consumers tend to like well-rounded logos, whereas U.S. consumers tend to like more angular logos. The authors speculate that cultural differences in preferences for design harmony might lie with angular shapes possibly generating confrontational associations, and rounded shapes eliciting compromise associations. Such an interpretation is consistent with findings that angular stimuli evoke feelings of conflict with Asian individuals (Schmitt & Simonson, 1997) who also rate graphics with rounded elements to be good, beautiful, and powerful (Tzeng, Trung, & Rieber, 1990). These studies imply that people may find visual forms more appealing when the salient qualities are congruent with their cultural values.

Perhaps most important to the present context, Zhang, Feick, and Price (2006) examined whether the individual-level factor self-construal affects people's preferences for angular and rounded shapes with logos. Their findings indicate that individuals with independent self-construals perceive angular shapes as more attractive, whereas individuals with interdependent self-construals find rounded shapes more attractive (Zhang, Feick, & Price, 2006). This finding is consistent with the expectation that the associations induced by rounded shapes (e.g. friendliness, harmony) are congruent with traits and aspects of an interdependent self-construal (e.g. maintain warm relationships, sense of belonging). Conversely, the associations induced by angular shapes (e.g. toughness, confrontation) are congruent with aspects of an independent self (e.g. self-referred, need for differentiation from others). Readers should note, though, that Zhang, Feick, and Price's (2006) findings are not in line with those reported by Pittard, Ewing, and Jevons (2007) who did not find differences in preferences for the divine proportion (1.618:1 ratio, a facet of harmony) across Australian, Singaporean, and South African samples. The explanation offered states that some preferences (i.e. the one for harmony in visual proportion) may be hardwired or innate (Pittard, Ewing, & Jevons, 2007).

In sum, while researchers have examined how harmony-related design elements such as shape or proportion affect consumer response to specific visual categories such as abstract forms, logos, or icons (Zhang, Feick, & Price., 2006; Pittard, Ewing, & Jevons, 2007), Gestalt theory suggests that examining higher-level design factors may be valuable for better understanding consumer reactions across categories. Despite the limitations inherent to available studies on holistic design harmony, it appears that harmonious visuals should appeal more to interdependents than independents because people holding an interdependent self-construal tend to maintain harmonious relationships to a greater extent than those holding an independent self-construal.

Synthesizing the literature on the role of self-concept in consumer response to visual design implies an interdependent self-construal to enhance the positive effect of visual harmony on consumer evaluation of a design's attractiveness as (visual) harmony is more consistent with interdependents' collective self, to view oneself in agreeable relationships with others. To test this prediction, we conducted an online empirical study with more than 800 participants recruited in Australia, Brazil, China, France, and Germany. The countries were chosen to represent low and high scores, respectively, on Hofstede's (1983) individualism-collectivism scale. Collecting data in such a culturally diverse setting serves to increase variance in self-construal as individuals in any culture can have both an independent and interdependent self-construal but one tends

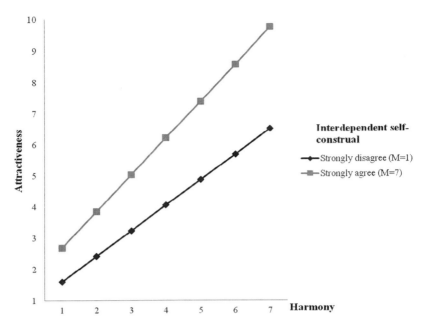

FIGURE 4.2 Illustrating the Interactive Effect of Harmony and Interdependent Self-Construal on Attractiveness.

to be predominant (Singelis, 1994). Stimuli for the study were logos, typefaces, kettles, and wine packages, preselected to score high and low, respectively, in design harmony. Participants submitted ratings of stimulus visual harmony, prototypicality (Kumar & Garg, 2010), and attractiveness (Hirschman, 1986), and indicated their self-construal (Singelis, 1994). Pooled across cultures and stimuli types, the results of moderating analysis show a significant (p >.05) harmony × interdependent self-construal interaction effect on attractiveness. As can be seen in Figure 4.2, harmony has a strong positive influence on attractiveness evaluation at high levels of interdependent self-construal, whereas the effect becomes less pronounced when interdependent self-construal was low. The independent self-construal × design harmony interaction effect was not significant. These findings provide initial evidence that an individual's self-construal interacts with design's harmony to influence individual evaluation of a design's attractiveness.

General Discussion

This chapter provides a comprehensive overview of the literature on the concept and consequences of harmony in visual design, reports empirical studies that focus on self-construal and its impact on consumer behavior, and introduces an exploratory study examining how self-construal influences attractive consumers find visual design low versus high in visual harmony across different types of marketing stimuli and countries. Because an interdependent self-construal is associated with a sense of belonging and social harmony (whereas an independent self-construal is associated with uniqueness and autonomy), we predicted and found that people with interdependent self-construals perceive harmonious design as more attractive than people with independent self-construals. As such, our results provide initial evidence that individual values related to social harmony transfer to consumer evaluation of visual stimuli.

The reviewed literature further indicates that material objects and possessions (such as visually appealing products) can serve as symbols or signs, representing socially constructed meanings and effectively reflecting their owners' self-identity including social aspects such as relations to others (Dittmar, 1992). It is noteworthy that an interdependent self-construal influences the aesthetic perception of design harmony even without explicit possession or consumption of the visual. Marketers and design professionals may find the insights useful for optimizing products, packages, logos, and typefaces, for better tailoring them to cultures varying in values and self-concepts, and thus for more effective positioning. Future research might then help to clarify why these findings occur, specifically, addressing the question of whether it is, in fact, congruity that plays a mediating role.

References

Ahluwalia, R. (2008). How Far Can a Brand Stretch? Understanding the Role of Self Construal. *Journal of Marketing Research*, 45 (June), 337–350.

Ahuvia, A. C. (2005). Beyond the Extended Self: Loved Objects and Consumers' Identity Narratives. *Journal of Consumer Research*, 32 (1), 171–184.

Algesheimer, R., Dholakia, U. M., & Herrmann, A. (2005). The Social Influence of Brand Community: Evidence from European Car Clubs. *Journal of Marketing*, 69 (3), 19–34.

Batra, R., Homer, P. M., & Kahle, L.R. (2001). Values, Susceptibility to Normative Influence, and Attribute Importance Weights: A Nomological Analysis. *Journal of Consumer Psychology*, 11 (2), 115–128.

Baumeister, R. F. (1986). *Public Self and Private Self*. New York, NY: Springer.

Belk, R. W. (1988). Possessions of the Extended Self. *Journal of Consumer Research*, 15 (2), 139–168.

Bloch, H. P. (1995). Seeking the Ideal Form: Product Design and Consumer Response. *Journal of Marketing*, 59 (3), 16–29.

Bloch, H. P., Brunel, F. F., & Arnold, T. J. (2003). Individual Differences in the Centrality of Visual Product Aesthetics: Concept and Measurement. *Journal of Consumer Research*, 29 (4), 551–565.

Chitturi, R., Raghunathan, R., & Mahajan, V. (2008). Delight by Design: The Role of Hedonic Versus Utilitarian Benefits. *Journal of Marketing*, 72 (3), 48–63.

Cho, H. & Schwarz, N. (2010). I Like Those Glasses on You, But Not in the Mirror: Fluency, Preference, and Virtual Mirrors. *Journal of Consumer Psychology*, 20 (4), 471–475.

Creusen, M. E. H., & Schoormans, J. P. L. (2005). The Different Roles of Product Appearance in Consumer Choice. *Journal of Product Innovation Management*, 22 (1), 63–81.

Crilly, N., Moultrie, J., & Clarkson, P.J. (2004). Seeing Things: Consumer Response to the Visual Domain in Product Design. *Design Studies*, 25 (6), 547–577.

Dion, K., Berscheid, E., & Walster, E. (1972). What Is Beautiful Is Good. *Journal of Personality and Social Psychology*, 24 (3), 285–290.

Dittmar, H. (1992). *The Social Psychology of Material Possessions*. New York, NY: St. Martin's Press.

Elliott, R., & Wattanasuwan, K. (1998). Brands as Symbolic Resources for the Construction of Identity. *International Journal of Advertising*, 17 (2), 131–144.

Escalas, J. E., & Bettman, J. R. (2005). Self-Construal, Reference Groups and Brand Meaning. *Journal of Consumer Research*, 32 (3), 378–389.

Eysenck, H. J. (1942). The Experimental Study of the 'good Gestalt' – A New Approach. *Psychological Review*, 49 (4), 344–364.

Gaertner, L., Sedikides, C., Luke, M., O'Mara, E. M., Iuzzini, J., Eckstein Jackson, L., et al. (2012). A Motivational Hierarchy Within: Primacy of the Individual Self, Relational Self, or Collective Self? *Journal of Experimental Social Psychology*, 48 (5), 997–1013.

Giese, J. L., Malkewitz, K., Orth, U. R., & Henderson, P. W. (2014). Advancing the Aesthetic Middle Principle: Trade-offs in Design Attractiveness and Strength. *Journal of Business Research*, 67 (6), 1154–1161.

Graham, L. (2008). Gestalt Theory in Interactive Media Design. *Journal of Humanities & Social Sciences*, 2 (1), 1–12.

Grammer, K., & Thornhill, R. (1994). Human (Homo sapiens) Facial Attractiveness and Sexual Selection: The Role of Symmetry and Averageness. *Journal of Comparative Psychology*, 108 (3), 233–242.

Gudykunst, W. B., Matsumoto, Y., Ting-Tommey, S., Nishida, T., Kim, K., & Heyman, S. (1996). The Influence of Cultural Individualism-Collectivism, Self-Construals, and Individual Values on Communication Styles across Cultures. *Human Communication Research*, 22 (4), 510–543.

Hahn, K. H. Y., & Kean, R. (2009). The Influence of Self-construals on Young Korean Consumers' Decision-making Styles. *Journal of Fashion Marketing and Management*, 13 (1), 6–19.

Heine, S. J. (2008). *Cultural Psychology*. New York, NY: W.W. Norton.

Hekkert, P., & Leder, H. (2008). Product Aesthetics. In H. N. J. Schifferstein & P. Hekkert (Eds.), *Product Experience* (pp. 259–285). San Diego, CA: Elsevier.

Henderson, P. W., & Cote, J. A. (1998). Guidelines for Selecting or Modifying Logos. *Journal of Marketing*, 62, 14–30.

Henderson, P. W., Cote, J. A., Leong, S. M., & Schmitt, B. (2003). Building Strong Brands in Asia: Selecting the Visual Components of Image to Maximize Brand Strength. *International Journal of Research in Marketing*, 20 (4), 297–313.

Henderson, P. W., Giese, J. L., & Cote, J. A. (2004). Impression Management Using Typeface Design. *Journal of Marketing*, 68 (4), 60–72.

Hirschman, E. C. (1986). The Effect of Verbal and Pictorial Advertising Stimuli on Aesthetic, Utilitarian and Familiarity Perceptions. *Journal of Advertising*, 15 (2), 27–34.

Hofstede, G. (1980). *Culture's Consequences: International Differences in Work-related Values*. Beverly Hills, CA: Sage.

Hofstede, G. (1983). National Cultures in Four Dimensions: A Research-based Theory of Cultural Differences among Nations. *International Studies of Management and Organization*, 13 (1–2), 46–74.

Hollins, B., & Pugh, S. (1990). *Successful Product Design*. London: Butterworths.

Homer, P. M., & Kahle, L. R. (1988). A Structural Equation Test of the Value-Attitude-Behavior Hierarchy. *Journal of Personality and Social Psychology*, 54 (4), 638–646.

Jacobsen, T., & Höfel, L. (2003). Descriptive and Evaluative Judgment Processes: Behavioral and Electrophysiological Indices of Processing Symmetry and Aesthetics. *Cognitive, Affective, & Behavioral Neuroscience*, 3 (4), 289–299.

Kahle, L. R., Beatty, S. E., & Homer, P. M. (1986). Alternative Measurement Approaches to Consumer Values: The List of Values (LOV) and Values and Lifestyles (VALS). *Journal of Consumer Research*, 13 (3), 405–409.

Kahle, L. R., & Kennedy, P. (1988). Using the List of Values (LOV) to Understand Consumers. *Journal of Services Marketing*, 2 (4), 49–56.

Kamakura, W. A., & Novak, T. P. (1992). Values-System Segmentation: Exploring the Meaning of LOV. *Journal of Consumer Research*, 19 (1), 119–132.

Kanagawa, C., Cross, S. E., & Markus, H. R. (2001). "Who am I?" The Cultural Psychology of the Conceptual Self. *Personality and Social Psychology Bulletin*, 27 (1), 90–103.

Kim, N. (2006). A History of Design Theory in Art Education. *The Journal of Aesthetic Education*, 40 (2), 12–28.

Kim, H., & Markus, H. R. (1999). Deviance or Uniqueness, Harmony or Conformity? A Cultural Analysis. *Journal of Personality and Social Psychology*, 77 (4), 785–800.

Kim, J.-O., Forsythe, S., Gu, Q., & Moon, S. J. (2002). Cross-cultural Consumer Values, Needs and Purchase Behavior. *Journal of Consumer Marketing*, 19 (6), 481–502.

Koffka, K. (1935). *Principles of Gestalt Psychology*. New York, NY: Harcourt, Brace & World.

Kumar, M., & Garg, N. (2010). Aesthetic Principles and Cognitive Emotion Appraisals: How Much of the Beauty Lies in the Eye of the Beholder? *Journal of Consumer Psychology*, 20 (4), 485–494.

Lalwani, A. K., & Shavitt, S. (2013). You Get What You Pay For? Self-Construal Influences Price-Quality Judgments. *Journal of Consumer Research*, 40 (2), 255–267.

Lam, S. K., Ahearne, M., Mullins, R., Hayati, B., & Schillewaert, N. (2013). Exploring the Dynamics of Antecedents to Consumer–brand Identification with a New Brand. *Journal of the Academy of Marketing Science*, 41 (2), 234–252.

Levy, S. J. (1959). Symbols for Sale. *Harvard Business Review*, 37 (July/August), 117–124.

Limon, Y., Kahle, L. R., & Orth, U. R. (2009). Package Design as a Communications Vehicle in Cross-cultural Values Shopping. *Journal of International Marketing*, 17 (1), 30–57.

Lin, J. (2013). Development of Scales for the Measurement of Principles of Design. *International Journal of Human-Computer Studies*, 71 (12), 1112–1123.

Locher, P., & Nodine, C. (1989). The Perceptual Value of Symmetry. *Computers & Mathematics with Applications*, 17 (4–6), 475–484.

Lowe, A. C-T., & Corkindale, D.R. (1998). Differences in "Cultural Values" and Their Effects on Responses to Marketing Stimuli – A Cross-cultural Study Between Australians and Chinese from the People's Republic of China. *European Journal of Marketing*, 32 (9/10), 843–867.

Markus, H. R., & Kitayama, S. (1991). Culture and the Self: Implications for Cognition, Emotion, and Motivation. *Psychological Review*, 98 (2), 224–253.

Muniz, A. M., & O'Guinn, T. C. (2001). Brand Community. *Journal of Consumer Research*, 27 (4), 412–432.

Orth, U. R., Campana, D., & Malkewitz, K. (2010). Formation of Consumer Price Expectation based on Package Design: Attractive and Quality Routes. *Journal of Marketing Theory and Practice*, 18 (1), 23–40.

Orth, U. R., & Crouch, R. C. (2014). Is Beauty in the Aisles of the Retailer? Package Processing in Visually Complex Contexts. *Journal of Retailing*. DOI: 10.1016/j.jretai.2014.05.004.

Orth, U. R., & Malkewitz, K. (2008). Holistic Package Design and Consumer Brand Impressions. *Journal of Marketing*, 72 (3), 64–81.

Orth, U. R., & Malkewitz, K. (2012). The Accuracy of Design-based Judgments: A Constructivist Approach. *Journal of Retailing*, 88 (3), 421–436.

Oyserman, D. (2009). Identity-based Motivation: Implications for Action-readiness, Procedural Readiness, and Consumer Behavior. *Journal of Consumer Psychology*, 19 (3), 250–260.

O'Donohoe, S. (1994). Advertising Uses and Gratifications. *European Journal of Marketing*, 28 (8/9), 52–57.

Pieters, J. M. (1979). A Conjoint Measurement Approach to Color Harmony. *Perception & Psychophysics*, 26 (4), 281–286.

Pieters, R., Wedel, M., & Batra, R. (2010). The Stopping Power of Advertising: Measures and Effects of Visual Complexity. *Journal of Marketing*, 74 (5), 48–60.

Pittard, N., Ewing, M., & Jevons, C. (2007). Aesthetic Theory and Logo Design: Examining Consumer Response to Proportion across Cultures. *International Marketing Review*, 24 (4), 457–473.

Plug, C. (1980). The Golden Section Hypothesis. *The American Journal of Psychology*, 93 (3), 467–487.

Reber, R., Schwarz, N., & Winkielman, P. (2004). Processing Fluency and Aesthetic Pleasure: Is Beauty in the Perceiver's Processing Experience? *Personality and Social Psychology Review*, 8 (4), 364–382.

Rokeach, M. (1973). *The Nature of Human Values*. New York, NY: The Free Press.

Rose, G. M., Shoham, A., Kahle, L. R., & Batra, R. (1994). Social Values, Conformity, and Dress. *Journal of Applied Social Psychology*, 24 (17), 1501–1519.

Schmitt, B. H., & Simonson, A. (1997). *Marketing Aesthetics*. New York, NY: The Free Press.

Schwartz, S. H. (1992). Universals in the Content and Structure of Values: Theoretical Advances and Empirical Tests in 20 Countries. *Advances in Experimental Social Psychology*, 25, 1–65.

Singelis, T. M. (1994). The Measurement of Independent and Interdependent Self-Construals. *Personality and Social Psychology Bulletin*, 20 (5), 580–591.

Solomon, M. R. (1983). The Role of Products as Social Stimuli: A Symbolic Interactionism Perspective. *Journal of Consumer Research*, 10 (3), 319–329.

Stoll, M., Baecke, S., & Kenning, P. (2008). What They See Is What They Get? An fmRI-Study on Neural Correlates of Attractive Packaging. *Journal of Consumer Behaviour*, 7 (4–5), 342–359.

Sung, Y., & Choi, S. M. (2012). The Influence of Self-Construal on Self-Brand Congruity in the United States and Korea. *Journal of Cross-Cultural Psychology*, 43 (1), 151–166.

Sung, Y., Choi, S. M., & Tinkham, S. F. (2012). Brand-Situation Congruity: The Roles of Self-Construal and Brand Commitment. *Psychology & Marketing*, 29 (12), 941–955.

Tajfel, H., & Turner, J. C. (1979). An Integrative Theory of Intergroup Conflict. In S. Worchel, & W.G. Austin (Eds.), *The Social Psychology of Intergroup Relations* (pp. 33–47). Monterey, CA: Brooks/Cole.

Tinio, P. L., & Leder, H. (2009). Just How Stable are Stable Aesthetic Features? Symmetry, Complexity, and the Jaws of Massive Familiarization. *Acta Psychologica*, 130, 241–250.

Trafimow, D., Triandis, H. C., & Goto, S. G. (1991). Some Tests of the Distinction Between the Private Self and the Collective Self. *Journal of Personality and Social Psychology*, 60 (5), 649–655.

Triandis, H. C. (1989). The Self and Social Behavior in Differing Cultural Contexts. *Psychological Review*, 96 (3), 506–520.

Tzeng, O. C. S., Trung, N. T., & Rieber, R. W. (1990). Cross-Cultural Comparisons on Psychosemantics of Icons and Graphics. *International Journal of Psychology*, 25 (1), 77–97.

Van der Lans, R., Cote, J. A., Cole, C. A., Leong, S. M., Smidts, A., Henderson, P. W., et al. (2009). Cross-National Logo Evaluation Analysis: An Individual-Level Approach. *Marketing Science*, 28 (5), 968–985.

Veryzer, R. W. (1993). Aesthetic Response and the Influence of Design Principles on Product Preferences. *Advances in Consumer Research*, 20, 224–228.

Veryzer, R. W., & Hutchinson, J. W. (1998). The Influence of Unity and Prototypicality on Aesthetic Responses to New Product Designs. *Journal of Consumer Research*, 24 (4), 374–394.

Vieira, V. A. (2010). Visual Aesthetics in Store Environment and Its Moderating Role on Consumer Intention. *Journal of Consumer Behaviour*, 9(5), 364–380.

Wheeler, S. C., Petty, R. E., & Bizer, G. Y. (2005). Self-Schema Matching and Attitude Change: Situational Dispositional Determinants of Message Elaboration. *Journal of Consumer Research*, 31 (4), 787–797.

Wei, S. T., Ou, L. C., Lou, M. R., & Hutchings, J. B. (2014). Package Design: Colour Harmony and Consumer Expectations. *International Journal of Design*, 8 (1), 109–126.

Wertheimer, M. (1925). *Drei Abhandlungen zur Gestalttheorie.* Erlangen: Philosophische Akademie.

Wong, W. (1993). *Principles of Form and Design.* New York, NY: Van Nostrand Reinhold.

Zhang, Y., Feick, L., & Price, L. J. (2006). The Impact of Self-Construal on Aesthetic Preference for Angular Versus Rounded Shapes. *Personality and Social Psychology Bulletin*, 32 (6), 794–805.

5

SUBCULTURAL ETHOS

The Dynamic Reconfiguration of Mainstream Consumer Values

Emre Ulusoy and Paul G. Barretta

Introduction

Consumer value is a critical and fundamental subject matter in the field of marketing and consumer research. Since consumption has become the key tenet of social organization in contemporary society, values constituting the ideology of consumption have increased in importance. Research on consumer values is relatively scarce and largely takes on a monolithic approach, perceiving culture as a homogeneous entity. Therefore, extant studies on consumer values overlook the growing impulse for fragmentation of the culture and thus fail to acknowledge the different and alternative value systems, discourses, and experiences outside of the mainstream culture. This chapter presents subcultures as discursively constituted social groups emerging largely as a reaction to the dominant values and discourses of mainstream modern culture. Since culture is arguably increasingly fragmented via constantly burgeoning subcultures, this chapter aims to unearth and highlight the values coalescing around subcultures that have long been overlooked in marketing and consumer research fields. To this end, we draw on extant studies in various disciplines to reveal the possible motivations behind the emerging subcultural ethos that indicate overt disjunction from that of mainstream culture.

Subcultures refer to social groups that are increasingly emerging as reactions against the mainstream culture and dominant social order by constituting their own alternative cultures and ethos largely on the basis of personal and collective choices and preferences pertaining to their worldviews, lifestyles, artistic interests, and ideological orientations (Gelder and Thornton 1997; Haenfler 2004; Hall and Jefferson 1976; Hebdige 1979; Williams 2011). A growing number of people are observed to participate in life through subcultures as they increasingly organize their worldviews, thoughts, ideologies, lifestyles, values, consumption activities, and construct their selves and/or identities in and through these subcultures in contemporary society. Therefore, studying subcultures can help to expose and understand the developments and transformations in the market and highlight the potential means and venues through which alternative identities, value systems, and cultural forms may emerge. Besides echoing the Hegelian dialectic, since subcultures are mainly considered to be the antithesis of mainstream culture (thesis), studying subcultures may provide us a broader picture and a more complete understanding with regard to the synthesis of our social world (Williams 2011).

Although research streams in consumer values and subculture have progressed, there is limited attention paid to how the List of Values (LOV) (Kahle et al. 1986) is seen from the lens of fragmented subcultures. Of particular interest, for example, is how *Sense of Belonging* is seen from a subculture lens. In the original description by Kahle and Kennedy (1988), people of this category are described as "housewives and clerical workers" who are dependent on others, representing a "home- and family-oriented value." Assessing this category from the lens of subculture, we find a sense of belonging not with mainstream society in general, but with coinciding fragments of society such as music based and other lifestyle subcultures (Cateforis and Humphreys 1997; Gardikiotis and Baltzis 2011; Haenfler 2006; Hebdige 1979; Hodkinson 2011; Miklas and Arnold 1999; Muggleton 2000).

Similarly, the description of self-respect is one that is described in Kahle and Kennedy (1988) as an "ALL American" value (quotation marks in original text). From the lens of subculture as a response to mainstream, self-respect is found not in conformity to an "American Dream" but instead in opposition to that dream. Other distinctions that are similar to these are seen when looking at the LOV through the lens of subculture emerge.

It is important to note that these distinctions are not a reflection of the appropriateness or viability of the original LOV; instead, they are an indication of societal changes that have occurred in the 30 or so years since LOV was published. Of particular interest will be the indications of these distinctions. How much of the distinction is due to changes in how values are viewed versus changes in how society has progressed; is subculture becoming more mainstream, or is mainstream becoming so fragmented that one can have membership in enough subcultures that the values need a new lens? Kahle's LOV is used as an important representation of a typography of society. Society undergoes change, and subculture is treated as a mechanism for identifying some of those changes.

Theoretical Overview

The main purpose of this chapter is to explore the dynamic value systems that may affect the process of fragmentation in the culture and the development of the subcultural ethos in various forms in contemporary society. Understanding of the underlying factors that may generate, cultivate, and/or motivate such complex phenomena is crucial. As a result of reviewing the literature, the

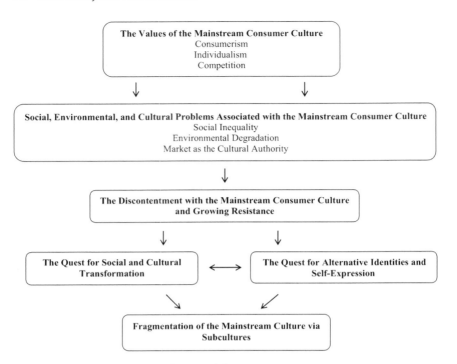

FIGURE 5.1 The Theoretical Flow Model.

underlying factors that seem to make the key contributions to the understanding of the process of fragmentation via subculture as well as the negotiation of dominant value systems and emerging subcultural ethos are found to be: (1) the values of the mainstream consumer culture; (2) the social, cultural, and environmental problems associated with the mainstream culture; (3) growing discontent with, and resistance to, the mainstream consumer culture; (4) quest for social and cultural changes as well as alternative identities (see Figure 5.1).

The Values of the Mainstream Consumer Culture

Since subcultures are presented in this research to be largely emerging in re-action to the mainstream consumer culture and dominant social order, it is crucial to have a broad understanding of the value systems and the underlying social, historical, and political factors of the mainstream consumer culture and dominant social order, which are reflected in Kahle's original LOV. Since the Industrial Revolution, production has mainly occupied the center of industrial societies in modernity (cf. Marx 1990). However, with the cultural turn from modern to postmodern (Fırat and Venkatesh 1995; Hassan 1987; Jameson 1985, 1991; Slater and Tonkiss 2001), rapid technological changes and advancements (e.g. computer technologies) (Harvey 1990; Poster 1990, 2006), and the proliferation of mass media (Schor 1998), consumption has arguably replaced production and thus taken center stage in contemporary Western postindustrial societies (Baudrillard 1998; Bocock 1993; Featherstone 1991, 1995; Fırat and Venkatesh 1995; Harvey 1990). In other words, we are said to be living in a society where the centrality of the organizing tenets of production in social life is rapidly replaced by the centrality of the organizing tenets of consumption.

In contemporary society, the centrality of consumption is woven into the very fabric of everyday life as a key element of culture, and plays a significant role in molding and influencing many aspects of lives of many people at both the individual and the collective level (Baudrillard 1998; Featherstone 1991; Fırat and Dholakia 1998). In other words, consumerism is now a key element of mainstream culture that has a considerable impact on a common set of attitudes, values, goals, ideals, norms, rituals, habits, behaviors, and identities shared by members of a society (Lury 1996). Thus, consumerism represents a way of life for citizens and is considered to be the essential component of contemporary culture (Miles 1998). Furthermore, consumerist values that mainly revolve around the notion of consumption-oriented means for happiness seeking are spreading from the West to the other parts of the world as the impact of globalization becomes more omnipresent (Belk 1985). Along these lines, whilst spirituality, frugality, simplicity, community, integrity, and production were espoused as the central virtues and values of the traditional and modern societies, these virtues and values have been arguably discarded and replaced in consumer culture with (over)consumption, material accumulation, and spectacle in pursuit of material pleasure as well as aesthetic and sensual experiences (Bocock 1993; Ger 2005).

While cultural spheres are said to be increasingly monopolized and dominated by the ideology of consumerism that is disseminated by corporate culture producers (also known as culture industry) through controlling the means of communication, Honea (2009, p. 6) contends that "media representations of popular culture provide examples of which consumer goods are considered 'hip' or 'cool' and encourage individuals to shape their identities through the consumption of these goods and services." Therefore, consumption works as a catalyst for individuals and groups not only in defining and extending their self-concepts (Belk 1988), but also in constructing their identities, constituting their value systems, and organizing their social structure (Beck 1992; Giddens 1991). Therefore, consumerism is acknowledged for being the social and economic order as well as the collective system of attitudes and practices that pervade the value structure of a society, which, in turn, constitutes a central part of the ideological elements of contemporary societies. As Kahle and Kennedy (1988) point out, the LOV is a tool which can help segment consumer markets. If a portion of that market has changed as a result of the consumerism that is the basis for segmentation, then it seems like a natural step to analyze that portion through the lens of subculture.

It has been argued that the ideology of consumerism, which is reinforced, disseminated, and perpetuated by neoliberal institutions of consumer capitalism (Heath and Potter 2004), requires the values of self-interest and materialism as the main pillars of the prevalent value system in contemporary societies (Slater and Tonkiss 2001). For instance, materialism includes mainly material objects and considerations in scope and refers to the importance consumers attach to these objects and worldly possessions (Belk 1985). In an attempt to disseminate this new value system to the members of contemporary societies, the pursuit of accumulation of material possessions, (over) consumption activities, and utility maximization acts is depicted not only as more desirable than the pursuit of higher spiritual goals or social relationships, but also as a means to bring about prosperity, seductive good life, and improved quality of life for everyone (Beruchashvili and Arnould 2005). Along these lines, neoliberalism takes aim at relocating the power to the individual (Hayek 1976; Ricardo 1817; cited in Slater and Tonkiss 2001)—more specifically to the consumer—by promoting the notion of individuals' freedom to choose at the expense of sociality that is to be eroded. In other words, neoliberal political economy grounds its ideology through the narrative of the values of freedom and autonomy. In so doing, it acknowledges and advocates the capitalistic order as the only essential and necessary component in providing freedom to individuals due to its provision of choice to consumers (Shankar et al. 2006). According to Shankar et al. (2006, p. 1015), consumer choice has become "a manifestation of people's ability to exercise free-will," as well as the means of improving quality of life within contemporary societies.

The marketing institution, as the promotion tool of consumer capitalism (Heath and Porter 2004), is said to play a key role in promoting the ideology of consumerism as the primary means of achieving quality of life (Kilbourne et al. 1997) along with the values of individualism and competition (Honea 2009). That is, marketing institution, as one of the key components of social control, is said to play a critical role in converting society from a producer to a consumer culture (Lazer 1969) and make consumption an ideological necessity to sustain a market economy (Cochoy 1998; Shankar et al. 2006).

Consumerism, however, has been increasingly criticized and problematized due to various negative social, environmental, and cultural consequences it is said to cause and thus gave way for some groups of people (e.g. subcultures) to quest for sociocultural transformation and alternative identity construction (Bocock 1993; Cherrier 2009; Hebdige 1979; Lasn 1999). As a result of growing critiques, subcultures arise as reactions against the mainstream consumer culture where the cultural sphere is claimed to be occupied and monopolized to a greater extent by the "sphere of circulation" (Marx 1990) and "culture industry" (Adorno 2001; Horkheimer and Adorno 2007). The next section provides an overview of the literature on these problems largely associated with consumerism and mainstream consumer culture. It then outlines the growing critiques from subcultural groups in relation to these problems, and the need for additional exploration.

The Discontentment with the Mainstream Consumer Culture

Consumerism as a way of life and an ideology is not without its critics. The ideology of consumerism is largely problematized due to its detrimental consequences for the society, environment, and culture. These consequences revolve mainly around the issues of social and economic inequalities, personal debt, and environmental degradation on the rise (Iyer and Muncy 2009; Kilbourne et al. 1997; Schor 1998; Schor and Holt 2000), as well as growing market authority in most cultural spheres (Firat and Venkatesh 1995; Firat and Dholakia 1998; Honea 2009; Slater and Tonkiss 2001). Furthermore, since some social groups are said to emerge in the form of subcultures as reactions against the problems largely associated with consumerism and mainstream consumer culture, we outline the major critical standpoints—societal, environmental, and cultural—in an attempt to address these problems and provide a more profound insight into the emergence of subcultures.

From a societal critique standpoint, the ideology of consumerism is problematized mainly for permeating and instilling the values of "living to consume" (Kilbourne 1997, p. 5), and for paying little or no attention to distributive justice and, thus, income and consumption inequalities (Fisk 1999). The dynamic dyadic relationships of the producers and consumers are to bring equality in the current power structure in the marketplace (Hollenbeck and Zinkhan 2006; Holt 2002). Yet, there exist growing inequalities in the marketplace reflected mainly by rapidly growing multinational and transnational corporations in power and size (Klein 2009; Lasn 1999; Ozanne and Murray 1995). For many, individuals and social organizations need to adopt a novel attitude toward the meaning of consumption (Fisk 1973) in order to bring about transformations within the existing value systems and, thus, move toward a more just society. The relationship between consumption and quality of life has long been investigated. For instance, Kilbourne et al. (1997) state that there is a decline in the quality of life in Western societies, where the prevailing belief of achieving happiness is based merely on consumption (Hetrick 1989). Similarly, Durning (1992, 2009) reveals that greater material consumption does not bring about greater happiness. Belk (1985) provides empirical evidence regarding the negative relationship between materialism and happiness. Furthermore, Firat and Dholakia (1998) claim that many powerless consumers either indicate imbalance in their satisfaction of their basic needs or overspend and go into debt and financial dependency. Along these lines, De Graaf et al. (2001) claim that such materialistic tendencies yield a lower quality of life satisfaction for generating more debts, bankruptcies, stress, and less savings and time for family and friends. Furthermore, individuals who espouse consumerist values tend to strive for more material acquisition and are said to be in a state of permanent dissatisfaction (Fromm 1979). On the other hand, consumption has taken a role in consumer society of satisfying the needs to be valued and respected by others. Hence, it has become a means to gain self-esteem and social acceptance. Even success has been assessed relative to the ability of consumers to consume (Fırat and Dholakia 1998). Consumers are aware that they are judged by what and how they consume in a society where the opportunity of consumption is not evenly distributed (Schor 1999). Therefore, those who are disadvantaged and have less access to resources, thus cannot consume as others around them, are said to feel oppressed and disappointed (Fırat and Dholakia 1998).

According to Bourdieu (1984), consumption reinforces power structures by reproducing class inequality, status, and alienation in everyday life. Schor (1999) claims that if consumption practices reproduce and reinforce social and consumption inequalities, then consumption patterns need to be changed in an attempt to achieve equality. As such, she adds, consumers should look for quality of life rather than quantity of commodities and avoid unregulated consumption that may pave way to the erosion of societal welfare. Schor (1999, p. 5) points out that "the aspirational gap has been created by structural changes–such as the decline of community and social connection, the intensification of inequality, the growing role of mass media, and heightened penalties for failing in the labor market." Therefore, Schor (1999, p. 2) claims that we need cultural change and new policies that will turn consumption into a more "democratic, egalitarian, and available to all" phenomenon. She goes on to state that "we need independent organizations of consumers to pressure companies, influence the political agenda, provide objective product information, and articulate a vision of an appealing and humane consumer sphere" (ibid: 12).

In sum, all these critical studies seem to imply and reinforce the notion that the grand universal happiness promises of the consumerism project cannot be accomplished (Alvesson 1994; Bauman 1992). Besides, the neoclassical assumptions that the maximum social good is achieved with the sum of individual assets is said to be a failure due to the non-egalitarian structure of capitalism (Bauman 1992; Bocock 1993; Slater and Tonkiss 2001). Therefore, emergence of subcultures as a reaction against mainstream culture seems to be an inevitable process.

From an environmental critique standpoint, the ideology of consumption is said to affect the environmental sustainability of present consumption as existing consumption patterns are increasingly viewed to be problematic (Kilbourne et al. 1997). Durning (1992) claims that population growth and consumption are two primary factors that yield environmental degradation. He goes on to state that although population growth has started to be perceived as a problem by both citizens and governments, consumption is still viewed by them to be critical and beneficial for national economic policy and well-being.

It has been argued that a mere focus on financial and economic growth and the rising intensity of competition in the market give way to a rise in unethical, socially irresponsible, and even abusive marketing practices in contemporary societies (Preston and Richard 1986; Sirgy and Lee 1996). This pursuit of mere economic growth, which encourages values to be eroded and degraded, is claimed to also have a damaging impact on the environment (Humphery 2010; Kilbourne et al. 2007; Schor 1998). That is, pollution, global warming, poverty, extinctions of species, and resource depletion are considered to be the consequences of the very failures of consumer capitalism (Bocock 1993; Kilbourne et al. 1997; McIntosh 1991; Schor 1998, 1999). On the other hand, there is a growing environmental concern among some individuals and social groups in contemporary society (Alwitt and Pitts 1996; Humphery 2010; Schwepker and Cornell 1991). This growing public awareness and concern for social and environmental issues as well as pressures from social movements push organizations and marketers to transcend their economic oriented boundaries (Schor 1998).

Kilbourne et al. (1997) argue that since the ideology of consumerism takes aim at disseminating the anthropocentric and egocentric values, consumption decision is reflected mainly in the private realm of self-interest. Therefore, emphasizing the importance of social and environmental values, Kilbourne et al. (1997, p. 11) point out that

> in any consumer decision, the dilemma ought to be whether to act as a self-interested consumer and get what one wants, or to act as a responsible citizen and do what ought to be done in consideration of what one wants.

That is, consumers must be aware of the social and environmental crises in order to respond with appropriate behavior and to balance the public and private interests in individual decision-making (Humphery 2010). For instance, some consumers cast their economic votes in an attempt to help save the environment and improve society (Frank 1988). These socially conscious consumers either "purchase products and services which they perceive to have positive (or less negative) impact on the environment or use their purchasing power to express current social concerns" (Roberts 1995, p. 140) or reduce their consumption level to protect the natural environment (Lee et al. 2009).

For many, resistance to the allure of the consumer society is not futile, but achievable (Elgin 1993; Hall and Jefferson 1976; Hebdige 1979; Humphery 2010; Lasn 1999; Schor 1998). However, it has been argued that many consumers are still yet to be sufficiently aware about the social and environmental impacts of their daily consumption habits (Schor 1998). Therefore, consumers should cooperate with environmentalist groups, civil society organizations, social movements, and NGOs—which are said to be more credible than the other institutions of the civil society—to provide alternative solutions to the problems caused by mainstream culture (Schor 1999).

From a cultural critique standpoint, mainstream culture is problematized for instilling the values of consumer culture into the very fabric of everyday life and, thus, making the culture very advertising and brand friendly (Lasn 1999). In other words, all facets of culture are said to revolve around the activities of selling, buying, promoting, and consuming the products and services as well as the experiences, images, and meanings largely associated with them. One of the key criticisms to consumer culture is raised by Frankfurt School scholars who argue that consumers are manipulated into participating in an artificial consumer culture (Fromm 1979; Habermas 1991; Horkheimer and Adorno 2007; Marcuse 1969). Likewise, Schor (2007, p. 22) states that "capitalist production creates capitalist culture and a passive citizenry, in which cultural consumption is used to reproduce an exploitative economic system." Furthermore, consumers are said to be forced to conform to the spoon-fed identities preestablished by the actors of the culture industry (Binay 2005). Since most of the social relations have been constructed through the consumption paradigm in contemporary societies, consumers who don't want to be excluded or discriminated against feel the need to conform, those who cannot afford this conformity feel oppressed and depressed (Fırat and Dholakia 1998), and those who refuse to conform feel marginalized in contemporary society (Honea 2009).

The market is claimed to dominate all facets of life by acting as a cultural authority, dictating its own preferences and values in contemporary society (Fırat and Venkatesh 1995). In other words, it monopolizes, governs, and dominates the cultural sphere via control of the means of communication and the popular culture to disseminate the values of the dominant ideology of consumer capitalism (Honea 2009). In so doing, it also seeks to appropriate, transform, and assimilate all the oppositional and antithetical cultures and values into the mainstream consumer (Fırat and Venkatesh 1995).

While some consumers conform to the significations developed in marketing practices and use the meanings so created in living their lives, other consumers find possibilities to refuse and resist marketing's cultural authority and its consumption codes through producing their own meanings and experiences (Fırat and Venkatesh 1995; Holt 2002). While the former may represent mainstream consumers, the latter may represent subcultural consumers. In contemporary societies, a growing number of people resist the market hegemony, consumer culture, and capitalism in an agentic way (Hollenbeck and Zinkhan 2006; Lee et al. 2009; Penaloza and Price 1993). While some attempt to bring about structural change, others strive for a cultural change relying on the notion that cultural change will eventually result in a healthier structural change (Duncombe 1997; Shukaitis and Graeber 2007).

In sum, a proposition in this research is that these social, environmental, and cultural problems, which are examined in detail in this section, largely associated with consumerism and mainstream consumer culture may pave the way to the rising critiques from different perspectives, including subcultures, which will be examined in the next section in more detail.

The Quest for Social and Cultural Changes and Alternative Identities

Consumers who have antagonistic stances against consumerism mainly stress the values of frugality, simplicity, community, integrity, anti-materialism, environmentalism, humanism, animal rights, social equality, pacifism, and the like (Bocock 1993; Humphery 2010; Schor 1998). They may take a critical stance not only against the activities of consumption that may represent profanity (Belk et al. 1989), greed, waste, and self-indulgent hedonism (Belk 1983), but also against the ideology of consumerism in general (Kozinets and Handelman 2004) for promoting materialistic values, self-interested efforts of material accumulation, overconsumption behavior, and the notion that accumulation of materials and possessions would lead to subjective well-being, happiness, and common prosperity (Belk 1983; Kilbourne et al. 1997; Slater and Tonkiss 2001).

Consumer resistance can take various forms of subcultures such as anti-consumerism (Humphery 2010; Lee et al. 2009; Zavestoski 2002), culture jamming (Lasn 1999), voluntary simplicity (Cherrier 2009; Elgin 1993), boycotting (Kozinets 1998), consumer activism (Kozinets and Handelman 2004), anti-brand communities (Hollenbeck and Zinkhan 2006), countercultural movements (Hall and Jefferson 1976; Hebdige 1979), and the like. In so doing, these consumers construct alternative identities mainly antithetical to the mainstream culture (Cherrier 2009; Hebdige 1979; Humphery 2010); produce their own cultural products, artifacts, positions, expressions, meanings, and the like; create an independent media largely driven by do-it-yourself ethic (Biel 2012; Moore 2007); and/or develop anti-consumerist tendencies that reflect in movements such as frugality, simple living, downshifting, voluntary simplicity, and the like (Elgin 1993; Humphery 2010; Schor 1998).

For instance, frugality refers to an escape from consumerism in contemporary society and represents an effort to achieve greater fulfillment through reducing working hours and the level of consumption and material possessions (Dominguez and Robin 1999). In line with this, consumers who are in pursuit of simple living seek meaning and fulfillment through enriching their inner selves and experiences rather than through the materials they accumulate (Elgin 1993). Therefore, they take frugality, sufficiency, and simple living as positive values and life statements (Schor 1998). Downshifting represents a disbelief in the values of materialism and consumerism and places the emphasis on "soul-searching" and a "coming to consciousness" (Schor 1998). It is mainly considered to be a process of trading off money for time and quality of life (Humphery 2010). Voluntary simplicity is considered to be a constructive alternative to consumerism and a more politicized form of downshifting

(Doherty and Etzioni 2003; Humphery 2010; Schor 1998). However, similar to downshifting, consumers who engage in the voluntary simplicity movement also consciously take aim at taking control of their behaviors, thoughts, and desires through putting some restrictions on their own consumption behaviors and patterns in an agentic and voluntary way (Schor 1998). Furthermore, the mediation of self-reliant communities in holding the balance between material and spiritual needs and in fostering inner growth and spiritual development is another trait of the voluntary simplicity movement (Doherty and Etzioni 2003; Humphery 2010). In addition to such developments, subcultures also emerge as a reaction toward hegemony as a resistance strategy to exercise their resistance to the dominant structure and the hegemony through style and rituals associated with subversive qualities (Hall and Jefferson 1976; Hebdige 1979).

Contrary to the thesis of passive consumers of mainstream culture, those who are discontent with the mainstream consumer culture may attempt to create their own alternative modes of living and being that espouse mainly antithetical values to the mainstream culture by playing an active and creative role in contemporary society. Along these lines, subcultures provide these consumers with venues or "public spheres" where they can freely articulate and express themselves, discuss critical sociocultural issues, speak their antagonistic voices to the existing socioeconomic structure, imagine alternative social orders and relationships, and attempt to bring about different social and cultural organizing and individual and collective identities.

Consequently, mainstream consumer culture fosters its own opponents in various subcultural forms. Subcultures are considered to be "a resource from which to develop a positive self-concept, a confidence in non-normative thinking, and a network of support in a world that often feels alienating and unfulfilling" (Williams 2011, p. 2). Therefore, subcultures emerge as a reaction against the mainstream culture and, thus, they are the key manifestations of the fragmentation. Subcultures adopt alternative sets of attitudes and value systems for a cultural change. Therefore, subcultures are actively sought out by some individuals and social groups who quest for alternative value systems and reliable information as to what is really happening in the society. Through subcultures, consumers aim to bring about challenges to the mainstream practices and status quo which is perceived to hinder societal and environmental well-being, even though some consumers might be slower to let go of materialistic behaviors they have developed as part of their consumerism-based values (Roberts and Manolis 2012).

Subcultures are venues where members are considered to be the active producers of their own cultures, cultural artifacts, products, symbols, experiences, and meanings (Hebdige 1979; Honea 2009; Muggleton 2000; Ulusoy and Fırat 2010; Williams 2011), mainly as reactions against the mainstream cultural sphere that is largely monopolized and dominated by the ideology of consumerism (Honea 2009). Subcultures tend to resist the prefabricated identities manufactured by corporate culture producers (Hebdige 1979) and tend to reject corporations, as the main actors of the dominant structure, mainly for conducting unethical practices around the world through violating human and animal rights, exploiting the natural sources, and damaging the environment and mental health (Haenfler 2006; Klein 2009; Lasn 1999). The clash also arises when the market institution tends to co-opt and appropriate the expressions of these subcultures and present them as commodities to wider audiences through mainstream means, and thus empty the meanings of their critical and oppositional stances (Heath and Potter 2004; Marcuse 1969).

Subculture and LOV

Kahle and Kennedy (1988, p. 53) point out that "LOV will not always be the optimal segmentation instrument, but it will often help one to understand the nature of the consumers one wants to reach." It lives on in textbooks and research not only in terms of segmentation, but in understanding the relationship between values and consumer behavior. The fact that segmentation and purchasing patterns are identified with the consumerism perspective which has led to the strengthening presence of subculture is supportive of the importance that consumer values play in understanding culture, and an indication that further attention should be paid to subcultural studies.

Thompson and Troester (2002) problematize the coexistence of fragmentation and personal values and offer an analysis through the lens of a microculture, which they compare to a subculture and determine that microculture "implies a theoretical relationship to the broader culture." Our conceptual perspective of subculture, particularly framed as anti-consumerism, offers a theoretical window of opportunity to further examine the importance of subculture, personal values, and how they have developed over the past 30 or so years. Earlier mention of the All-American, well-respected value being considered mainstream leads us now to consider two important conceptual questions: first, what does the impact of subculture have on mainstream culture, and second, if our society has become fragmented, and consumers who relate to a subculture value are anti-mainstream, where would they fit?

In terms of the alleged impact of music-based subcultures—specifically punk subculture—on society, Biel (2012; back cover), based on the interviews he conducted with subcultural members, states that

> punk is notorious for its loud music, aggressive attitude and safety-pinned style. Less well known is the radical values system that has emerged hand-in-hand with the sound and aesthetic. Since the 1970s, punks have built their music, fashion and lifestyles around core values of social justice, creative freedom, community integrity, fiercely democratic politics and do-it-yourself ingenuity. From journalism to psychology, graphic design to alternative fuel, bodybuilding to the Occupy movement, these interviews show just some of the ways that punk values continue to shape mainstream American life.

Concerning where subculture consumers fit in the LOV framework, subcultures have come to provide a venue or a way for people to find anchors and feel empowered to generate more dynamic, fluid, and organic identities and modes of life (Bennett 1999; Maffesoli 1996; Ulusoy and Fırat 2010). Subcultural engagement can be considered to be a form of consumer resistance as it arguably largely espouses the values of anti-consumerism and/or ethical consumerism. Subcultural consumers refuse the ideology of consumerism and the market hegemony and express their antagonism toward such forces that are deemed to be oppressive (Holtzman et al. 2007). Therefore, in addition to the motives of identity-seeking, resistance toward hegemonic market structure also appears to be one of the key motives for consumers who participate in subcultures and thus manifest the fragmentation in culture (Holtzman et al. 2007).

The "Fun and Enjoyment in Life" value category of the LOV would seem to be the mid-1980s version of what we now think of as subculture, described in Kahle et al. (1986, p. 51) as "(y)oung people who appreciate life especially like this value… They dislike family roles, religion, and children." From 1976 to 1986, the percentage of people choosing this value rose from 4.5% in 1976 to 7.2% in 1986, indicating an upward trend. While these value traits seem to relate to members of subcultures, there are some that would need updating in today's subculture society—and we take the perspective that the "Fun and Enjoyment in Life" value category may be one category that included a subset that has now grown. For example, in 1986, members of this type were described as "often unemployed or work in sales or labor, but they are optimistic and well adjusted." Under the lens of subculture, some of these consumer types may now be more dedicated to their anti-consumption beliefs, older, and hold down professional jobs. As indicated by Hodkinson (2011, p. 281), members of the Goth subculture maintain their identity as they age; however, they adapt through the "development of somewhat reduced intensity and more 'comfortable' forms of goth participation which complemented a greater emphasis on work, long-term friendships, committed relationships and children, while also accommodating physical changes to the body." From a conceptual perspective, one could see such consumers as having been categorized in the "Fun and Enjoyment of Life" category in 1986, but through the lens of subculture, we would argue that they are their own category.

References

Adorno, Theodor W. (2001), *The Culture Industry: Selected Essays on Mass Culture*, New York, NY: Routledge.

Alvesson, Mats (1994), "Critical Theory and Consumer Marketing," *Scandinavian Journal of Management*, 10 (3), 292–313.

Alwitt, Linda F. and Robert E. Pitts (1996), "Predicting Purchase Intentions for An Environmentally Sensitive Product," *Journal of Consumer Psychology*, 5 (1), 49–64.

Baudrillard, Jean (1998), *The Consumer Society: Myths and Structures*, Newbury Park, CA: Sage.

Bauman, Zygmunt (1992), *Intimations of Postmodernity*, London: Routledge.

Beck, Ulrich (1992), *Risk Society: Towards a New Modernity*, London: Sage Publications.

Belk, Russell W. (1985), "Materialism: Trait Aspects of Living in the Material World," *Journal of Consumer Research*, 12 (3), 265–280.

———— (1988) "Possessions and the Extended Self," *Journal of Consumer Research*, 15, 139–168.

Belk, Russell W., Melanie Wallendorf, and John F. Sherry (1989), "The Sacred and the Profane in Consumer Behavior: Theodicy on the Odyssey," *Journal of Consumer Research*, 16 (June), 1–39.

Bennett, Andy (1999), "Subcultures or Neo-Tribes? Rethinking the Relationship between Youth, Style, and Musical Taste," *Sociology*, 33 (3), 599–617.

Beruchashvili, M. and Eric J. Arnould (2005), "Negotiating Competing Dogma: Religion and Mundane Consumption," in Religion and Consumption: The Profane Sacred Special Session, *Advances in Consumer Research*, 32, 79–80.

Biel, Joel (2012), *Beyond the Music: How Punks Are Saving the World with Diy Ethics, Skills, & Values*, Oregon: Microcosm.

Binay, Ayse (2005), *Investigating the Anti-Consumerism Movement in North America: The Case of Adbusters*. Ph.D. Thesis, University of Texas at Austin.

Bocock, Robert (1993), *Consumption*, London: Routledge.

Bourdieu, Pierre (1984), *Distinction: A Social Critique of the Judgment of Taste*, Cambridge, MA: Harvard University Press.

Cateforis, Theo and Elena Humphreys (1997), "Constructing Communities and Identities: Riot Grrrl," in *Musics of Multicultural America: A Study of Twelve Musical Communities*, ed. Kip Lornell and Ann Rasmussen, New York, NY: Schirmer Books, 317–342.

Cherrier, Hélène (2009), "Anti-Consumption Discourses and Consumer-Resistant Identities," *Journal of Business Research*, 62, 181–190.

Cochoy, Franck (1998), "Another Discipline for the Market Economy: Marketing As a Performative Knowledge and Know-how for Capitalism," in *The Laws of the Markets*, ed. Michel Callon, Oxford: Blackwell, 194–221.

De Graaf, John, David Wann, and Thomas H. Naylor (2001), *Affluenza: The All-consuming Epidemic*, San Fransisco, CA: Berrett-Koehler.

Doherty, Daniel and Amitai Etzioni (2003), *Voluntary Simplicity: Responding to Consumer Culture*, Lanham, MD: Rowman & Littlefield.

Dominguez, Joe and Vicki Robin (1999), *Your Money or Your Life: Transforming Your Relationship with Money and Achieving Financial Independence*, New York, NY: Penguin.

Duncombe, Stephen (1997), *Notes from Underground: Zines and the Politics of Alternative Culture*, London: Verso.

Durning, Alan T. (1992), *How Much is Enough? The Consumer Society and the Future of the Earth*, New York, NY: W.W. Norton and Company.

———— (2009), *The Dubious Rewards of Consumption*, New Renaissance Magazine: Renaissance Universal.

Elgin, Duane (1993), *Voluntary Simplicity: Towards a Way of Life that is Outwardly Simple, Inwardly Rich*, New York, NY: Harper.

Featherstone, Mike (1991), *Consumer Culture and Postmodernism*, London: Sage.

———— (1995), *Undoing Culture: Globalization, Postmodernism and Identity*, London: Sage.

Firat, A. Fuat and Alladi Venkatesh (1995), "Liberatory Postmodernism and the Reenchantment of Consumption," *Journal of Consumer Research*, 22 (3), 239–267.

Firat, A. Fuat and Nikhilesh Dholakia (1998), *Consuming People: From Political Economy to Theaters of Consumption*, London: Routledge.

Fisk, George (1973), "Criteria for a Theory of Responsible Consumption," *Journal of Marketing*, 37 (4), 24–31.

——— (1999). "Reflection and Retrospection: Searching for Visions in Marketing," *Journal of Marketing*, 63 (1), 115–121.

Frank, Robert H. (1988), *Passions with Reason*, New York, NY: W.W. Norton.

Fromm, Erich (1979), *To Have or to Be?*, London: Sphere Books.

Gardikiotis, Antonis and Alexandros Baltzis (2011), "'Rock Music for Myself and Justice to the World!': Musical Identity, Values, and Music Preferences," *Psychology of Music*, 40 (2), 143–163.

Gelder, Ken and Sarah Thornton (1997), *The Subcultures Reader*, London: Routledge.

Ger, Guliz (2005), "Religion and Consumption: The Profane Sacred," *Advances in Consumer Research*, 32, 79–80.

Giddens, Anthony (1991), *Modernity and Self-Identity: Self and Society in the Late Modern Age*, Stanford, CA: Stanford University Press.

Habermas, Jurgen (1991), *The Structural Transformation of the Public Sphere: An Inquiry into a Category of Bourgeois Society*, Cambridge, MA: The MIT Press.

Haenfler, Ross (2004), "Rethinking Subcultural Resistance: Core Values of the Straightedge Movement," *Journal of Contemporary Ethnography*, 33 (4), 406–436.

——— (2006), *Straight Edge: Clean-Living Youth, Hardcore Punk, and Social Change*, New Brunswick: Rutgers University Press.

Hall, Stuart and Thomas Jefferson (1976), *Resistance through Rituals: Youth Subcultures in Post-War Britain*, London: Hutchinson.

Harvey, David (1990), *The Condition of Postmodernity: An Enquiry into the Origins of Cultural Change*, Oxford: Blackwell.

Hassan, Ihab H. (1987), *The Postmodern Turn: Essays in Postmodern Theory and Culture*, Columbus: Ohio State University Press.

Hayek, Friedrich August von (1976), *The Denationalization of Money*, London: Institute of Economic Affairs.

Heath, Joseph and Andrew Potter (2004), *Nation of Rebels: Why Counterculture Became Consumer Culture*, New York, NY: Harper Business.

Hebdige, Dick (1979), *Subculture: The Meaning of Style*, London: Routledge.

Hetrick, W. (1989), "The Ideology of Consumerism: A Critique," in Proceedings of the 1989 *AMA Winter Educators' Conference: Marketing Theory and Practice*, ed. R. Bagozzi and J. Peter, Chicago: American Marketing Association, 40–43.

Hodkinson, Paul (2011), "Ageing in a Spectacular 'Youth Culture': Continuity, Change and Community Amongst Older Goths," *The British Journal of Sociology*, 62 (2), 262–282.

Hollenbeck, Candice R. and George M. Zinkhan (2006), "Consumer Activism on the Internet: The Role of Anti-brand Communities," *Advances in Consumer Research*, 33, 479–485.

Holt, Douglas B. (2002), "Why Do Brands Cause Trouble? A Dialectical Theory of Consumer Culture and Branding," *Journal of Consumer Research*, 29 (1), 70–90.

Holtzman, Ben, Craig Hughes, and Kevin Van Meter (2007), "Do it Yourself... and the Movement Beyond Capitalim," in *Constituent Imagination: Militant Investigations // Collective Theorization*, ed. Stevphen Shukaitis and David Graeber, Oakland, CA, Edinburgh: AK Press, 44–61.

Honea, Jay C. (2009), *Sell-outs or Outsiders? Co-optation and Resistance in Action Sport Subcultures*, Germany: VDM Verlag Dr. Muller.

Horkheimer, Martin and Theodor W. Adorno (2007), *Dialectic of Enlightenment: Philosophical Fragments*, Redwood City, CA: Stanford University Press.

Humphery, Kim (2010), *Excess: Anti-Consumerism in the West*, Cambridge: Polity Press.

Iyer, Rajesh and James A. Muncy (2009), "Purpose and Object of Anti-Consumption," *Journal of Business Research*, 62, 160–168.

Jameson, Fredric (1985), "Postmodernism and Consumer Culture," in *Postmodern Culture*, ed. H. Foster, London: Pluto, 111–125.

——— (1991), *Postmodernism, or, the Cultural Logic of Late Capitalism*, Durham: Duke University Press.

Kahle, Lynn R., Sharon E. Beatty, and Pamela Homer (1986), "Alternative Measurement Approaches to Consumer Values: The List of Values (Lov) and Values and Life Style (Vals)," *Journal of Consumer Research*, 13 (3), 405–409.

Kahle, Lynn R. and Patricia Kennedy (1988), "Using the List of Values (Lov) to Understand Consumers," *Journal of Services Marketing*, 2 (4), 49.

Kilbourne, William, Pierre McDonagh, and Andrea Prothero (1997), "Sustainable Consumption and the Quality of Life: A Macromarketing Challenge to the Dominant Social Paradigm," *Journal of Macromarketing*, 17 (4), 4–24.

Klein, Naomi (2009), *No Logo: 10th Anniversary Edition*, New York, NY: Picador.

Kozinets, Robert V. (1998) "Ensouling Consumption: a Netnographic Exploration of the Meaning of Boycotting Behavior," *Advances in Consumer Research*, 25, 475–480.

Kozinets, Robert V. and Jay M. Handelman (2004), "Adversaries of Consumption: Consumer Movement, Activism, and Ideology," *Journal of Consumer Research*, 31 (December), 691–704.

Lasn, Kalle (1999), *Culture Jam*, New York, NY: HarperCollins.

Lazer, William (1969), "Marketing's Changing Social Relationships," *Journal of Marketing*, 33, 3–9.

Lee, Michael S.W., Judith Motion, and Denise Conroy (2009), "Anti-Consumption and Brand Avoidance," *Journal of Business Research*, 62, 169–180.

Lury, Celia (1996), *Consumer Culture*, New Brunswick: Rutgers University Press.

Maffesoli, Michel (1996), *The Time of the Tribes: The Decline of Individualism in Mass Society*, London: Sage.

Marcuse, Herbert (1969), *Negations: Essays in Critical Theory*, Boston: Beacon Press.

Marx, Karl (1990), *Capital: A Critique of Political Economy, Volume I*, London: Penguin Books.

McIntosh, A. (1991), "The Impact of Environmental Issues on Marketing and Politics in the 1990s," *Journal of the Market Research Society*, 33 (3), 205–217.

Miklas, Sharon and Stephen J. Arnold (1999), "'the Extraordinary Self': Gothic Culture and the Construction of the Self," *Journal of Marketing Management*, 15 (6), 563–576.

Miles, Steven (1998), *Consumerism: As a Way of Life*, London: Sage.

Moore, Ryan (2007), "Friends Don't Let Friends Listen to Corporate Rock: Punk as a Field of Cultural Production," *Journal of Contemporary Ethnography*, 36 (4), 438–474.

Muggleton, David (2000), *Inside Subculture: The Postmodern Meaning of Style*, Oxford: Berg.

Ozanne, Julie L., and Jeff B. Murray (1995), "Uniting Critical Theory and Public Policy to Create the Reflexively Defiant Consumer," *American Behavioral Scientist*, 38 (February), 516–525.

Penaloza, Lisa and Linda Price (1993), "Consumer Resistance: A Conceptual Overview," *Advances in Consumer Research*, 20, 123–128.

Poster, Mark (1990), *The Mode of Information: Poststructuralism and Social Context*, Cambridge: Polity Press.

————— (2006), *Information Please: Culture and Politics in the Age of Digital Machines*, Durham, NC: Duke University Press.

Preston, Ivan L. and Jef I. Richards (1986), "The Relationship of Miscomprehension to Deceptiveness in FTC Case," *Advances in Consumer Research*, 13, 138–142.

Ricardo, David (1817), *On the Principles of Political Economy and Taxation*, London: John Murray.

Roberts, James A. (1995), "Profiling Levels of Socially Responsible Consumer Behavior: A Cluster Analytic Approach and Its Implications for Marketing," *Journal of Marketing*, 97–117.

Roberts, James A. and Chris Manolis (2012), "Cooking up a Recipe for Self-Control: The Three Ingredients of Self-Control and Its Impact on Impulse Buying," *Journal of Marketing Theory & Practice*, 20 (2), 173–188.

Schor, Juliet B. (1998), *The Overspent American: Why We Want What We don't Need*, New York, NY: Harper Perennial.

————— (1999), "The New Politics of Consumption: Why Americans Want So Much More Than They Need," *Boston Review*. Available at: http://bostonreview.net/BR24.3/schor.html

————— (2007), "In Defense of Consumer Critique: Revisiting the Consumption Debates of the Twentieth Century," *The ANNALS of the American Academy of Political and Social Science*, 611, 16–30.

Schor, Juliet B. and Douglas B. Holt (2000), *The Consumer Society Reader*, New York, NY: The New Press.

Schwepker, Charles H. and Bettina T. Cornell (1991), "An Examination of Ecologically Concerned Consumers and Their Intention to Purchase Ecologically Packaged Products," *Journal of Public Policy & Marketing*, 10 (2), 77–101.

Shankar, Avi, Hélène Cherrier, and Robin Canniford (2006), "Consumer Empowerment: A Foucauldian Interpretation," *European Journal of Marketing*, 40 (9/10), 1013–1030.

Shukaitis, Stevphen and David Graeber (2007), *Constituent Imagination: Militant Investigation // Collective Theorization*, Oakland, CA: AK Press.

Sirgy, Joseph M. and Dong-Jin Lee (1996), "Setting Socially Responsible Marketing Objectives: A Quality-of-Life Approach," *European Journal of Marketing*, 30 (5), 20–34.

Slater, Don and Tonkiss, Fran (2001), *Market Society*, Cambridge: Polity Press.

Thompson, Craig J. and Maura Troester (2002), "Consumer Value Systems in the Age of Postmodern Fragmentation: The Case of the Natural Health Microculture," *Journal of Consumer Research*, 28 (4), 550–571.

Ulusoy, Emre and A. Fuat Fırat (2010), "Revisiting the Subculture: Fragmentation of the Social and the Venue for Contemporary Consumption," *Advances in Consumer Research*, 38, 558.

Williams, Patrick J. (2011), *Subcultural Theory: Traditions and Concepts*, Malden: Polity.

Zavestoski, Stephen (2002), "Guest Editorial: Anticonsumption Attitudes," *Psychology and Marketing*, 19 (2), 121–126.

6

HANDMADE

How Indie Girl Culture Is Changing the Market

Rachel H. Larsen and Lynn R. Kahle

One of us first encountered Indie Girl Culture (IGC) through the blog *A Beautiful Mess* in the summer of 2009. It was a part of a network of blogs that focused on all things girly, crafty, and pretty—all things that independent girls liked—proved fascinating, especially the influential, proactive community that was forming around interests that society at large might brush aside as trivial. IGC blogs with businesses were especially intriguing with their ability to naturally attract a customer base through their own self-promotion—an approach that is quite contrary to what most marketers employ, yet provides a customer response that is stronger and more favorable than most. What are the dynamics that comprised this culture and value system, and what makes it work?

The Independent DIY Lifestyle Blogging Business Model

The Independent DIY Lifestyle Blogging Business model embodies the three main elements of this paper: the Handmade movement's foundational ideas, progressive marketing theories, and the opportunities on the Internet for bloggers. These ideas work together to create a sustainable business model that focuses on fostering valuable relationship capital with the customer and empowering the individual, whether it be the customer or the business. Here are the terms defined to explain their significance in identifying this model:

- "Independent" refers to the individual's independence from big businesses and corporations. Through independence, bloggers have freedom in expression and creation. This independence also separates these individuals from corporations with strong focuses on the DIY culture, such as LifeHacker and Instructables.

- "DIY" also refers to the do-it-yourself lifestyle attitude where one approaches everything with a self-achieving attitude and values for the handmade quality.
- "Lifestyle" refers to the holistic appeal that blogging individuals create through their content by embodying an entire lifestyle, in both personal and business aspects (cf. Kahle & Valette-Florence, 2012).
- "Blogging" refers to the blog's essential role in this community as the primary social media platform. Elements of Permission and Relationship Marketing are inherent to the nature of blogs.
- "Business" refers to the business aspect of these blogs. Making money is a primary goal of these blogs, whether through selling advertising space or featured-content sponsorships.

By combining these elements, the Independent DIY Lifestyle Blogging Business model creates self-reliant, entrepreneurial individuals who appeal to their customer base through utilizing progressive marketing methods on their blogs. The subculture of young women that has developed around this model is a community called IGC. Often, culture and community are held together by values. We could define shared values as including culture and community (Kahle & Valette-Florence, 2012).

First, it is important to explore how the Arts and Crafts movement, punk subculture, and Handmade movements have led to the birth of IGC. On the business side, progressive marketing theories such as Permission and Relationship Marketing have offered a more sustainable, effective alternative to Interruption Marketing. These progressive marketing theories emphasize the customer's importance by fostering favorable relationship capital, which empowers the individual both as a customer and as a business. Finally, we'll show how the Internet has maximized the potential of the Permission Marketing and how blogs have fostered relationship capital. These elements all interact to create the success of the Independent DIY Lifestyle Blogging Businesses model and the IGC that uses it.

Handmade Culture and IGC

The Arts and Crafts Movement

The Handmade movement grew out of the Arts and Crafts movement, which started in the late nineteenth century in England. The Arts and Crafts movement was a "reformist phenomenon" (Bowman, 1990) led by three revolutionary thinkers who were frustrated with the Industrial Revolution and Victorian-era design (Koplos & Metcalf, 2010). These reformists contrasted current design trends with a style that emphasized "simplicity, revealed materials, and avoidance of ostentation," trademarks of what they considered "good design" (Bowman, 1990; Koplos & Metcalf, 2010, p. 83).

The Arts and Crafts movement was largely a reaction to the Industrial Revolution of the late eighteenth century, which had quickly spread to the United States from the United Kingdom. The Industrial Revolution rapidly pushed forward the creation of factories and automated production processes (Koplos & Metcalf, 2010). These monumental changes to production left behind certain laborers of the workforce, most notably the skilled craftsmen. These workers, in particular, lost the dignity of their work, which was now primarily left to automated processes (Koplos & Metcalf, 2010).

The Arts and Crafts movement was in part a reaction to these changes to production, and it attempted to revive the role of the craftsmen and elevated their status through this progressive reform. The craftsmen of this movement, artisans skilled in manual work, were empowered through their newfound ability to support themselves by selling their unique products infused with their personality. The opportunity to sell directly to customers created relationship capital, or trust, between the buyer and the seller—something that was lost in the Industrial Revolution. Work became a source of dignity again for the craftsmen as they began to counter the industrialization created by the Industrial Revolution.

The Arts and Crafts movement continued its emphasis on craftsmanship and building relationships with customers throughout the 1890s. The American soil provided a good place to plant the fundamentals of DIY with the country's fundamental beliefs in individualism and personal liberties. Moving into the postwar era and the development of the middle class, the understanding of craft and design grew. The results of this newfound understanding of the movement were an increased overall appeal and a larger market opportunity. The growth of the Arts and Crafts movement harbored a countercultural spirit of anti-corporation, which continued into the punk subculture.

Punk Subculture

The punk subculture grew out of the 1960's hippie movement, which provided an "alternative to the conventional social system" (Howard, 1969). Punk values were largely defined by the punk music scene that took shape during the 1970s and "boiled down to the idea that self-reliance was the key to expression" (Oakes, 2009, p. 44). These ideals created a strong, united community that would later become the basis for the Handmade movement. In *Punks: A Guide to an American Subculture*, Sharon M. Hannon (2010) notes that the punk music scene "broke down the barriers that separated the audience from the musicians and each other and helped a new community grow around two principles: individuality is paramount, and anyone can create great art" (Hannon, 2010, p. 2).

The roots of the modern Handmade community, of which IGC is an offshoot, grew out of this punk subculture. Local punk scenes were chronicled through individual zines, homemade versions of magazines. These zines brought DIY into "the realm of publishing" and created an active, supportive community that valued the importance of handmade craft (p. 2). Faythe Levine, a handmade crafter, advocate, author, and director of *Handmade Nation*, explains how the punk and zine communities helped her connect with DIY artists in the craft community (Oakes, 2009). Levine also emphasizes the influence of "riot grrrl," a subsection of punk that embraces feminist notions of DIY that has heavily influenced the Handmade community—and even more, the IGC (Oakes, 2009).

The Handmade Community

The idea of the modern Handmade community started with the local church bazaar craft fair. The simple craft fair has grown into large and influential events, with one of the biggest being the Renegade Craft Fair. As of 2017, Renegade showcases local makers in 12 different cities with around 300,000 attendees annually. The craft fair has also expanded to the Internet to create online marketplaces, Etsy being one of the most notable. These business venues empower individuals with their own storefront, allowing crafters to support themselves and become self-sufficient.

The Handmade community is built on the personal interactions that developed through craft fairs. Craft fairs emphasize the personal nature of handmade goods through the customer's buying directly from the maker and the handmade good itself. Oakes (2009) believes that there is an intrinsic value in handmade objects and that it "adds a layer of personal investment in the transaction that would be impossible to recreate on a mass-market level" (Oakes, 2009, p. 191). This personal investment can be considered relationship capital and is intimate and generally favorable. This personal investment and relationship capital also carries over to the Internet, as crafters share their stories, post pictures from their life, and interact with customers (Oakes, 2009).

The antiestablishment ideals behind the punk "riot grrrl" echo throughout the Handmade community. Oakes observed that "most of the vendors at Renegade are young women who are operating small businesses, a phenomenon that is still unique in the larger indie culture" and suggests that the art of craft is "inherently female" and notes that the sewing and knitting—crafting basics—are activities that women have done throughout history (Oakes, 2009, p. 191). Yet, these activities were traditionally used to occupy women's time at home. These female business owners have turned that notion on its head and are using those activities to support their livelihood. This female empowerment is a continuation of the individual empowerment created through the Arts and Crafts and punk movement and is echoed in the IGC.

Handmade Conclusion

Throughout the past 250 years, the same ideals have been translated through a number of different subcultures, each pushing for independence for makers within society. The ideals first embodied in the Arts and Crafts movement were echoed in the punk subculture and provided the building blocks of the Handmade movement. These movements aim to empower the individual against industrial society with craft. Craft has evolved into a powerful force that allows individuals to assert their independence from industrial society.

The Arts and Crafts reacted to the degradation of the craftsmen during the Industrial Revolution. It empowered the craftsmen by giving back their craft and independent livelihood. The punk subculture echoed this individual empowerment and advocated for DIY thinking and corporate independence. These ideals were largely evident through the punk zine community, which influenced the craft community and led to the modern Handmade movement. This movement is characterized by the fostering of strong relationship capital developed through personal interactions and female empowerment.

The individual empowerment and personal relationship capital that developed in the Handmade movement is consistent with the foundational nature of the Internet and embodies principles of Permission and Relationship Marketing. The characteristics of this movement heavily echo the IDLBB model and IGC. The details of these relationships will be elaborated in the following sections.

In this next section, we will see how the lack of efficiency of traditional Interruption Marketing methods led to the rise of Permission and Relationship Marketing methods as alternative practices. The IDLBB model combines these progressive marketing theories with the individual empowerment established by the Handmade movement to reverse the traditional customer–business relationship.

Marketing Theory

Interruption Marketing

Traditional advertising is based on the theory of Interruption Marketing. In *Permission Marketing*, Godin (1999) describes Interruption Marketing as the commonly used advertising approach where companies use advertisements to "interrupt what the viewers are doing in order to get them to think about something else" (Godin, 1999, p. 25). Interruption Marketing is used everywhere: in newspapers and magazines, by telemarketers, on billboards, the radio, the Internet, and most commonly on television. Godin (1999) argues that this method is focused on short-term value.

Interruption Marketing was effective when it first emerged during the growth of mass media. The lack of commercialized media gave published advertisements an opportunity to appeal to society at large. Commercial advertisements began to fuel the growth of mass media and an interdependent relationship grew between the two (Godin, 1999). The success of Interruption Marketing relies on capturing the customer's attention and persuading him or her to purchase the advertised product or service. The increased use of Interruption Marketing meant that more and more companies were competing for the limited amount of customer attention.

One of Interruption Marketing's limitations is that it assumes it has the viewer's permission to advertise when it does not. Not only do advertisers take this assumption for granted, the interaction's lack of anticipation and participation can even build resentment in consumers, which makes it harder for the advertiser to get their attention.

The abundance of advertisements also numbs consumers to the effects. Every time an advertiser develops an innovative, effective method within Interruption Marketing, it becomes less effective as other advertisers copy the approach. The increasing sexuality in ads is an example of this effect. Adding sex appeal to advertisements was an easy way initially to grab the consumer's attention, but as other advertisers adopted this method, the amount of sex appeal had to increase to gain the same amount of attention that their advertisements received when sex appeal was first used. The same evolution can be seen with comedy or violence in advertisements. Innovative approaches to Interruption Marketing are pushed to the extremes as their effectiveness is quickly exhausted through advertiser competition. Advertisers need an advertising approach that is effective and sustainable.

A more significant barrier to Interruption Marketing is the breakdown of mass media and the options that new media outlets present. Interruption Marketing worked well with limited media outlets—advertisers were able to reach a large audience when consumers had only a few television channels or radio stations from which to choose. But that approach has lost its effectiveness as society has diversified into many media, subcultural, value, and demographic subgroups. The individual's needs often cannot be addressed through impersonal advertisements tailored to mass media. This changing social landscape provides an opening for alternatives like Niche and Lifestyle Marketing. Niche Marketing focuses on reaching out to those people with a specific interest and Lifestyle Marketing (Kahle & Valette-Florance, 2012) consists of appealing to those people with a particular lifestyle.

Some large corporations moved to nontraditional marketing models such as product placement, which attempts to hide advertisements within content that consumers already desire. The shortcomings of Interruption Marketing have created opportunities for the IDLBB model to be successful. The increasing customer resistance set the stage for a new solution: a sustainable and effective method for companies to advertise to their target audience.

Permission Marketing

With advertising in need of a new approach, Godin presents Permission Marketing. Permission Marketing offers customers the opportunity to receive marketing material and only markets to them after receiving permission. A common example of Permission Marketing is e-mail newsletter sign-ups. The clothing store, Gap, has an e-mail list which customers can sign up for in exchange for "style, news and an exclusive offer" (Gap, 2012). When interested customers give their e-mail addresses to businesses to inform them about new products and sales, they are giving the businesses permission to advertise to them. This approach stands in stark contrast to the principles of Interruption Marketing. It utilizes the business' and customer's time most effectively, reduces media clutter, and puts the customer in charge of the relationship.

Permission Marketing utilizes everybody's time efficiently. Advertising funds and efforts are spent more effectively by initially asking permission of a large audience but then only proceeding with those consumers who grant it. This approach self-selects the appropriate target audience and results in a higher rate of return with engaged customers. Permission Marketing also eliminates clutter, in contrast to the media saturation created by Interruption Marketing. Advertisements are more impressionable when the customer does not have to worry about sifting through irrelevant advertisements. Advertisers can be confident that they are utilizing their marketing efforts efficiently when utilizing Permission Marketing. This modern approach recognizes that businesses can succeed by embracing niches and subcultures, not by rejecting them in favor of mass markets. This approach also allows companies to know its audience intimately and use their resources most effectively.

Customers in Control

Permission Marketing puts customers in control of the business relationship. By asking customers for their attention, businesses are reversing the traditional marketing relationship. Customers can grant permission, and businesses will pursue them, instead of advertiser's forcing their own agenda on customers. This change addresses one of the inherent flaws of Interruption Marketing: businesses who act as if they have obtained customer permission when they have not.

Permission Marketing honors the value of the customer's permission, which positively influences their relationship capital. This theory respects individuals and their time, and it works to build trust that results in loyal customer relationships. Obtained permission is the key to this loyalty, which is why businesses will heavily guard it. Taking advantage of customer permission and contact information by selling or sharing them only decreases the value of the permission and the relationship capital. By abusing its customer's trust, the business's ability to engage customers decreases. Relationship capital is tied directly to the value of a customer's permission and ensures that this permission is not abused. Violating the permission hurts the business as much as it bothers the customers, and it essentially becomes an internal control to ensure customer permission protection.

Permission Marketing is an effective alternative to Interruption Marketing that hinges on obtaining customer approval before expending additional marketing efforts. Permission Marketing emphasizes the importance of the customer and this relationship is elevated higher through Relationship Marketing.

Relationship Marketing

In *Winning the Customer*, Lou Imbriano, former Chief Marketing Officer for the New England Patriots, explains the value of customer relationships and satisfaction in Relationship Marketing. Relationship Marketing is an advertising approach that focuses on developing the long-term customer relationship to generate business, rather than the short-term value of a single sale to generate revenue (Imbriano, 2012, p. 95). Relationship Marketing realizes that revenue comes essentially from the customer relationship and accordingly elevates the importance of that relationship. To build strong relationships with customers, businesses need to focus on meeting the customer's needs. In Relationship Marketing, businesses do this task to build customers' trust and favor, which heavily contributes to achieving favorable relationship capital.

In *Digital Capital*, business strategy author Don Tapscott characterizes relationship capital as a company's "ability to engage customers, suppliers and other partners in mutually beneficial value exchanges" (Tapscott, Lowy, & Ticoll, 2000). Tapscott's definition is similar to how Imbriano describes Relationship Marketing: "creating and leveraging people and relationships for everyone's good" (Imbriano, p. 137). Relationship capital can broadly be termed as a measure of the customer's investment in a company, which is partially defined by the value the customer receives out of the relationship. If that value is significant and beneficial, the customer–business relationship will become mutually beneficial and can be considered successful.

Relationship Marketing can also be complicated when the line between the friendship and the business relationship begins to get blurry. Imbriano emphasizes building "unbreakable relationships" in the business context and explains how strong friendships often resulted. Sometimes, these friends asked favors that were not in his best business interest, but he granted them out of loyalty to his friends. It is difficult to determine if a business owner is going the extra mile out of pure friendship or to maintain a client. But Imbriano holds that this distinction between friendship and business does not matter as long as the goal is achieved.

To Imbriano, the ultimate intentions behind customer–business relationships do not matter as long as the customer's needs are met. Imbriano illustrates this point from a restaurant example: he wanted wasabi but the restaurant had just run out. Though slightly disappointed, Imbriano carried on with his meal until his waiter came back to his table, sweating with some wasabi. Imbriano was impressed and did not know if the waiter made the extra effort to go out and buy wasabi for him to receive a large tip, or if he was just really nice and wanted Imbriano to have his wasabi. But the reason for the waiter's effort does not matter to Imbriano because the results were delivered: he got wasabi. This example illustrates how focusing on the customer's needs naturally leads to a mutually beneficial relationship for the customer and business.

Marketing Conclusion

Permission and Relationship Marketing are viable alternatives in light of Interruption Marketing's ineffectiveness. The social landscape has become less compatible for Interruption Marketing to be successful. Permission and Relationship Marketing are more sustainable alternatives that value the customer relationship. Both marketing theories focus on building valuable relationship capital by being mutually beneficial for the buyer and seller and protecting the customer relationship. These progressive theories are the future standards of marketing on the Internet and are embraced by bloggers.

Blogs

This section explains how the nature of the Internet and blogs embraces the Handmade movement. This section also explains how progressive marketing theories function in the IDLBB model and how IGC utilizes them.

Indie Girl Culture

IGC is the cultural framework from which the IDLBB model developed. This independent, or "indie," value subculture is a primarily female community that was born on the Internet. IGC encompasses a wide range of media and topics including fashion, crafting, design, and photography. Although IGC is widespread across different social media platforms like Pinterest, Twitter, and Facebook, blogs are the central lifeblood of the culture where the primary interactions between bloggers and readers happen. Instagram is emerging as a significant platform for personalities to develop and personal interactions to materialize that uses the principles of the IDLBB model. Indie Girl bloggers are likely to share things as personal as the outfit they are wearing that day; pictures they took; their reasoning behind lifestyle or parenting choices; or things they've crafted, baked, or designed.

Primary Blog Case Studies

IGC can be represented through three influential Indie Girls and their blogs: *Designlovefest (DLF)*, *A Beautiful Mess (ABM)*, and *Fancy Treehouse (FTH)*. Each blog has a primary focus, but can still be classified as lifestyle blogs because they frequently feature personal pictures, crafts, outfits, recipes and more, and have an accompanying business.

- *ABM* is a lifestyle blog run by crafter Elsie Larson (2010). *ABM* consistently features an abundance of new DIY projects and lifestyle inspiration. Elsie used to run Red Velvet, an online and brick-and-mortar vintage boutique, but closed that down and now offers products through *ABM*'s online shop.
- *DLF* is a design blog run by graphic designer Bri Emery. *DLF* is a bright, positive blog where she posts "exquisitely curated layouts featuring bright colors and fabulous design, mixed with witty typography and a flair for the unexpected" (2012). Bri taught a traveling Photoshop class until the end of 2015 and now mainly focuses on creating original content in partnership with brands.
- *FTH* is a fashion blog run by Coury Combs. *FTH* documents Coury and her family's everyday outfits, which she pairs with some sweet sentiments about their daily adventures. Coury ran an accompanying online store where she sold self-altered thrifted clothing from 2008 until March 2017 (Combs, 2017). Now, Coury is focusing being an "influencer" and partnering with brands to represent them.

These blogs represent the epitome of IGC and illustrate the success of the IDLBB model. The next section explores how the Internet and blogs work together to advance the IDLBB model, with particular attention to these three blogs.

Individual Empowerment through Social Media Platforms

The Internet has maximized the ideals of individual empowerment rooted in the modern Handmade movement and changed the social landscape by offering new, accessible opportunities to interact. These opportunities allow individuals to voice their opinion and connect with others, expanding their circle of influence and connections. Users are realizing this power and are capitalizing on it to share knowledge, collaborate, empower themselves, and build creative communities.

Social media platforms accentuated the importance of the user and gave them a voice. These platforms were tailored to the individual and thrived on user content, encouraging individuals to share their opinion. Facebook, Twitter, Instagram, YouTube, and blogs exhibit the direct Network Effect, where the value of the platform increases with its network size. Because of the large amounts of content and users on these platforms, small businesses have the chance to compete with large corporations. This democratization of marketing echoes the ideals of individual empowerment and mainstream independence first popularized in the punk subculture.

The Internet created irreplaceable channels for opportunity that are now essential to the growth and continuance of the Handmade movement. The individual empowerment created through the Internet is not just limited to the business owner, but also extends to the customer. The Internet allows customers to search for a product's best price, a privilege that used to be limited to industry insiders. Airlines' fares and Amazon are examples of this competition.

The viral nature of the Internet embraces the reversal of the customer–business relationship introduced by progressive marketing theories. The individual's extended influence through social media platforms provides a trusting audience to make the individual's opinion more influential than ever before. This cultural change encourages businesses to guard the integrity of its work and customer relationships since it can be damaged easily through social media. The Internet's inherent empowerment of the individual through social media platforms proves to be an ideal place for Permission Marketing to play an influential role.

Blogs

Blogs play a powerful role in empowering individuals and establishing businesses. It is the primary tool propelling the growth of the IDLBB model and IGC. The personal disposition of blogs fits well with its high level of customizability. The blog's lack of restraint in its design and layout allows each blog to be personalized. Blog entries are referred to as posts and can include pictures, video, and sound in addition to standard text. Entries are displayed in reverse chronological order and users have the ability to comment on them. Individuals maintain most blogs, but blogging teams and contributors are becoming common. The ability to instantly publish or change content allows blogs to be very personalized and is in stark contrast to traditional media (i.e. books, magazines, and film). Readers can also subscribe to blogs and receive updates when there are new posts, which makes them a perfect vehicle for Permission Marketing. Readers give bloggers their permission to advertise to them when they subscribe to them, which allows bloggers to maintain a nonaggressive nature, even if they are promoting their own work.

The personal nature of blogs fosters relationship capital between the reader and the blogger more easily and quickly than a larger, corporate company could. The emotional connection that develops between reader and blogger is enhanced through potential further interactions, blog comments, and other social media. All of these elements combine to make blogs the primary tool for the IDLBB model.

Blogosphere Subcommunities

The blogosphere, or the collective network of blogs, has divided itself into subcommunities, which makes it easy to effectively utilize Niche and Lifestyle Marketing. Blogging niches have developed, like IGC which are built around similar interests and/or lifestyles. The dominating blogging subcommunities consist of news, politics, gossip, fashion, and food.

The blogosphere has incredible power through the Long Tail theory, an idea popularized by Chris Anderson of *Wired*, (2006), which refers to the potential lying in the larger population. According to the Long Tail theory, around 20% of blogs receive the majority of attention and the remaining 80% tend to stay out of the limelight and seem relatively insignificant. The Long Tail theory argues that the total amount of attention received by the top 20% and the remaining 80% is the same. This theory recognizes the significant role these non-dominating blogs play in keeping the community strong and active.

The Power of the Blogosphere against Mainstream Media (MSM)

The blogosphere empowers individuals by sidestepping the standard editor of traditional media that became our culture's tastemakers through their publishing and distributing power. Frank Warren, author of *PostSecret* (the blog and book), an ongoing community mail art project, spoke about indirect censorship when publishing one of his books. Warren's publishers forced him to omit some secrets from the book that they thought Walmart would deem as "inappropriate" and would keep them from purchasing the book, thus losing a significant portion of revenue from book sales. Warren stated that the threat of not being shelved by Walmart and other corporate giants is a subtle censorship that has been forced onto authors and artists.

Publishers and editors are playing a large role in shaping culture tastemakers, which can easily go unnoticed. Corporate giants offer large amounts of money and shelf space and play a huge role in determining content, as evidenced by Warren's experience. These corporate giants make their editorial decisions based on what they think will sell, which determines what people can and will buy. By removing the editors from the publishing process, society is allowed to become culture's tastemakers themselves. Blogs are what allow individuals to do this (Hewitt, 2005). For example, though the publishers determined the contents of Warren's book, he was able to freely publish any secret, including the rejected ones, on his *PostSecret* blog (Warren, 2005).

While corporations are driven by projected sales, bloggers are driven by audience reception. Bloggers know if their content resonates with their audience by the responses it receives through comments, views, or tweets. The reactions from a large collection of individuals can elevate self-published promotion to the forefront of society with a force similar to that of large corporations. For example, Justin Bieber's music on YouTube attracted so much attention that he was pursued for a recording contract. Instead of content being filtered through one person, social media platforms filter content through society at large. This change has allowed the blogosphere to become its own editor and to create a disruptive force to corporate tastemakers.

Blogosphere's Check on Itself and MSM

The blogosphere expects accuracy and integrity as a community. Blogs have shown that they are crucial to the new way in which information is spread through the Internet. Blogs attempt to represent the truth and carefully source information, and the blogosphere as a whole ensures the validity of any reported material. Other bloggers and individuals are more likely to call out discrepancies from bloggers due to the lack of business and political ties in the vast blogosphere and the instant nature of blogging and social media. This indirect accountability encourages bloggers to assert their own integrity and address inaccuracies from others on a regular basis.

Through the blogosphere, individuals also have an influence on MSM. In *BLOG*, Hugh Hewitt (2005) illustrates the credibility of the blogosphere. Focusing mainly on current events and politics, Hewitt contrasts the blogosphere with MSM. He argues that MSM do not cover all topics evenly and that society is subject to this bias. The blogosphere provides an alternative to this bias. It is a means for information acquisition, in-depth discussion, and activism so that important issues are brought to the MSM. Hewitt demonstrates this point with Jayson Blair, a journalist at the *New York Times* (NYT). Blair was caught plagiarizing and fabricating dozens of stories, but he was not fired when this problem was discovered. Although the MSM ignored the issue, the blogosphere realized the importance of this issue and maintained pressure on the situation until Blair was eventually fired. Individuals have gained a powerful voice against the MSM through blogs. Of course, sometimes misinformation spreads through the blogs as well.

In the blogosphere, relationship capital is fostered by accuracy, credibility, and transparency, which establish a blogger's trustworthiness and integrity, two influential factors in determining relationship capital. The overall feeling a company's general customer has toward a business is the most effective gauge of a company's relationship capital. It is important for blogs to know the nature of relationship capital to allow them to build and to maintain healthy business relationships.

Blogging vs. Advertising

Advertising often intends to persuade its audience to do something, while blogging more often focuses on sharing something. Bloggers become sponsors when they are paid to advertise, which covers activities such as educating about a product or company, motivating a purchase, or creating relationships. Bloggers must ethically disclose these sponsorships to their readers to maintain a transparent relationship with their audience and to keep any relationship capital they've built.

Maintaining transparency with one's audience allows blogs to grow freely, as *The Secret Diary of Steve Jobs* showed. *The Secret Diary* is a humorous blog written from the late Steve Jobs' imagined perspective (Lyons, 2012). *The Secret Diary* was clearly not real, but this content was effectively communicated to the audience, and they loved it (Schofield, 2007). This blog showed that audiences will respond positively if the author's intentions are clear and transparent, even if the content is not true. Transparent intentions between the blogger and the audience are essential to create and maintain valuable relationship capital.

Bloggers will lose credibility if they are not transparent with their audience. Walmart learned the importance of blogging with integrity from its traveling blog, *Wal-Marting Across America*. Walmart hired two writers to travel across the US in their RV and camp out in Walmart parking lots. The writers documented their trip in a blog, or a flog, an advertisement made to look like an authentic blog—a fake blog. They posted about all the friendly Walmart employees they met along their trip and how each of them loved their job with a passion. Although the couple first planned to take the trip on their own, they were subsequently financially supported by Walmart and did not reveal this funding on their blog (Gogoi, 2006). Walmart intended for the blog to improve customer perceptions about the controversial corporation, but once the undisclosed sponsorship got out, it hurt their reputation and credibility even more than before the blog started. The idea of trust and transparency is crucial to create favorable relationship capital with one's audience. As Godin (1999) points out in *Permission Marketing*, it is permissible to make a mistake, but deception is not tolerated.

Transparent Relationships

Within IGC, bloggers have needed to ensure transparency regarding sponsorships to respect the reader relationship and protect relationship capital. It is a common practice for companies to send products to popular bloggers to feature on their blogs as a form of discrete advertising. Bloggers realize this and have created some standard practices to protect their integrity. Most bloggers only accept products that they choose and/or fit into their personal style. It is also common for them to denote if a product is received from a company. Bloggers usually note gifts by crediting the product as "courtesy of" (c/o) the company or by thanking them in the post copy. By distinguishing sponsored products and posts, bloggers have maintained the value of their opinion and their reader relationship.

Blogger Naomi Davis of *Love Taza* recently posted about fashion-conscious maternity clothing and recommended some brands after clarifying that the post was not sponsored. This disclosure let her audience know that she was not recommending these specific brands because they were reimbursing her, but because she genuinely thinks they are good brands. Her readers value her opinion and she is protecting its value by clarifying that it is free from other influences. Bloggers who do not disclose when they are being sponsored for featuring content essentially destroy whatever relationship capital they have built up for a short-term gain. Once the audience discovers the hidden relationship, the audience's trust is broken, and the ability to advertise to them in the future is lost. It should also be noted that relationship capital is damaged even if the audience merely *thinks* the blogger is hiding something from them.

Along with disclosing business relationships, it is important for bloggers to note if their blogs are for-profit. For-profit blogging is common as it allows bloggers to devote adequate time to blogging. Featured-content sponsorships, advertisements, and affiliate programs are popular ways of generating blog revenue through advertisers. Featured-content sponsorships are posts in which companies pay bloggers to show off a product or service. Advertisements show up as pictures, sometimes videos, around the blog content. Affiliate programs generate revenue when readers click-through on a blog's link and/or make purchases. Ad-free blogging is a popular movement where bloggers believe that advertisements devalue the medium. Regardless, it has become important for bloggers to disclose any financial support to their readers so that the relationship is kept clear and transparent.

Sincere Personalities

When using the IDLBB model, blogging personalities have needed to maintain sincerity around their content, to ensure that it is not deceptively concocted to generate sales. Fake personalities can destroy relationship capital because it so strongly violates the audience's trust. Especially in the Handmade market, the customer usually makes a conscious decision to shop Handmade in an attempt to separate themselves from big corporations and support individuals. The collective blogosphere usually provides general assurance that blogging personalities are sincere and genuine through cross-checking them against other social media platforms and personal connections. Because this blogging approach is so holistic and interconnected with one's personal life, it prevents companies from creating a personality to represent their brand. In turn, companies need to seek out an already established personality to represent their brand.

Business Blogs

Personal blogs are powerful platforms for individuals that increase the extent of their influence. Blogs provide individuals with a platform to promote their opinions and represent themselves on the Internet. When blogging individuals have accompanying businesses, like within the IDLBB model, a business blog has become a powerful tool that can be used to foster strong relationship capital for the business.

Business blogs are categorized as blogs that communicate business-related information to their readership. Blogs provide businesses with a platform that allows them to compete with larger corporate sites, while also empowering small businesses to take full advantage of the personal relationship that they can provide the customer with. The personal nature surrounding blogs creates emotional investment which fosters relationship capital, as mentioned earlier. This relationship capital provides small businesses with an edge that enables them to compete with larger businesses.

Emotional Connection Fosters Relationship Capital

Elsie's blog, *ABM*, exemplifies how strong relationship capital can be developed through blogs. *ABM's* audiences became emotionally invested in her business through her blog, as they are nearly synonymous. In her e-course teaching the nuances of successful blogging, *Blog Love*, Elsie notes that her readers wanted to see posts about her shop, Red Velvet, which essentially served as self-promotion for her (Larson, 2010). In other words, her readers are so emotionally invested in her business that they are actually *requesting* more of her self-promotion; they want to know more about her business and what she is doing with it. This re-lationship capital that developed through her blog is highly valuable. Not only are her customers loyal—they are actively *pursuing* her business.

Coury of *FTH* also took advantage of her strong customer relationship by frequently promoting her online store. She would post a picture of the entire stock she had added to her store, often ten to twenty pieces, along with bigger pictures of her favorite pieces (Combs, 2012). Nevertheless, her audience did not generally feel exploited from this self-promotion. They wanted it to see how she styled the pieces. The self-promoting content fitted well within her own blog's character, because it was also personal and matched the overall IGC style. This relationship directly contrasts to Interruption Marketing, in which businesses are forcing their advertisements on customers.

The emotional connection between Elsie and Coury's business and their read-ers breaks down the barrier that corporations have built between the buyer and the seller. In fact, the buyer–seller relationship becomes reminiscent of the relation-ships that craftsmen cultivated during the Arts and Crafts movement. The indi-vidual is empowered with the craft and the purchase becomes an experience. The personal relationship is revived, and strong relationship capital is reestablished.

Lifestyle Approach Advantages

The IDLBB model capitalizes on self-promotion and expands its appeal through the lifestyle blogging approach. Even if potential customers are not interested in a business' products or services, they may still connect with the blogger's lifestyle or personality. This connection allows bloggers to appeal to a wider audience who can still engage with the content provided, even if it is not in-terested in the business product or service. It also creates an opportunity for this audience to be exposed to potentially relevant products that are introduced later. In an *Interview with Emma and Elsie from Red Velvet*, Emma Chapman, Elsie's sister and *ABM* co-owner, states that monetizing their blogs through sponsors has been a big help to their business, but that being able to connect with their audience has been even better (Parry, 2011). By sharing their lifestyle and interests, in addition to promoting their business, they are creating more opportunities to connect with customers.

Blogging Personality

With any blog, the ability to determine whose preferences are primary has become important, but most notably for business blogs that are dealing with audiences who also serve as their primary customer base. Some marketers argue that the business should appeal to one's audience, but others argue that the business should stay true to the owner's own preferences. In *Romancing the Customer*, Paul Temporal (Temporal & Trott, 2001) argues that businesses utilizing Relationship Marketing should prioritize activities of value to the customer. In *The Age of Engage*, Denise Shiffman (2008) speaks against that approach and argues, "Your company's voice is defined through the narrative you create, and that narrative encompasses your company style, tone, view of the marketplace, vision of the future, and passion" (p. 87). Shiffman's approach focuses on the company's ability to represent itself accurately to the customers, not on how to please the customer. If people do not engage with the vision a business presents, Shiffman believes that "they don't associate with your vision, passion, and creed," and that they are not your target audience anyway (Shiffman, 2008, p. 95).

Compelling support for this view comes from Bri of *DLF*. In a post from November 2011, she wrote, "I saw my blog grow when I started to become more picky...only post what you REALLY LOVE. if *you* are obsessed with it, they probably will be too [sic]" (Emery, 2011). Bri encouraged appealing to one's own preferences before the audience's, as this approach will help one gain an audience with similar tastes (2008, p. 95). From this perspective, catering to the audience is not an essential part of the success of the IDLBB model. Meeting the audience's needs is not as important as developing the blog or company's brand to attract the right audience.

The Blog Brand

Within the IDLBB model, the blogging personality becomes the business' brand. The distinction between a personal or business blog becomes blurry because the two have become so intertwined. For Bri, her personality, her design style, and her business are almost indistinguishable on *DLF*. Speaking of her readers, Bri says that she "started getting comments like 'this is so design-lovefest!' or 'bri would love this!' and that's because they start to get a sense of who I am and what my brand is all about [sic]" (Emery, 2011). Bri's blogging personality and her brand have essentially merged into DLF and created such a strong brand that readers use it to define things.

Defining a business with one's blogging personality has become a significant way to differentiate a business. Imbriano (2012) briefly touched upon this point in regards to Relationship Marketing: your personality is completely unique to you and is a legitimate way to differentiate your business. The business offerings are defined by the blog's personality and the values it reflects. These qualities are a valid way to distinguish businesses and choose favorites. In IGC, there are many businesses that have similar products and approaches to their work. Although overall style and price are still defining purchase points, brand personality is increasingly becoming important in the purchase decision. For example, a number of blogging vintage clothes retailers like FTH, Liebemarlene Vintage, and MouseVox Vintage. While they had similar products and prices, their blogging personalities differed and distinguished each respective brand.

Personal Representatives

Businesses with personality brandings create a personal connection to increase their relationship capital through customer engagement. Larger businesses realize this and try to create that personal connection through a company spokesperson. Well-known spokespeople include Dennis Haysbert for Allstate Insurance and LeBron James for Nike. It is important to distinguish that Lebron *represents* the Nike brand, while Bri is *becoming* the DLF brand. Even with spokespeople, the IDLBB model still offers a more direct personal relationship with their customers than corporations.

With bloggers becoming brands, readers are pursuing and consuming a brand without even realizing it. Readers are invested in the blogger and the content they provide, without recognizing that they have become emotionally invested in the brand in addition to the blogger. By consistently reading or subscribing, readers are partaking in Permission Marketing by supporting a lifestyle and embracing a personality, which both encompass the business brand. It is a successful advertising approach, but it is fundamentally different than more traditional methods of advertising, such as Interruption Marketing, because of its nonaggressive delivery through blogs and the relationship capital cultivated through its personal nature. Readers are pursuing the brand because they like and enjoy it. The business blogger has created a scenario where their customers enjoy their self-promotion and seek it out. They have created an effective pull-relationship where they are not pushing advertisements on customers.

Blog Conclusion

The Internet provides a platform to emphasize the importance of individuals and empower them against large corporations, echoing the same ideals that began in the Arts and Crafts movement. The blogosphere has become a powerful force against MSM and allows individual's more influence. The blog's personal and nonaggressive nature includes elements of Permission Marketing, making it an effective vehicle to promote individual businesses and products. The success of blogs depends entirely on positive relationship capital. When substantial relationship capital develops, bloggers' personalities have the chance to develop into fleshed-out brands, which gives these small businesses a distinct advantage over large businesses.

Conclusions

IGC is an offshoot community of the modern Handmade movement, which has its roots in the Arts and Crafts movement and punk subculture. The Arts and Crafts movement revived the role of the craftsman and the craft, empowering the individual in light of the Industrial Revolution, and developed a simple style that favored handmade qualities. The punk subculture built the roots of the DIY attitude, which led to the development of the modern Handmade movement. The Handmade movement echoes the individual empowerment created through craft and fosters a strong sense of community through the revival of personal purchases.

Interruption Marketing is less appropriate for the social landscape. This change in social landscape allowed progressive marketing theories to flourish. Permission Marketing's emphasis on meeting the customer's needs echoed the Handmade movement's individual empowerment ideals. Relationship Marketing embodied the attitude behind the personal purchases that were reoccurring. The success of these theories depended on creating favorable relationship capital among its customers.

The Internet embraces and furthers individual empowerment through new media outlets and social media platforms. This effect is especially embraced through blogs, which naturally encourage the development of relationship capital through their personal nature. Businesses took advantage of this relationship capital and created blogs that directed the posts toward themselves. Once sustainable relationship capital developed, blogging personalities began to define businesses. Personalities were becoming brands and readers were consuming them. IGC is an illustration of this phenomenon, which uses the IDLBB model as a basis for its success. This theory embodies the dynamics of this culture and extends them to subcultures and industries.

From this analysis, the successful implementation of the IDLBB model ultimately lies in its ability to foster favorable relationship capital through individual empowerment. The growth and success within IGC highlight innovative approaches that are influencing the marketing industry and prove the IDLBB model to be an effective, sustainable form of small business marketing.

References

Anderson, C. (2006). *The long tail*. New York: Hyperion.

Bowman, L. G. (1990). *American arts & crafts: Virtue in design*. Los Angeles, CA: Los Angeles County Museum of Art.

Combs, C. (2012). "New in Store," Fancy Treehouse (blog), May 4, 2012, http://fancytreehouse.blogspot.com/2012/05/new-in-store.html, accessed May 2012.

Emery, B. (2011). "You Gotta Start Somewhere!," *Designlovefest* (blog), November 21, 2011, www.designlovefest.com/2011/11/you-gotta-start-somewhere/, accessed April 2012.

Gap. "Gap," www.gap.com/, accessed May 2012.

Godin, S. (1999). *Permission marketing: Turning strangers into friends, and friends into customers*. New York: Simon & Schuster.

Gogoi, P. (2006). "Wal-Mart's Jim and Laura: The Real Story," *Bloomberg Businessweek*, www.bloomberg.com/news/articles/2006-10-09/wal-marts-jim-and-laura-the-real-storybusinessweek-business-news-stock-market-and-financial-advice, accessed May 2017.

Hannon, S. M. (2010), *Punks: A guide to an American subculture*. Santa Barbara, CA: Greenwood Press.

Hewitt, H. (2005). *Blog: Understanding the information reformation that's changing your world*. Nashville, Tenn: T. Nelson Publishers.

Howard, J. (1969). *Protest in the sixties* (Annals of the American Academy of Political and Social Science, Vol. 382, March 1969), PDF e-book, 48, www.jstor.org/stable/1037113, accessed May 2012.

Imbriano, L. (2012). *Winning the customer: Turn consumers into fans and get them to spend more*. New York: McGraw-Hill.

Kahle, L. R., & Valette-Florence, P. (2012). *Marketplace lifestyles in an age of social media: Theory and method*. Armonk, NY: M. E. Sharpe.

Koplos, J., & Metcalf, B. (2010). *Makers: A history of American studio craft*. Chapel Hill, NC: University of North Carolina Press.

Larson, E. (2010). "Session 1: What's the Point?" Blog Love (blog e-course), November 26, 2010, http://abeautifulmess.typepad.com/bloglove/2010/11/whats-the-point-.html, accessed April 2012.

Lyons, D. (2012). www.fakesteve.net/, accessed April 2012.

Oakes, K. (2009). *Slanted and enchanted: The evolution of Indie culture*. New York: Henry Holt and Co.

Parry, B. (2011). "Interview with Emma and Elsie from Red Velvet," *Ozarks News Journal*, March 3, 2011, news video, www.youtube.com/watch?v=zGsZ-C-LNBY, accessed April 2012.

Schofield, J. (2007). "Who is the real Fake Steve Jobs?" *The Guardian*, August 8, 2007, www.guardian.co.uk/technology/2007/aug/09/guardianweeklytechnologysection.stevejobs, accessed April 2012.

Shiffman, D. (2008). *The age of engage: Reinventing marketing for today's connected, collaborative, and hyperinteractive culture*. Ladera Ranch, CA: Hunt Street Press.

Tapscott, D., Lowy, A., & Ticoll, D. (2000). *Digital capital: Harnessing the power of business webs*. Boston, MA: Harvard Business School Press.

Temporal, P., & Trott, M. (2001). *Romancing the customer: Maximizing brand value through powerful relationship management*. Singapore: Wiley.

Warren, F. (2005). "PostSecret," www.postsecret.com/, accessed May 2012.

7

UNDERSTANDING THE VOTER DECISION TRADE-OFF ANALYSIS AS A FOUNDATION FOR DEVELOPING MORE PREDICTIVE POLLING METHODOLOGIES

Thomas J. Reynolds

Introduction

By the time you read this, Donald Trump's surprising win in the 2016 primaries and in the general election will have been analyzed by many. In January 2017, a Google search with the words "why did Donald Trump win the election" got more than 44 million hits. On November 10, 2016, CNN's Gregory King published an article enumerating 24 "theories" that attempted to explain the event (http://edition.cnn.com/2016/11/10/politics/why-donald-trump-won/). In December, Salon.com posted an article, originally appearing on Alternet.com, with 13 more. NPR.org had seven; BBC offered five.

Theories—well, not really theories in any strict sense, but explanations—abound, and some of these explanations seem more plausible than others. Many pundits have exactly opposite viewpoints. It was racism, said one; it wasn't, said another. It was Comey; no it wasn't. It was sexism; no it wasn't. The bottom line is that the failure of Team Clinton and her band of non-questioning media supporters to correctly identify the key target market of swing states, which would ultimately determine the election outcome, in combination with their desire to favor her perceived status ultimately led to consistent reporting of incorrect polling results. This resulted in de-energizing her base, by their belief that "the election was in the bag."[1] Thus, the purpose of this piece is to posit a theory-based framework that can improve prediction of an observable, future event, in this case the outcome of an election, which was in fact the Achilles's heel of Mrs. Clinton and her band of media support staff in 2016.

As noted, Trump's win was so surprising in that it was not predicted by traditional polling data. None of the well-known national polling organizations put Trump's chances as high as 50–50. Was this a failure of the pollsters (read as: is polling science really science)? To be clear, this is not about

Monday-morning quarterbacking, claiming that we knew the outcome *a priori*. While the necessary data in the requisite format from a statistically representative sample by state may have been in someone's possession, most of us didn't have it. The intent of this piece is to introduce for future investigation a new decision framework extending prior work that has served as the cornerstone of the political strategy development process (Wirthlin, 2004, p. 142). The questioning methodology fueling this strategy model has been implemented via the Internet for the 2008 election, providing a baseline set of data (Reynolds, 2014) which will be extended here to illustrate this new conceptual approach to polling—framed in a new decision model for political application.

The specific data that go to the heart of the election contain information that aids in understanding the voter decision process. It is the understanding of the decision-making process that leads to optimizing strategy. And thus, it is this understanding that leads to the development of more accurate polling methods. That is because understanding the cognitive process underlying voter decision-framing—how voters gather and structure information personally relevant to their decision process—gives insight into what questions will best predict voting behavior. This understanding of the decision process is also central to assessing and strategizing about how best to affect voting likelihood. That decision is important to a candidate's strategy and to the predictive polling process; understanding voters who are predisposed to vote for a given candidate ("leaning toward" a candidate) is often the swing factor determining the election outcome. It is a strategic goal of a candidate to get Leaners in the candidate's favor to vote, and opposing Leaners not to vote. Therefore, the likelihood of success in this regard must be factored into the strategy development and polling process.

The specific intention of this work is to outline a detailed explanation of how political strategy is developed and its effect assessed which, in turn, will provide the framework for developing more predictive polling methods. Understanding how different voter segments frame their decisions (e.g. voting vs. not voting, Candidate A vs. Candidate B) that will provide the theory-based model required to identify the most predictive measures of voting behavior.

Background

Traditional polling methods involve three factors: the sampling plan (in this case, respondents who are registered voters, qualification of prior voting behavior, and time of day implemented), the administration framework (live telephone interview, an automated interview delivered over the phone, or responding directly to questions delivered via the Internet—by voice or in text), and the types and wording of the questions asked. There is inherent bias in each of these factors, and each has been known to influence the results.

To better predict voting behavior, one must predicate the research methods on the underlying decision processes of key voter segments. That is the same basis upon which strategy is developed. Conventional polling data will certainly gather background specifics like demographics and voter history including likelihood of voting, perceptions of the candidates with their positions on voter-relevant issues, and, if people are honest with their answers, likelihood of voting for a given candidate. Many of these types of data are relevant; however, on the subject of understanding the underlying manner in which the voting decision is framed, conventional polling data provide no more than fodder for speculation. Thus, the observed result is the overwhelming abundance of conjectural postelection theory generation following the unpredicted 2016 outcome of the Trump victory. Clearly, the answer lies in understanding the cognitive processes underlying voting intent. Moreover, since affecting voting intent is the express goal of research to develop political strategy, it makes sense to apply the theoretical underpinnings of the strategy development methodology to improve polling accuracy.

Strategy Development Optimization

Formulating and executing political strategy follow a general strategy development paradigm (Reynolds, 2017). This paradigm outlines how a successful strategy should be based on a thorough understanding of three things: (1) the problem framing parameters, (2) the underlying decision trade-off cognitive processes, and (3) an analytic model to develop and to serve as a basis to assess strategic options. The fundamental proposition here is that political strategy can be treated in the same way as many business strategies, analyzed in a similar way, and executed in a similar way. Moreover, many of the really interesting marketing problems— Coke vs. Pepsi, Miller Lite vs. Bud Light, Chevy vs. Ford—can be thought of similar to political campaigns. The common answer to all marketing problems, and the development of an optimal marketing strategy, is to understand the decision processes of the target customers. The simple bottom line is that if you know how folks think, you can greatly increase the likelihood of a successful sale.

Problem Framing

So let's take a look for a moment at the formulation of business strategy. The first step is to frame the problem space (Olson & Reynolds, 2001) by answering the following questions:

- What are the choice alternatives? (the candidates)
- Decisions about what? (what decision do we need to understand…To vote? For whom?)
- Who are the relevant customers? (your target market of potential "buyers")
- What is the decision context? (the key influencing environmental variables)

Choice alternatives? For the 2016 general election, the two are Hillary Clinton (D) and Donald Trump (R). More specifically, Mr. Trump was in reality a third-party alternative candidate, with no political experience, who successfully gained the Republican nomination.

<u>Decisions about what</u>? For the purpose of understanding how to best address improving polling accuracy, the decision process framing voting intent for the 2016 presidential race will be the focus.

<u>Who are the relevant customers who define the target market</u>? Some voters are committed *a priori* and their decisions are not subject to change… they state they will definitely vote for one candidate. Some, for example, vote for the party, not the person; others are single-issue voters, and a hardline position on an issue such as abortion or gun control would require heroic efforts to change. Some voters, however, are uncommitted or "soft identifiers" who lean in favor of one candidate but may be open to reassessing their position (including whether to vote or not).

True undecideds who intend to vote, commonly known as swing voters, may have one or more of the following attitudes:

1   I think the country is on the "wrong track."
2   I'm dissatisfied with Congressional ineffectiveness and Washington "gridlock."
3   I'm generally dissatisfied with current political environment.

Note that such voters can identify with either party. These negative attitudes regarding political theatre, however, serve to define the lens through which they view the competing candidates, which, in turn, guides their decision-making. The significant negative sentiment which existed throughout the nation regarding the political system presented Mr. Trump, the outsider, with a potentially significant advantage.

Likely recognizing this, for example, Hillary Clinton's attempt to refocus voters to the positive with the phrase, "You need someone to vote for, not someone to vote against" was tantamount to pushing a chain uphill. Once a negatively valenced, candidate-defining perception is established, it is nearly impossible to turn it into a positive. This fact is clearly evidenced by the significantly more effective role of negative political advertising, with negative advertising being as much as five times as effective as positive messages (Phillips, Urbany & Reynolds, 2008).

The target market, defined in its broadest sense, is undecided voters (including leaners). In a practical sense, because of the way the electoral college works and the ways the states allocate electors, each state constitutes its own unique target market (and a truly "national" campaign is only useful primarily in establishing very high-level, party-line positions). For that reason, the national polling that we often hear and see reported is likely to be misleading. The real strategic question is which states are "in the bank" and which states are "in play," meaning there exists reasonable potential to carry them in the election. This type of analysis for the 2016 election is presented in Table 7.1, which contains voting history by state over the

TABLE 7.1 Target Market "Equity" Electoral Analysis Including Negative Sentiment Index

| 206 | | 121 | | 211 |

Republican Base

C-Rep%	Elections 2012	2004	2000		Electoral	C-Rep%
64				Arizona	11	
67				Montana	3	83
67				North Dakota	3	78
67				South Dakota	3	77
70				Missouri	10	62
71				Texas	38	56
75				Georgia	16	
80				Nebraska	5	
80				West Virginia	5	
82				Tennessee	11	
88				Kentucky	8	
88				Louisiana	8	
89				Alabama	9	
100				Oklahoma	7	
100				Arkansas	6	
100				Kansas	6	
100				Utah	6	
100				Idaho	4	
100				Alaska	3	
100				Wyoming	3	
					165	

Former Obama Fans=41 Electoral

C-Rep%				State	Electoral
73				Indiana	11
79				South Carolina	9
80				North Carolina	15
83				Mississippi	6
					41

Swing States: GOP Congressional Majority

C-Rep%	Elections 2012	2004	2000		Electoral
				Obama "Effect"=75 Electoral	
				Iowa	6
				ohio	18
				virginia	13
				Florida	29
				Colorado	9
					75

C-Rep%				In Play (C-Rep%)=46 electoral	Electoral
70				Pennsylvania	20
60				Wisconsin	10
56				Michigan	16
					46

Negative Sentiment:
(on both measures)

⇒ US on the "Wrong Track"

⇒ Dissatisfied with Political Environment

Republican Base:	>55%
Swing States:	>52%
Democrat Base:	>42%

Democrat Base

	Elections 2012	2004	2000	State	Electoral	C-Rep%
				Illinois	20	45
				New Jersey	14	43
				New York	29	34
				Washington	12	33
				Minnesota	10	30
				Maine	4	25
				New Mexico	5	20
				California	55	18
				Oregon	7	14
				Maryland	10	10
				Massachusetts	11	0
				Connecticut	7	0
				Hawaii	4	0
				Rhode Island	4	0
				Delaware	3	0
				District of Columbia	3	0
				Vermont	3	0
					201	

Very Likely Clinton=10 Electoral

				State	Electoral	C-Rep%
				Nevada	6	67
				New Hampshire	4	75
					10	

Note: C-Rep% is the percentage of Republicans in Congress (prior to the 2016 election).

last four presidential elections (with electoral votes) and the percentage of Republicans in Congress at the time of the election.[2]

The red top left block seen in Table 7.1 indicates that there are 206 electors "in the bank" for Republicans, if the "Likely Republican" group is included. Similarly, the top right blue box indicates that there are 211 electors "in the bank" for the Democrats. The electoral votes being fairly close, attention turns to the swing states in the middle. If the candidates win their likely leaning states, the undecided states and their 121 electors will determine who wins the election. For that reason, polling should focus on a combination of both the likely leaning states and the swing states.

Although all of the states identified earlier as swing states have consistently voted for the Democratic candidate in the last two election cycles, they have a significant Republican base given their percentage representation in Congress. Clearly, the candidates and their strategy teams understand this. That is why the candidates focused on those states, and why neither candidate spent much or makes much effort to sway voters in states such as New York or California, or in locations such as Washington, D.C.; the outcome was too well-known in advance.[3] But the national polls are heavily influenced by those locations in state-specific polling.

> Assuming polling is analyzed by state by what methods do polls gain an in-depth understanding of what is underlying the voting-decision trade-off?

What is the decision context? Democratic-friendly mass media combined with frequently outlandish behavior of Candidate Trump creates a negative environment for the Republican candidate. The general, negative perception of the overall political environment, as noted in Table 7.1, favors his nonpolitical background. From a strategic perspective, Mr. Trump's trademark demonizing of his opponents, be they political, the media, or even the entire political system as a whole, serves to leverage his position in the political marketplace. Why? Because this emotion-activating descriptor is more likely to be the defining, top-of-mind association in the voters' minds. The relevance of this fact will become clear shortly.

Decision Theory

Once the target market is defined as voters in swing states, understanding the bases of their political decision process by voting intent segments serves as the basis for strategy development. And, traditional polling methods typically involve some form of importance assessment of issues and candidate traits relative to each of the candidates which serves as the foundation for strategy development. However, there are multiple, leap-of-faith assumptions underlying this form of polling questioning that are frequently ignored. The accuracy and honesty of the respondent, not to mention the lack of a theoretical model upon which these questions and their responses relate to the actual voting decision process. It is the specification of the latter that offers insight into the strategy development process (i.e. what you are trying to affect) which can serve as the basis for reconfiguring more insightful and thus predictive polling methods.

At the heart of gaining true insight into voter decision-making is the underlying decision model. One recently explored model involves asking a respondent for top-of-mind (ToM) associations with respect to both candidates. What has been found is that if there exists a clear preference or strong voting intent, a voter is very likely to provide a positive attribute for a preferred candidate, and a negative attribute for the less-favored candidate. It is this method for tapping into the association networks that frame the decision process that offers potential for polling that leads to strategy development. Thus, building a polling methodology based upon this understanding should provide a superior option to the existing methods.

To illustrate, suppose the Respondent was asked: "What is the first thing that comes to mind when I say Hillary Clinton?" The respondent says, "First woman president." Asking directly, "Is that a positive or a negative, to you?" obtains that valence of the response. If the respondent says, "a positive," the respondent is then asked: "What is the personally relevant implication to you of her becoming the first woman president?" The likely response is either some version of social equality or a leadership trait, such as "can better deal with the social problems facing the US." And to complete the decision network, the respondent is asked: "Why do you think it's important that the candidate will be able to deal with social problems facing the US?" The response in this example is "a family orientation will guide her decision making." What has been identified in this example is the underlying decision network underlying preference for Hillary Clinton.

In the example presented in Figure 7.1, the question, "What is the first thing that comes to mind when I say Donald Trump?" elicits "He will repeal Obamacare." The respondent views that as a negative, and the leadership trait associated with that attribute is "Caring/Concerned," in this case to be understood as "Uncaring or Unconcerned." "Why do you think it's important that the candidate be a Caring leader?" elicits "It will make this a better country." So, this negatively valenced decision-framing for Mr. Trump is that "this will NOT be a better country" because of his desire to repeal Obamacare.

The secondary valence ToM decision networks are also presented, along with the summary codes for the verbatim responses that are used in the analysis, in Figure 7.1. These secondary networks are required for the developing of strategic options premised on the principle of leveraging the determinant the respective decision equities and supplanting the decision disequities.

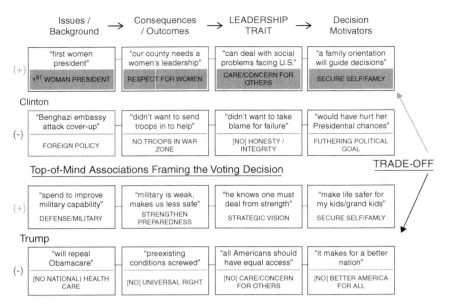

FIGURE 7.1 CODED Pro-Clinton Voting Decision Trade-off (+ vs. −) (*Note*: Decision Framework Adapted from Reynolds (2005)).

This tailored-questioning process to elicit both the positive and negative decision networks via the Internet was first implemented for the 2008 election (Reynolds, 2014). (Noteworthy is that a reliability estimate of self-coding of the levels obtained in this manner compared to the actual elicited verbatim responses was quite high.) A summary of the 2008 data of the 2×2 valence combinations for each voting intention classification with parallel estimates derived from small samples for the 2016 election is presented for illustrative purposes in Table 7.2. The estimates of the relative sizes of the voting intent groups were derived from information provided by one of the candidate's polling results. It is apparent that this database can and would be broken down by demographic targets for optimizing both candidates positioning communications (advertising and speeches) and media strategy.

The consistency of (+,−) decision contrasts for the "Very Likely" voters is quite substantial (82% and 89%, respectively). This construct is known as confirmation bias (Nickerson, 1998) which is the tendency to search for, interpret, favor, and recall information in a way that confirms one's preexisting beliefs or preconceptions, while giving disproportionately less consideration to alternative possibilities—and the avoidance of processing conflicting information. It is this principle that frames much of our decision-making. It is basically a type of cognitive bias resulting from a systematic error of inductive reasoning. And, this effect is stronger for emotionally charged issues and for

TABLE 7.2 Summary of Top-of-Mind Valences by Voting Likelihood: 2008 (National) and 2016 (Swing States Estimate)

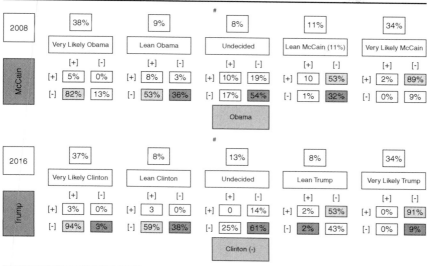

deeply entrenched beliefs, which politics clearly engenders. This method of obtaining the primary voting decision-framing networks is consistent with this theory of cognitive processing underlying the decision process. Extending the method to discover the attributes associated with the opposite valences for both candidates provides the necessary data to optimize political strategies. Given that this framework serves as the basis for strategy development, it makes sense to use this decision understanding to designing polling methods. Importantly, there are two primary differences between traditional means-end theory and laddering research methods (Reynolds & Gutman, 1988) underlying decision-making are (1) instead of focusing directly on the voter's values (terminal and instrumental), this approach focuses on the perception of the candidate's motivating end-goals (e.g. values) and (2) the instrumental belief in relevant leadership traits that lead the voter to believe that the end-goal can be achieved by this candidate.

In the 2008 data for the Obama vs. McCain election, there were 8% "undecideds" as compared to the estimated 13% for the 2016 data. Remarkably, this difference combined with the percentage of dual ToM negatives (people whose first response to each candidate was negative) indicates that 61% of "undecideds" fall within a "voting for the lesser of two evils" designation.

To build a strategic "game board" for the purpose of developing positioning communications (both positive and negative—primarily in the form of "attack ads"), a summary of the valenced codes for the potentially key sway-able groups is performed (see Table 7.3).

TABLE 7.3 Undecided Voters (16%) across All Swing States

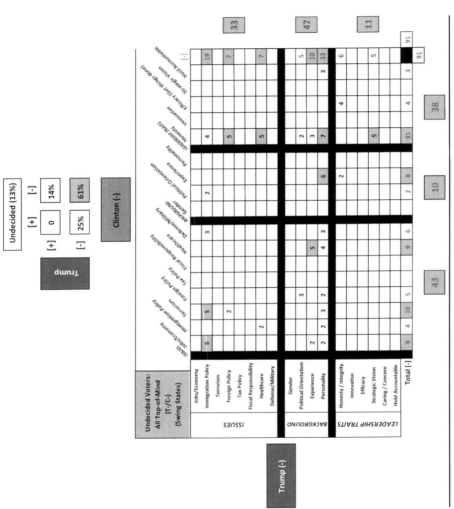

Note: [1] To be included, the percentage has to be greater than 1.49%.
[2] Brown checked-call measure used for both candidates.

This ToM summary represents the "best estimates" for the 61% hypothetical sample of "swing state undecideds" which is substantial and key to the "lesser of two evils" segment. So, to illustrate the strategy development process if you were part of Team Trump, you would first develop the optimal strategy for Mrs. Clinton, following war game precepts. The big negatives representing 66% of the total negatives for Mr. Trump which can be reinforced by attack ads are: 32% Personality; 10% Experience; 10% Immigration Policy; 7% Foreign Policy; and 7% Health care.

To maximize effectiveness, linking the very significant negative of Personality (e.g. crude, arrogant, egotistical, narcissist, and bully) to each of the issues offers a sound strategic opportunity. To round out the strategy development framework with high potential positive messages for Mrs. Clinton is a summary across all of the swing voters, which includes both "leaner" groups with the "undecideds," and is presented in Table 7.4. Leveraging the positive strategic equities of Political Orientation (21%), Gender (14%), and Immigration Policy (12%) appears to have the most potential for reinforcing the base supporters and appealing to a broader segment of the electorate. (For those unfamiliar, the "strategic game board" of the decision networks used to form each strategy, with examples, is detailed in the Appendix.)

Given that optimal strategies can be developed for the opposition (Mrs. Clinton), then anticipating that, optimal strategies can be developed for Mr. Trump using the decision networks summarized in the form of a "strategic game board" as a basis.

Implications for Polling Research

Current polling practice typically asks some form or the following question:

> If the election was held today would you vote for Candidate A or B?

Framing the issue in this way fails to provide an option for a probabilistic weighting, which is more reflective of the true nature of the voting decision. The following outlines a questioning process that provides the basis to develop and assess different weighting options.

The cognitive process underlying decision-making that underlies the strategy development process outlined here is based upon the first, valenced associative meaning for ToM associations for each candidate. The summary 2×2 tables of these valenced combinations broken down by key voting intent segments, as outlined earlier, serve as the foundation for developing political strategy and both positive and negative communications. The issue, then, is how can this understanding of the framing of the voting decision be used in political polling? The potential answer lies in determining the magnitude of the difference by asking the respondent for the relative importance of the first ToM

TABLE 7.4 Leaners and Undecided Voters (16%) across All Swing States

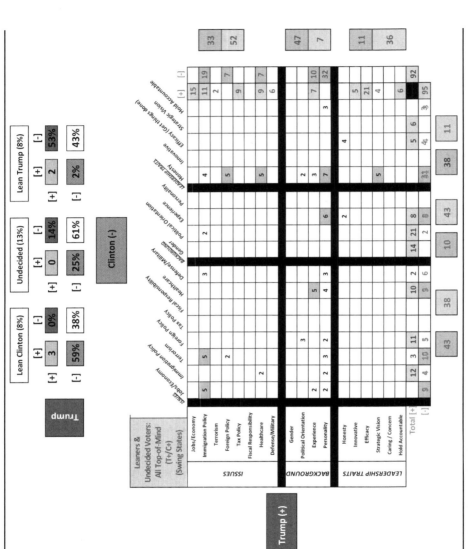

Note: [1] To be included, the percentage has to be greater than 1.49%.
[2] Brown shaded cell means used for both candidates

descriptors for each candidate. This difference can be obtained by asking the subject the following:

> Please allocate 7 points between the top-of-mind associations you men-
> tioned for each candidate which reflects how important they are with
> respect to determining your voting decision.

The resulting majority weighting identifying the most important criteria allows for a reliability assessment with regard to the voting intent classification
question. And, internal consistency with respect to confirmation bias can be
assessed for the opposite valence combinations of (+,−) and (−,+). Of particular
interest for the same valence combinations of (+,+) and (−,−) is the magnitude
of the difference between the point allocations. These differences offer the
basis to assign a probability for directional movement in terms of likely voting
behavior. For example, the assignment of descriptor importance points for
the same valences of 5:2, 6:1, or 7:0 would suggest a very reasonable, possibly
differential, likelihood of directional movement (implied weighting) to the
candidate who received the highest allocation. Thus, the clear opportunity
exists to develop a weighting system based upon assessing the basis of decision-
framing process. (The valenced pairwise classification types—i.e. issue, background, or leadership trait—may well have an interaction effect which should
be investigated.)

Suggested, then, is the following sequence of polling questions.

1   (a) ToM association and corresponding valence as well as the secondary
    valence ToM association. (b) Seven-point allocation question using the
    initial valenced ToM associations for each candidate as the basis.
2   Past voting behavior and likelihood to vote in the upcoming contest.
3   Likelihood of voting.
4   Demographics.
5   If the election was held today, what would you do? (Vote for Candidate A,
    Vote for Candidate B, or Not vote.)

The analysis of data from this question format should provide both the reliability estimates, already noted, and the basis for developing a differential weighting model based upon the point allocation question (1b) which can be directly
contrasted to the deterministic voting question format (5).

Likely the best format to explore this suggested polling approach would be
to follow one representative group of voters, sampling subgroups of them to
determine their changes over time. To minimize potential method bias, it is
further suggested that no subgroup is subjected to this method of polling more
than a very few times.

Summary

It has been posited that a successful business development strategy should be based on a thorough understanding of three things: (1) the problem framing parameters, (2) the underlying decision trade-off cognitive processes, and (3) an analytic model to develop and to serve as a basis to assess strategic options. The problem framing exercise clearly led to a determination of the key states that had potential for Mr. Trump. The fact that all but one of the states (Colorado) with more than 50% of Republicans in Congress at the time of the 2016 election was won by Mr. Trump was not focused upon or reported by any national media. This understanding clearly helps define the primary sample of voters to be focused upon by polling.

A decision model that identifies the framing of voter preference and voting intent grounded in the concept of neural networks provides a system to develop strategic communication positioning options (pro- and con-attack) which can be extended directly to the polling process. A suggested approach is outlined with further research ideas. The validation of this neural network approach underlying decision-making has recently been shown to be highly predictive with respect to the prediction of advertising creating purchase intent for a wide range of consumer products (Reynolds, in press). A recommendation is to extend this type of advertising research to assess the strength of neural connections to predicting changes in decision intent to political ads, both positive and attack-oriented.

Implication

In a small political study with undecided voters, it has been found by activating with a self-questioning online program using ToM associations to "ladder" (Reynolds & Gutman, 1988) to higher levels of abstraction for a combination of positive network for one candidate and a negative network for the other has moved voting intent significantly in the direction of the candidate with the positive ToM and away from the negative. This preliminary finding further supports the effect of confirmation bias in framing the voting decision.

Speculation

A logical extension of confirmation bias activated by a dual presentation, at the same time, of both positive and negative (attack) political advertising as part of the research format (Reynolds & Rochon, 1991; Reynolds, Westberg & Olson, 1997) by simultaneously activating the decision-framing function is that this would have a highly influential, directionally predictive effect.

Notes

1 There were three tempestuous factors that set the stage for the perfect storm for Mr. Trump in 2016; namely, the failure of President Obama to convince undecided voters that his views would be channeled through Mrs. Clinton, the significant effect of Mr. Trump's negative labeling of his opponent (Crooked Hillary) in terms of the key leadership trait of honesty, and the innovative media strategy of Mr. Trump to use Twitter and his "rally strategy" to gain both media coverage and energize his supporters.
2 The percentage of Republicans in Congress for a given state predicted the winner of every state but one, that being Colorado.
3 It was an apparent failed assumption by the Clinton campaign that the 4-election blue, consistently Democrat states of Pennsylvania, Wisconsin, and Michigan were "in the bank," ignoring the majority percentage of the Republicans in Congress for each.

References

Nickerson, R.S. (1998). Confirmation Bias: A Ubiquitous Phenomenon in Many Guises. *Review of General Psychology*, 2, 175–220.

Olson, J. P. & Reynolds, T. J. (2001). The Means-End Approach to Understanding Consumer Decision Making. In *Understanding Consumer Decision Making: The Means-End Approach to Marketing and Advertising Strategy*. (eds.) Reynolds, T. J. & J. P. Olson, Mahwah, NJ: Lawrence Erlbaum Associates.

Phillips, J., Reynolds, T. J. & Reynolds, K. (2010). Decision-Based Voter Segmentation: An Application for Campaign Message Development. *European Journal of Marketing*, 44, 310–330.

Phillips, J., Urbany, J. & Reynolds, T. J. (2008). Confirmation and the Effects of Valenced Political Advertising: A Field Experiment. *Journal of Consumer Research*, 34, 794–806.

Reynolds, T. J. (2005). LifeGoals: The Development of a Decision-Making Curriculum for Education. *Journal of Public Policy and Marketing*, 24, 75–81.

Reynolds, T. J. (2014). *Political Candidates and Means-End Strategy*. Presentation given at the Marketing Educators' Conference, San Francisco.

Reynolds, T. J. (2017). Strategic Marketing Imperatives and Insights: Common Pitfalls and Solutions. In *Consumer Social Values*. (eds.) Gurel-Atay, E. & L. R. Kahle, New York: Routledge.

Reynolds, Thomas J, & Phillips, Joan M. (in press). The Strata Model Predicting Advertising Effectiveness: A Neural Network Approach to Enhancing Predictability of Consumer Decision Making. *Journal of Advertising Research*.

Reynolds, T. J. & Gutman, J. (1988). Laddering Theory, Method, Analysis and Interpretation. *Journal of Advertising Research*, 28, 11–31.

Reynolds, T. J., & Rochon, J. P. (1991). Means-end based Advertising Research: Copy Testing is not Strategy Assessment. *Journal of Business Research*, 22, 131–142.

Reynolds, T. J., Westberg, S. & Olson J. P. (1997). A Strategic Framework for Developing and Assessing Political, Social Issue, and Corporate Image Advertising. In *Values, Lifestyles and Psychographics*. (eds.) Kahle, L. & L. Chiagouris, Mahwah, NJ: Lawrence Erlbaum Associates.

Wirthlin, D. (2004). *The Greatest Communicator: What Ronald Reagan Taught Me about Politics, Leadership, and Life*. Hoboken, NJ: John Wiley & Sons.

APPENDIX

The goal here is to review the process of the development and interpretation of the "game board" to develop the anticipated + and − strategies for Mrs. Clinton which can then be addressed by Mr. Trump in the development and implementation of his own strategy. To accomplish this, the connections of top-of-mind (ToM) associations to the higher-level meanings that underlie their respective decision networks must be developed. It is this "strategic game board" that permits the development and assessment of potential strategic options, both positive and negative. This game board is referred to as the Voter Decision Map (VDM is presented in Figure A.2) which is constructed from the methodologies introduced from voter decision segmentation (Reynolds, 2005; Phillips, Reynolds & Reynolds, 2010).

After the VDM is constructed, the next step is to reference the respective key percentages in the summary tables of positives and negatives of the key target groups defined by their respective voting intent. The game board, then, is used to summarize and prioritize the likely strategies of the opposition, in this case, Hillary Clinton (see Figure A.3). What follows is simply intended to illustrate the ideation process underlying the strategy of developing strategic options.

To illustrate, having the strategic game board in place, one should identify your own key negatives which serve as the basis for your opposition to attack you. In this case, the large Trump negatives which will serve as the basis for the anticipated (−) attack ads are:

- 32% Personality
- 10% Experience
- 10% Immigration Policy
- 7% Foreign Policy

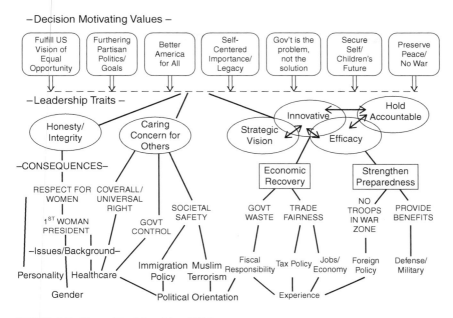

FIGURE A.2 Voter Decision Map 2016.

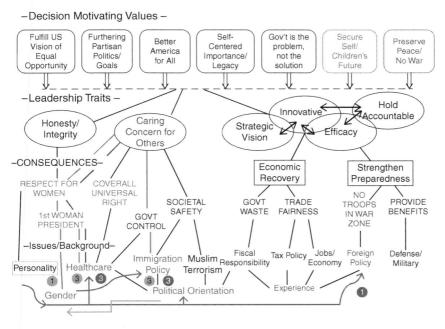

FIGURE A.3 Voter Decision Map 2016 [purple (−); blue (+)].

From a strategic perspective, to be maximally effective, attack ads should be linked where possible with reference to specific Issues (−). To illustrate how this is executed, consider the following likely attack strategies with references to specific target groups which would likely be proposed by Team Clinton:

1   "Personality" linked with "Foreign Policy" to "Military"... (through Experience)....threat Troops in War Zone—increasing the chances of leading US to War (threat of pissing off adversaries leading to war—NO Leadership-No Strategic Vision) General target.
2   "Personality" linked with (Political Orientation) to "Immigration Policy" .... To "Leadership Trait" of Non-Caring...to Self-Centered Arrogance (women and Hispanics are the primary targets).
3   "Personality" linked to "Healthcare".... Double here: Non-caring + no sensitivity for the needs of women—Female Health Services [Planned Parenthood issue clinic]) (women primary target).

As is obvious, this process of playing "what if" games with strategy development is greatly facilitated by this game board approach which is predicated on understanding the underlying decision processes of the key target groups. Continuing, then, the next step is to outline with the accompanying rationales what is anticipated as the most likely positive strategies that will be targeted at the Undecideds (including Leaners) by Team Clinton. These are:

1   "Political Orientation" (Democrat—I think leaning Progressive because of Bernie)—I agree, the map must connect "Respect for Women" to Caring Concern for Others—to a combo of Equal Opportunity and Secure Self....Children's Future—with emphasis on the latter (women primary target).
    "Gender" (<u>combine with one above</u>) (needs to be connected to Issues...like Personality above')—linking to Progressive makes sense "First Woman President"...finally break glass ceiling, etc. (your daughter could be the next one) (primary target of women, especially younger ones).
2   "Immigration Policy"—linking to Gender...Caring/Concerned about families. Targets of Hispanics and especially woman.
    ["Foreign Policy" (NOTE: sizeable negative of 5%)...so reject using this].
3   "Healthcare" (personal history of primary focus)...Caring / Concern is the linchpin of the Democratic Party.

Given the likely Clinton strategies outlined earlier, the question is: What should Team Trump strategize to counter these? Just to further illustrate this strategy development process, consider the following example logic offering a rationale for a series of rather obvious positionings.

First for the potential negative, attack ad, strategies (rule: always try to get double usage...connecting ideas) which can be summarily developed using the "strategic game board."

> Honesty (family history, Benghazi, etc.) ... Tie to Foreign Policy and to Defense (strengthen preparedness...) which go to Hold Accountable (Benghazi), Efficacy (get things done) (innovative-new ideas rather than the same old thing)...idea maybe we don't draw to all the Leadership Traits as it is now rather we draw a like above for the Decision Motivating Values)
>> Rationale.....Honesty / Integrity negates First Women/Respect for Women and to some degree Caring Concern...thus it is blocking... because one would question that HRC is telling the truth...or is she motivated by political gain (which should be directly implied)...with historical linkages
> Terrorism (Muslim)—both overseas (call a shit head a shit head) and at home in US
>> Play the "Societal Safety" card...linkage directly...to Immigration Policy as well
> Question Caring Concern directly (–)...would one who really cares put our society at risk with unlimited immigration (actually raising the number from Obama's days)?
>> Experience (Benghazi-related, re-set with Russia)...tie to Leadership... failure

Now for the potential positive positioning strategies...for ads and the cornerstone of speeches...

Efficacy (Leadership)...centerpiece of all....so, this should be the key leverage in all of the three following positive policy-related strategies (with key "connections" and general notes).

> Jobs / Economy...tax strategy to bring manufacturing home...trade fairness....economic recovery...link to strategic vision / innovative / efficacy – get things done (per above)
>> Tax Policy...reduce on middle class (democratic target) and simplify....can get it passed, stopping lobbyists for special interests... explain like Reagan move money in citizens pockets, they can choose how to spend it...reduce gov't size (add in), budget connection

Healthcare…repeal Obamacare…gov't control not Efficient (thus to be Efficacious…'Innovative' solution to foster competition—the underlying rationale); linking to Better America for All…and tying it to "Gov't is the problem"…

(ala Reagan)

The topline summary of this process is that understanding in a graphic format the decision-making processes of key groups (from supporting ToM data), the development of both positive and negative strategies with their corresponding rationales is straightforward.

8

MONEY ATTITUDES AND SOCIAL VALUES

A Research Program and Agenda

*Gregory M. Rose, Altaf Merchant, Mei Rose,
Aysen Bakir, and Drew Martin*

Attitudes toward money are complex and motivate action. Values are abstract
constructs that impact more concrete attitudes and behaviors, including attitudes toward money. Rose and Orr (2007) initially developed a four-
dimensional symbolic money attitudes scale (achievement, status, worry, and
security), closely aligned with personal values. Two additional dimensions,
evil and budgeting, respectively, explored an ethical-evaluative and behavioral
aspect of money. Subsequent research has explored money meanings among
Hindu families (Merchant, Rose, and Gour 2014), attitudes among French and
American adolescents (Rose, Bakir, and Gentina 2014), and other issues.

Collectively, this body of research has produced a diverse set of findings that
compliment personal values research. Research in India, for example, highlights the pervasive role of money, the fleeting nature of prosperity, the primacy
of "dharma" (duty), and the rapid and burgeoning development of a consumer
culture. This chapter summarizes this and other research on money and suggests directions for future research.

"Brother, can you spare a dime" and "We're in the money" are Depression-Era
songs, by Harburg and Gorney, and Dubin and Warren, respectively, describing economic frustration and seeking greater prosperity (Lavender n.d.). These
songs represent polar ends of the economic spectrum. Begging for a dime
represents desperation for basic needs, while sunny skies and spending money
freely suggest a potentially more carefree life. Arguably, both songs describe the
feelings of a struggling middle class. These songs suggest that attitudes toward
money are complex, personal, and subjective. Individual actions are enabled
or disabled by money or the lack of it. Money's resource flexibility provides a
means of exchange that is imbued, valued, and sought for its symbolic aspects.
Central to modern life, money is one of the most meaningful and arguably "the

most emotionally meaningful object in contemporary life" (Krueger 1986, p. 3). Gellerman (1968) describes money as a projectable field for individual hopes, strivings, desires, and fears (Rose and Orr 2007).

Conceptually, understanding money's meaning to consumers helps to visualize cultural values. Values are desirable end-states that guide consumers' actions (Rokeach 1973). Personal values are complex, abstract constructs that link to more concrete attitudes and behaviors, including cognitive, affective, and behavioral reactions toward money. Prior research establishes money's impact on personal values as well as attitudes and behaviors, including natural food shopping (Homer and Kahle 1988), genetically modified food (Honkanen and Verplanken 2004), conformity in dress (Rose, Shoham, Kahle, and Batra 1994), e-shopping tendencies (Jayawardhena 2004), service quality perceptions (Ladhari, Pons, Bressolles, and Zins 2011), and mall shopping behavior (Cai and Randall 2012). Values impact and align closely with symbolic attitudes toward important objects, especially money.

This chapter outlines a series of studies exploring money attitudes, discusses the link between personal values and money attitudes, suggests avenues for future research, and discusses multiple methods of exploring the symbolic meanings of money. Initially, our exploration of attitudes toward money emerged from a cross-cultural study of personal values (Rose et al. 1994, Rose and Orr 2007). This research stream examined objects and attitudes with strong symbolic connotations that were closely tied to personal values. Examining the existing money attitude scales (Furnham 1984, Yamauchi and Templer 1992) revealed the need for the careful psychometric development of a theoretically grounded and empirically valid scale (Rose and Orr 2007). Subsequent research explored money attitudes toward Hindu couples in India (Merchant, Rose, and Gour 2015), contrasted the symbolic money meanings of Korean and Indian middle-class couples (Merchant, Rose, Martin, Choi, and Gour 2016), and explored money attitudes among French and American adolescents (Rose, Bakir, and Gentina 2016). Collectively, this research employs a variety of qualitative and quantitative techniques, including focus groups, depth interviews, folktale elicitation, exploratory and confirmatory factor analysis, cluster analysis, and structural equation modeling. This research has produced a rich and diverse set of findings that compliment and supplement the findings of research on personal values.

This chapter begins by discussing alternative scales for assessing attitudes toward money. The link between money meanings and personal values follows, including a brief discussion of research examining the development of money meanings among children and adolescents. As sociocultural differences exist, the next section explores cultural differences in money meanings and methods for exploring these meanings. This discussion, by necessity, will be brief and focus on potential means for examining the symbolic meanings and cultural sources of cognitive, affective, and behavioral reactions toward money (Tang 1992, Tang and Liu 2012).

Scales for Measuring Attitudes toward Money

Several scales exist for measuring attitudes toward money. One widely used measure is Yamauchi and Templer's (1982) four-factor money attitude scale. Initially, they generated 63 items to measure three content domains: (a) security, described as concerning "optimism, confidence, comfort, and its reverse, pessimism, insecurity, and dissatisfaction," (b) retention, "which includes parsimony, hoarding, and obsessive personality traits," and (c) power-prestige, "which comprises aspects of status, importance, superiority, and acquisition" (Yamauchi and Templer 1982, p. 522). Empirically, their analysis generated a four-factor 29-item scale (power-prestige, retention-time, distrust, and anxiety), after dropping a fifth factor labeled quality. The first two factors, power-prestige and anxiety, examine "the use of money to impress and influence others" (Yamauchi and Templer 1982, p. 523) and as "a source of anxiety." The other two factors, retention-time and distrust, empirically amalgamated items originally intended to measure security and retention. Retention-time involves "planful preparation" behaviors (Yamauchi and Templer 1982, p. 523), such as financial planning and budgeting, while distrust examines "hesitant, suspicious, and doubtful attitudes" (Yamauchi and Templer 1982, p. 524), such as complaining about cost and thinking that the item purchased could have been obtained elsewhere for less.

Other studies show similar perceptions and motivational characteristics for some of these dimensions (see Engelberg and Sjoberg 2006). For example, Goldberg and Lewis (1978) describe security collectors, power grabbers, and autonomy worshipers. Furnham's (1984) money belief and behavior scale contains dimensions relating to obsession, power, retention, security/conservation, inadequacy, and effort/ability. Tang and his colleagues extensively examine money attitudes relating to ethics (Tang 2016, 1995, 1992, Tang and Liu 2002). Their initial scale consists of six subscales, Good and Evil, Budget, and Achievement, Respect/Self Esteem, and Freedom/Power, focusing on money attitude's affective, behavioral, and cognitive components. This research stream advanced into a number of short-form scales, including a six-item, three-factor scale which comprised evil (affective), budget (behavioral), and success (cognitive) (Tang, Tang, and Luna-Arocas 2005). Tang's recent research also focuses on the affective Love of Money (LOM) (Tang and Liu 2012) and examines several dimensions, including the degree to which money is seen as important (importance), motivates an individual to work hard (motivator), and affects individual desires for personal wealth accumulation (rich).

Collectively, these scales demonstrate money meaning's complex, multidimensional nature, and highlight the importance of affective, symbolic, and behavioral components of related attitudes. Affectively, some consumers see money as important, good, and attractive, while others perceive money as evil, useless, or shameful (Mitchell and Mickel 1999). Symbolically, "money is often associated with four of the most important symbolic attributes that humans strive for: (1) achievement and recognition, (2) status and respect, (3) freedom and control, and (4) power" (Mitchell and Mickel 1999, p. 569). Behaviorally, money associates with specific actions such as budgeting and investing.

The literature shows that methods to measure money attitudes have evolved over time. Mitchell and Mickel (1999) describe the early measures of money attitudes (Wernimont and Fitzpatrick 1972, Yamauchi and Templer 1982) as idiosyncratic, with little theory, and lacking sufficient assessment and attention to reliability and validity. Subsequently, scales are more systematic in developing measures (Furnham 1984, Mitchell, Dakin, Mickel and Gray 1998, Tang 1992, 1995). For example, Mitchell et al. (1998) focus on "behaviors and beliefs that indicate that money is important to an individual" (Mitchell et al. 1998, p. 573). Specific subscales focus on the importance or value placed on money, involvement, and time spent on financial affairs, knowledge of financial affairs and skill at handling money, comfort in taking risks, and the perception that money is a source of power. Thus, prior research identifies numerous dimensions relating to money, with varying degrees of attention paid to theoretical development and empirical validation.

Rose and Orr (2007) develop four scales to measure symbolic money meanings with motivational properties: achievement, status, worry, and security.

> Achievement and status, respectively, examine the extent that an individual perceives money as a marker of accomplishment or prestige. Worry examines the extent that a person feels anxious about money, while security examines the extent that a person values money as a means of protection from an uncertain future.
>
> *(Rose and Orr, p. 743)*

Seven studies validate these scales including the measures' content validity; reliability; factor structure; and discriminant, predictive, nomological, and convergent validities. For example, one study assesses convergent validity by comparing married couples' evaluations of their own and their spouse's money attitudes, while another employed known group differences by assessing the attitudes of the Yahoo! Frugal Folks and the Yahoo! Frugal living clubs. Thus, several scales exist for assessing money attitudes.

Consumer-Oriented Money Attitude Scales

Table 8.1 presents sample scales and items related to consumption. Several scales assess various aspects of attitudes toward money. Idiosyncratic, less theoretically grounded scales (e.g. some subscales of Wernimont and Fitzpatrick 1972; Yamauchi and Templer 1992) are not included. Other dimensions of money attitudes potentially relate to various aspects of consumer behavior. The choice of specific scale(s) depends on the study's purpose. Tang et al.'s (2005) LOM scale, for example, provides an interesting set of scales relating to affective evaluations of money and related ethical behaviors. Belief about the degree to which money promotes evil provides an interesting means of assessing overall affective evaluations of the impact of money on individuals and society (Tang 1995). For examining the symbolic, motivational aspects of money, Rose and Orr (2007) provide an interesting set of scales (i.e. Worry, Status, Achievement, and Security). Tang's (2016) Budget and Mitchell et al.'s (1998) Skill at Handling Money scales offer methods for assessing specific behavioral aspects of an individual's use of money. Other scales such as Obsession (Furnham 1984), Knowledge of Financial Affairs (Mitchell et al. 1998), and Contribute—the Mathew Effect (i.e. compensation should relate to merit/performance) (Tang 2016) offer alternatives which may be relevant in some situations. Table 8.1 provides a starting point for research requiring money attitude scales. The next section briefly

TABLE 8.1 Sample Consumer Money Attitude Scales and Items

Component/Scales/Authors	Sample Item
Symbolic Money Meaning	
Status (c.f., Mitchell et al. 1998, Power-Prestige, Yamauchi and Templer 1982, Rose and Orr 2007[a])	I must admit that I purchase things because I know that they will impress others
Worry (Rose and Orr 2007)	I worry a lot about money
Achievement (Rose and Orr 2007)	Money is a symbol of success
Security (Rose and Orr 2007)	Saving money gives me a sense of security
Happiness (Tang 2016)	Money can buy happiness
Power (Tang 2016)	Money is power
Affective Evaluations of Money	
Importance (Tang and Chiu 2003, c.f., Mitchell et al. 1998, Value importance of money)	I value money very highly
Motivator (Tang and Chiu 2003)	I am motivated to work hard for money
Rich (Tang and Chiu 2003)	Having a lot of money (being rich) is good
Evil (Tang 1995)	Money is the root of all evil
Behaviors Related to Money	
Budget (Tang 1995)	I budget my money very well
Give/Donate Money (Tang 2016)	I give generously to charitable organizations
Skill at handling money (Mitchell and Mickel 1999)	I never have checks that bounce

Note
a   items frequently are utilized in multiple scales and selective instances may be cited.

discusses the development of money attitudes and behaviors among children and adolescents. The relationship between money attitudes and personal values will be discussed in this chapter's summary and conclusion section.

The Development of Money Attitudes among Children and Adolescents

Several studies examine the development of money attitudes among children and adolescents (Beutler, Beutler, and McCoy 2008, Beutler and Gudmunson 2012, Rose et al. 2016). This research area is gaining more attention with growing concerns about consumption and materialistic value trends in society, particularly among children and adolescents (Blazquez and Bonas 2013).

As children and adolescents become competent consumers, a variety of factors shape their attitudes, skills, and knowledge toward consumption. Consumer socialization, the process by which children learn to become consumers (Rose 1999, Ward 1974), includes the skills and knowledge children acquire during their development of consumer behavior, and the acquisition of values, motives, and knowledge related to consumption behavior. Children also develop attitudes and behaviors related to materialism and impulsive consumption behavior (Roedder John 1999). "One of the most enduring concerns about consumer socialization is that our culture encourages children to focus on material goods as a means of achieving personal happiness, success, and self-fulfillment" (Roedder John 1999, p. 202).

Understanding how and when children start developing materialistic values is at the center of consumer socialization research (Roedder John 1999). Research shows that children at a very young age start to value material possessions (Goldberg and Gorn 1978, Roedder John 1999). As children get older and move into elementary school, these materialistic values mature and crystallize. By the time children are in fifth or sixth grade, they develop an understanding of the social significance of material possessions. These differences also exemplify the changes that occur in moving from the perceptual (3–7 years old) to the analytical stage (7–11 years old) of development. Children initially view possessions by quantity. They develop better social comparison skills as they age and an understanding of the social status that comes with material possessions as they move into the analytical stage of development. Changes in their perceptions of social status impact their judgments of and their valuation of the material possessions that influence their personal satisfaction and self-fulfillment as they grow older (Roedder John 1999). Previous research further shows that teenagers hold strong materialistic values (Chaplin and John 2007). Adolescents attach great importance to materialistic possessions and view consumption as a way to define happiness and success in life (Dittmar and Pepper 1994, Isaksen and Roper 2012).

Numerous studies also discuss materialism's impact among adolescents. While a full discussion of the literature on adolescent materialism is beyond the scope of this chapter, the materialism literature shows positive correlations between the children and their parents' level of materialism (Adib and El-Basssiouny 2012, Goldberg, Gorn, Peracchio, and Bamossy 2003), specifically among mothers and adolescents (Flouri 2007). Adolescent materialism has also been linked to family communication patterns, high levels of television viewing, and peer communication (Chaplin and John 2007). Other studies show a negative relationship between materialism and self-esteem among 12–18-year olds, suggesting that self-esteem mediates the relationship between children's materialism, and parent' and peer' influence (Chaplin and John 2007).

Previous research has also examined several issues regarding adolescent consumption behavior. This research has developed a retail shopping typology of American teenagers (Breazeale and Lueg 2011), examined country-of-origin's effect on product consumption (Goldberg and Baumgartner 2002), identified the dimensions of adolescent consumption autonomy (Palan, Gentina, and Muratore 2010), and evaluated the impact of teenagers' self-perceptions on their attitudes toward luxury brands (Gil, Kwon, Good, and Johnson 2012). Collectively, this research shows that consumption and material possessions play a pivotal role in adolescents' lives (Isaksen and Roper 2012, Piacentini and Mailer 2004).

Adolescent consumption behavior and materialistic values are influenced by a variety of socialization agents, including peers (Roedder John 1999). Peers significantly impact young adults' materialistic attitudes (Duh, Benmoyal-Bouzagio, Moschis, and Smaoui 2014). Teenagers that are more susceptible to peer influence tend to have lower self-esteem and a greater lack of self-confidence than those that are less susceptible to peer influence (Achenreiner 1997). Accordingly, individuals who are high on self-monitoring tend to exhibit materialistic values (Browne and Kaldenberg 1997).

Given this background and the importance that adolescents place on consumption for self-definition (Beutler, Beutler, and McCoy 2008), a recent study explores the money meanings of French and American adolescents (Rose et al. 2016). Initially, a qualitative analysis helped to better understand the money attitudes of these adolescents and provide guidance for developing measures of money meanings. The results suggested that modifying existing adult scales for measuring the symbolic (achievement, status, security, and worry), behavioral (budget), and affective (evil) aspects of money attitudes could successfully capture adolescents' attitudes toward money. Additional quantitative research further assessed similarities and differences in French and American attitudes toward money and segmented adolescents based on their money attitudes. Both individual differences and cultural proclivities shaped adolescent money attitudes. In general, anxiety relating to money (worry) is an individual difference, although French teens on average worry slightly more than their American counterparts. American teens, in contrast, place a greater value on the achievement, status, and security aspects of money, reporting higher levels of budgeting than French teens. Interestingly, perceptions of the evils of money suggest no significant difference across nations. Cluster analysis of the six money attitude scales identified three segments. These segments further highlight the importance of both cultural proclivities and individual differences. The first segment, *no worries*, places less importance on money and was similar to the proportion of American and French teens contained in the sample. The second and third segments, *success* and *security*, in contrast, highlight the increased importance of success and security, respectively, found among the American and French samples of adolescents, respectively.

As expected, the three segments differed on the importance they placed on price, brand, and novelty. The security-oriented cluster (segment) placed the greatest value on price, the achievement group considered brand name and novelty most important, and the no worries group felt that novelty and price are less important than the security group, and brand name is less important than reported by the achievement group.

Overall, Rose et al. (2016) illustrate the importance of simultaneously examining both individual and cultural differences. Some attitudes toward money (e.g. the extent that money is perceived as evil) tend to vary more among individuals than across cultures, at least among adolescents. Other dimensions (e.g. worry) appear to vary primarily among individuals, but also exhibit differences that are consistent with larger cultural differences in values. Specifically, French adolescents as a whole exhibit higher level of worry, which is consistent with a higher uncertainty avoidance score in France than in the U.S. (Hofstede 2001). Differences in money attitudes toward achievement and status (e.g. American teens placing a higher value on symbolic money meanings) are consistent with high materialism levels previously discussed in the U.S. (Richins and Dawson 1992, Schor 1998, Tocqueville 2000). Complex interactions between cultural and individual money perceptions remain important for future research. Symbolic money meanings are complex, nuanced, rich, and inherently related to cultural perceptions and associations toward money. The next section discusses the usefulness and importance of qualitatively evaluating cultural money meanings through techniques such as in-depth interviews, narrative evaluations, and folktale elicitation. These techniques begin with rich, individual, particular emic perceptions and move toward a more general etic understanding of national cultures and behaviors.

Qualitative Evaluations of Cultural Associations toward Money

Quantitative approaches to understanding money attitudes are useful and help define the various dimensions of the construct as well as gauge differences among different groups of consumers. Insights are not channeled through graphs and statistical tables; instead, they evolve as researchers interpret data and interact with consumers. Qualitative research is known to throw light on the consumption of market-made commodities and desire-inducing symbols that are central to consumer culture (Holt 2002). Consumer culture represents interconnected systems of commercially produced images, texts, and objects that groups use—through the construction of overlapping and even conflicting practices, identities, and meanings that help the consumers make cumulative sense of their environments and orient their experiences and lives (Kozinets 2001). These meanings are embodied and negotiated by consumers in social situations, family roles, and relationships (Arnould and Thompson 2005). Instruments, such as surveys, questionnaires, and interviews, are focused and generally directed toward more specific research questions. As a consequence, these traditional tools are most effective in examining predefined research questions and testing hypotheses. Qualitative research techniques, in contrast, are particularly effective for examining consumer attitudes in a natural setting. These methods reveal novel ideas, themes, topics, and insights difficult to capture using positivist research methods.

Collecting data as stored by consumers provides an opportunity to broaden the scope of inquiry and uncover behavioral insights inaccessible by employing traditional survey instruments. Stories are common forms for people to catalog and retrieve memories representing their lives (Adaval and Wyer 1998, Shank 1999). As individuals find difficulty explaining their behavior (Rapaille 2006), asking respondents to explain and reflect on their behavior (i.e. emic interpretations) unlocks information stored in their adaptive unconscious (Wilson 2002). Keeping in mind the multiple, varied, and diverse meanings and attitudes consumers have toward money, qualitative research provides a lucrative forum to unlock and explore the richness of such meanings among consumers. Qualitative research helps delve beneath the surface. Well-structured studies yield a holistic overview of consumer behavior, providing insights into emotions, motivations, metaphors, culture, and beliefs. Most importantly, the achievement of understanding happens in real time through direct interactions with consumers.

Etic or researcher analysis of qualitative results offers additional insights obtained from emerging qualitative techniques. These interpretivist and naturalistic inquiries are used to study consumer culture and gauge human behavior in conjunction with traditional research methods, like surveys and experiments (Arnould and Thompson 2005). Similarly, Mahrer and Boulet (1999) suggest that combining observational or naturalistic research with experimental testing of hypotheses can provide unique insights. Keeping in mind these assertions, employing qualitative research programs to understand money attitudes will further nurture the development of robust epistemologies incorporating information missed through pure positivist research techniques.

Recently, two papers examining money meanings and attitudes employ qualitative research. Merchant et al. (2015) examine this topic in the context of an emerging market—India, whereas Merchant et al. (2016) contrast the attitudes toward money in India and South Korea. Merchant et al. (2015) use in-depth interviews to facilitate the ease with which informants could relate their views on money and money management and also because the method accommodated probing to understand more fully their thoughts. They conducted 24 semi-structured (12 married couples) audio-taped interviews across three Indian cities—Delhi, Hyderabad, and Bhubaneshwar. They sampled different family structures (joint/nuclear) and family working statuses (dual income/single income). Broad questions probed respondent's views on money (such as, What comes to your mind when you think of money?), then moved to questions about married life (for example, What are the roles of the husband and wife in marriage?), and then discussed money management in the household with questions such as How do you and your spouse decide to spend money? Data analysis followed the hermeneutic approach, moving from a part-to-whole mode of interpretation. An interpretative group derived themes emerging from the transcripts and moved from an emic view (focusing on the informant's point of view) to an etic framework (examining broader/cultural meanings, reflective meanings of the respondents' experiences, and the patterns discerned across all interviews) (Thompson, Locander, and Pollio 1989). Study findings demonstrate the importance of money for living, the fickle nature of prosperity, the worship of money through the Hindu goddess Lakshmi, the limitations of money, the need for saving, and the role of dharmatic duty in people's perception and attitudes toward money. Results show a substantial variation in how money was managed within families. Joint families where the husband was the sole wage earner reflected more traditional patterns in which the wife's role was mainly taking care of the house, whereas nuclear families where the wife also worked outside the home had more egalitarian attitudes toward money management. Father/mother in laws also frequently exerted an influence (direct and indirect) over how money was spent within the household.

Merchant et al. (2016) expand on these insights in two ways. They contrast the findings from in-depth interviews in India with a more developed Asian country—South Korea, and elicit attitudes toward money by a novel innovative technique—folktale elicitation. Their findings show interesting similarities and differences across the two countries. Respondents from both nations emphasize the importance of consuming to convey status and keeping up with their neighbors. Koreans focus less on saving and exhibit more focus on spending to enjoy their life than Indians. Indians link saving to dharma (doing their duty) and supporting their children. Koreans also place a high value on family and supporting their children, but appear less focused on saving to ensure the success of future generations than Indians. Both samples also reflect the need to share money. However, the Korean sample expresses social balance motives by emphasizing reciprocation, whereas Indian respondents also state that moral balance drivers such as tradition and religion affect their decisions (Zaltman and Zaltman 2008).

As mentioned earlier, another new contribution of Merchant et al. (2016) introduces folktale elicitation to uncover underlying meanings of money. They asked husband–wife dyads to write down stories they may have heard about money. These stories depicted unconscious memories and cultural values associated with the meaning, use, importance, and limitations of money. Study findings uncover some differences across the two countries. While the Indian stories had both positive and negative themes, the Korean stories generally depict a more positive outlook toward money. Korean stories focus more on earning and spending money, while Indian stories center more specifically on earning (rather than spending) and the problems associated with money.

Discussion

Attitudes toward money as depicted by the song lyrics in the opening paragraph, as well as stories portrayed by respondents in the series of studies in this chapter are complex, personal, and subjective. This chapter outlines a series of studies exploring money attitudes, discusses the link between personal values and money attitudes, explains multiple methods of exploring the symbolic meanings of money, and suggests avenues for future research. Money has myriad symbolic meanings; it conveys feelings of future security, serves as a marker of achievement and/or status, and can be a source of worry or anxiety (Merchant, et al. 2016, Rose and Orr 2007). Money meanings are related to materialism, consumer susceptibility to interpersonal influence, quality consciousness, compulsive buying, budgeting, and the importance one places on price versus prestige in making purchases (Rose and Orr 2007). The symbolic meanings associated with money should mediate the relationship between values (personal and cultural) and consumer behaviors (Homer and Kahle 1988, Rose and Orr 2007). Future research could further examine and better articulate the relationship between personal values, money meanings, and various consumer behaviors, including the importance of brands, prestige products, brand meanings, and pro-social behaviors.

Money meanings are socially constructed, pervasive, and enacted within a cultural context (Merchant et al. 2015). Attitudes toward money vary among individuals and across culture. In the U.S., the Protestant Ethic provides a traditional, pervasive influence on consumers. It involves hard work, self-sacrifice and conscientiousness, and portrays self-indulgence and selfishness as evil (Belk and Wallendorf 1990, Goldberg and Lewis 1978). American culture values autonomy, exhibits a willingness to take risks (as evidenced by low scores on uncertainty avoidance), and emphasizes uniqueness and individuation (Gentina, Butorib, Rose, and Bakir 2014, Hofstede 2005, Kitayama and Markus 1992).

French culture, in contrast, focuses on close personal contacts, strong connections and obligations, exhibits less tolerance for ambiguity (high scores on uncertainty avoidance), and demonstrates a preoccupation with the perceptions and judgments of others (Hall and Hall 1990, Hofstede 2001).

Similarities in specific age segments, such as adolescents, as well as individual differences also influence perceptions of money. American and French teens, for example, express anxiety and worry about money; associate money with achievement, status, and security; and sometimes believe that money promotes evil. Some similarity in money attitude across cultures is expected, given the importance that adolescence places on achieving independence and moving into adulthood (Erikson 1968, Palan et al. 2010); their preoccupation with material possession to assimilate and differentiate themselves from their peers (Gentina et al. 2014, Palan et al. 2010); and their view of consumption as a way to define happiness and success in life (Dittmar and Pepper 1994, Isaksen and Roper 2012). At the cultural level, French teenagers worry more about money on average than American teens, which is consistent with the high degree of uncertainty avoidance imbued in French culture (Hall and Hall 1990, Hofstede 2001). American teens, on the other hand, place a higher value on the symbolic money meanings of achievement and status, which is consistent with American national culture's being achievement-oriented, driven to succeed, and focused on acquiring material possessions and wealth (Hofstede 2001, Tocqueville 2000). In addition, American adolescents also demonstrated higher levels of budgeting than French teens. This is consistent with differences in American and French parental styles. French parents foster dependence and influence their teens' money and spending by giving them an allowance (Gollety 1999), while American parents emphasize developing independence and consumption autonomy in their children (Mangleburg and Brown 1995, Rose 1999).

Research has also examined collectivist cultures, including Hindus in the developing nation of India. Hindus account for 80.5% of India's population (827 million people) (India Census 2011). Attitudes toward Dharma (doing one's duty) are inextricably linked to Hindu attitudes toward money and thus utilized to facilitate the education and future success of subsequent generations, Hindu children. Money is further valued for both its utilitarian and symbolic properties and perceived as a marker of status (Merchant et al. 2015). Indians embrace spending to maintain relationships and delineate and maintain status. This acceptance of status-oriented spending contrasts sharply with the traditional Christian premise of humility and the Protestant notion of frugality. Although differences exist in the treatment of spending, both the Protestant Ethic found in America and the Hindu' notion of dharma embrace duty and purpose beyond oneself (Merchant et al. 2015). Additional research should further examine the impact of the Protestant Ethic in the U.S. and other individualist countries, the impact of emerging and long-established norms of materialism, and the potential decline of the Protestant Ethic, as well as generational differences in money attitudes. Differences between the Protestant Ethic and the Catholic Ethic of charity and their impact in various western cultures on attitudes toward money could also be assessed. Additional research could also be conducted in collectivist nations, such as China and Japan that have unique cultural and ethical influences, such as Confucianism Shintoism, and Buddhism.

To date, we have examined similarities and differences between the collectivist nations of Korea and India. Both are horizontal collectivist nations; India is in the mid- to early stages of economic development, while Korea is a developed nation where economic success and consumption are more widespread. Buddhism (43%) and Christianity (55.1%) are South Korea's primary religions (Korea.net 2005). While respondents in India often referred to mythological and religious stories to make sense of their desire and sharing of money, these stories were not predominant in Korea. Korean respondents often discussed the desire of sharing money with their parents, but there were no mentions of other extended family members. Money was associated with security, social legitimacy, and respect in both India and Korea. However, Korean respondents place a higher value on spending and immediate gratification than Indian respondents. These differences may be attributed to the economic development of these nations and religious differences.

Symbolic money meanings are socially constructed from personal and cultural values and affect consumer behaviors (Homer and Kahle 1988, Rose and Orr 2007). Examining the complex interactions between individual and cultural values, as well as differences across various demographic groups, including age-cohorts, family lifecycle (particularly the presence of children), and social class provide an interesting avenue for future research into consumer money meanings.

Research on money attitudes has employed a variety of qualitative and quantitative techniques, including focus groups, depth interviews, folktale elicitation, narrative evaluation, exploratory and confirmatory factor analysis, cluster analysis, and structural equation modeling. Quantitative approaches to understanding money attitudes are useful and help define the various dimensions of the construct as well as explicate differences among different groups of consumers. Several scales exist for measuring attitudes toward money and may be categorized as symbolic, affective, and behavioral. Behavioral assessments of money attitudes are associated with specific actions such as budgeting and investing. Affective evaluations of money include the degree to which money and being rich is an important motivator, and the degree to which individuals believe that money promotes evil. Symbolic meanings of money are associated with symbolic attributes that humans strive for such as achievement, status, freedom, and power (Mitchell and Mickel 1998, Tang 1995, 1992, Tang et al. 2005). Quantitative research has successfully measured these dimensions of money meanings.

Qualitative research, such as in-depth interview and folktale elicitation, is particularly effective for examining consumer money attitudes in a natural setting. Stories are common forms for people to catalog and retrieve memories representing their lives (Adaval and Wyer 1998, Shank 1999). The symbolic meaning of money is embodied and negotiated by consumers in social situations, family roles, and relationships (Arnould and Thompson 2005). Qualitative methods reveal novel ideas, themes, topics, and insights difficult to capture using quantitative research methods. These techniques begin with narrative evaluations of rich, individual, particular emic perceptions, and move toward a more general etic understanding of national cultures and behaviors. Merchant et al. (2015) uncover the importance of money for living, the fickle nature of prosperity, and the role of dharmatic duty in people's perception and attitudes toward money among Hindus in India. Results further show a substantial difference in money management between joint (extended) families, where the husband was the sole wage earner, and nuclear families, especially when the wife also worked outside the home. Joint and nuclear families had more egalitarian attitudes toward money management.

Folktale elicitation provides a novel innovative research technique that could be utilized in subsequent research. Folktales are traditional stories displaying mythological patterns that Jung (1948/1990) identifies as archetypes. These archetypes serve as both inner guides to the unconscious and external anchors for myths, legends, art, literature, and religion (Pearson 1991). Folktale elicitation techniques allow informants to share stories about money that provide metaphoric, thematic narrative content that can reveal deep-seated and unconscious attitudes. Stories from India and Korea in Merchant et al. (2016), for example, highlight the importance of and the need for money, and the limits and dangers of excessive desire for money and greed. The benevolent and just use of money to support others (particularly one's family) leads to positive outcomes for the protagonist and provides a didactic portrait of the correct use of money, in contrast to stories of selfishness, which produces more negative outcomes.

The findings from the series of studies discussed in this chapter only examine the tip of the iceberg. Future research can contribute to the literature by further examining stories of money and folktales in a variety of cultures and contexts, including children's stories, folktales, religious texts, popular cultural references in music and media, and advertisements. Further examining money attitudes and values among different consumer groups (individuals, couples, and families) of different social classes, in other nations with different cultures (e.g. individualistic versus collectivist cultures) and predominant religions (such as Muslim, Jewish, or no religious affiliation) should also provide valuable insight into money meanings. The complex interactions between cultural and individual money perceptions remain an important avenue for future research. Finally, future research building on these findings could further examine innovative research techniques to elicit unconscious thoughts and metaphors relating to money. Some suggestions include asking respondents to put together collages, drawings, photographs, adages, movie scenes, and dialogues related to the meanings, use, and importance of money.

References

Achenreiner, G. B. (1997). Materialism Values and Susceptibility to Influence in Children. *Advances in Consumer Research*, 24, 82–88.

Adaval, R. and Wyer, R. S. (1998). The Role of Narratives in Consumer Information Processing. *Journal of Consumer Psychology*, 7(3), 207–245.

Adib, H. and El-Bassiouny, N. (2012). Materialism in Young Consumers An Investigation of Family Communication Patterns and Parental Mediation Practices in Egypt. *Journal of Islamic Marketing*, 3(3), 255–282.

Arnould, E. J. and Thompson, C. J. (2005). Consumer Culture Theory (CCT): Twenty Years of Research. *Journal of Consumer Research*, 31(4), 868–882.

Belk, R. W. and Wallendorf, M. (1990). The Sacred Meaning of Money. *Journal of Economic Psychology*, 11, 35–67.

Beutler, I. F., Beutler, B., and McCoy, K. (2008). Money Aspirations about Living Well: Development of Adolescent Aspirations from Middle School to High School. *Journal of Financial Counseling & Planning*, 19(2), 67–82.

Beutler, I. F. and Gudmunson, C. G. (2012). New Adolescent Money Attitude Scales: Entitlement and Conscientiousness. *Journal of Financial Counseling & Planning*, 23(2), 18–31.

Blazquez, J. F. D. and Bonas, M. C. (2013). Influences in Children's Materialism: A Conceptual Framework. *Young Consumers*, 14(4), 297–311.

Breazeale, M. and Lueg, J. E. (2011). Retail Shopping Typology of American Teens. *Journal of Business Research*, 64(6), 565–571.

Browne, B. A. and Kaldenberg, D. O. (1997). Conceptualizing Self-Monitoring: Links To Materialism And Product Involvement. *Journal of Consumer Marketing*, 14(1), 31–44.

Cai, Y. and Randall, S. (2012). Personal Values and Mall Shopping Behavior. *International Journal of Retail & Distribution Management*, 40(4), 290–318.

Chaplin, L. N. and Roedder John, D. (2007). Growing Up in a Material World: Age Differences in Materialism in Children and Adolescents. *Journal of Consumer Research*, 34(4), 480–493.

Dittmar, H. and Pepper, L. (1994). To Have Is To Be: Materialism And Person Perception In Working-Class And Middle-Class British Adolescents. *Journal of Economic Psychology*, 15(2), 233–251.

Duh, H. I., Benmoyal-Bouzaglo, S., Moschis, G. P., and Smaoui, L. (2014). Examination of Young Adults' Materialism in France and South Africa using Two Life-course Theoretical Perspectives. *Journal of Family and Economic Issues*. [Available online] http://link.springer.com/article/10.1007/s10834-014-9400-9.

Engelberg, E. and Sjöberg, L. (2006). Money Attitudes and Emotional Intelligence. *Journal of Applied Social Psychology*, 36(8), 2027–2047.

Erikson, E. H. (1968). *Identity: Youth and Crisis*. New York: Norton.

Flouri, E. (2007). Exploring the Relationship between Parenting and Materialism in British Mothers and Fathers of Secondary School Age Children. *Journal of Socio-Economics*, 26(6), 167–176.

Furnham, A. (1984). Many Sides of the Coin: The Psychology of Money Usage. *Personality and Individual Differences*, 5, 501–509.

Gellerman, S. W. (1968). Motivating Men with Money. *Fortune* (March), 144–146, 179–180.

Gentina, E., Butorib, R., Rose, G. M., and Bakir, A. (2014). How National Culture Impacts Teenage Shopping Behavior: Comparing French and American Consumers. *Journal of Business Research*, 67(4), 464–470.

Gil, L. A., Kwon, K., Good, L. K., and Johnson, L. W. (2012). Impact of Self on Attitudes toward Luxury Brands among Teens. *Journal of Business Research*, 65(10), 1425–1433.

Goldberg, M. E. and Baumgartner, H. (2002). Cross-Country Attraction as a Motivation for Product Consumption. *Journal of Business Research*, 55(11), 901–906.

Goldberg, M. E. and Gorn, G. J. (1978). Some Unintended Consequences of TV Advertising to Children. *Journal of Consumer Research*, 5(June), 22–29.

Goldberg, M. E., Gorn, G. J., Peracchio, L. A., and Bamossy, G. (2003). Understanding Materialism among Youth, *Journal of Consumer Psychology*, 13(3), 278–288.

Goldberg, H. and Lewis, R. T. (1978). *Money Madness: The Psychology of Saving, Spending, Loving and Hating Money*. New York: William Morrow and Company.

Gollety, M. (1999). Lorsque Parents et Enfants S'apprennent Mutuellement À Consommer, *Décis Mark*, 18, 69–80.

Hall, E. T. and Hall, M. R. (1990). *Understanding Cultural Differences*. Yarmouth, Maine: Intercultural Press.

Hofstede, G. (2001). *Culture's consequences: Comparing Values, Behaviors, Institutions, and Organizations across Nations*. Thousand Oaks, CA: Sage.

Holt, D. B. (2002). Why Do Brands Cause Trouble? A Dialectical Theory of Consumer Culture and Branding. *Journal of Consumer Research*, 29(June), 70–90.

Homer, P. M. and Kahle, L. R. (1988). A Structural Equation Test of the Value-Attitude-Behavior Hierarchy. *Journal of Personality and Social Psychology*, 54(4), 638–646.

Honkanen, P. and Verplanken, B. (2004). Understanding Attitudes towards Genetically Modified Food: The Role of Values and Attitude Strength. *Journal of Consumer Policy*, 27(4), 401–420.

India Census. (2011). The Census of India, http://censusindia.gov.in/.

Isaksen, K. J. and Roper, S. (2012). The Commodification of Self Esteem: Branding and British Teenagers. *Psychology and Marketing*, 29(3), 117–135.

Jayawardhena, C. (2004). Personal Values' Influence on E-Shopping Attitude and Behavior. *Internet Research*, 14(2), 127–138.

Jung, C. G. (1948/1990). The Phenomenology of the Spirit in Fairytales (R. F. C. Hull, trans.). In H. Read, M. Fordham, and G. Adler (Eds.), *The Archetypes and the Collective Unconscious*, Vol. 9. Princeton, NJ: Princeton University Press, 207–254 (Original work published 1959).

Kitayama, S. and Markus, H. R. (1992). Construal of the Self as Cultural Frame: Implications for Internationalizing Psychology. Paper presented at the *Symposium on Internationalization and Higher Education*. Ann Arbor: University of Michigan.

Korea.net. (2005). *Religion*. Accessed on 23 May 2016.

Kozinets, R. V. (2001). Utopian Enterprise: Articulating the Meaning of Star Trek's Culture of Consumption. *Journal of Consumer Research*, 28(June), 67–89.

Krueger, D. W. (1986). Money, Success, and Success Phobia. In D. W. Krueger (Ed.), *The Last Taboo: Money As Symbol And Reality In Psychotherapy And Psychoanalysis*, New York: Brunner/Mazel, 3–16.

Ladhari, R., Pons, F., Bressolles, G., Zins, M. (2011). Culture and Personal Values: How They Influence Perceived Service Quality. *Journal of Business Research*, 64(9), 951–957.

Lavender, C. (n.d.), *Songs of the Great Depression*. Retrieved from http://csivc.csi.cuny.edu/history/files/lavender/cherries.html.

Mahrer, A. R. and Boulet, D. B. (1999). How to Do Discovery-Oriented Psychotherapy Research. *Journal of Clinical Psychology*, 55(12), 1481–1493.

Mangleburg, T. F. and Brown, J. J. (1995). Teens' Sources of Income: Jobs and Allowances, *Journal of Marketing Theory and Practice*, 3(1), 33–46.

Merchant, A., Rose, G., and Gour, M. (2015). Meanings of Money Among Middle Class Hindu Families in India. In L. Marsh and H. Li (Eds.), *The Middle Class in Emerging Societies: Consumers, Lifestyles and Markets*, Routledge: Georgia State University, 161–183.

Merchant, A., Rose G., Martin, D., Choi, S., and Gour, M. (2016). Cross-cultural folk-tale-elicitation research on the perceived power, humanistic and religious symbolisms, and use of money. *Journal of Business Research*, doi: 10.1016/j.jbusres.2016.10.021.

Mitchell, T. and Mickel, A. (1999). The Meaning of Money: An Individual-Difference Perspective. *The Academy of Management Review*, 24(3), 568–578.

Mitchell, T. R., Dakin, S., Mickel, A., and Gray, S. (1998). The Measurement of Money Importance. Paper Presented at the Annual Meeting of the *Academy of Management*, San Diego.

Palan, K., Gentina, E., and Muratore, I. (2010). Adolescent Consumption Autonomy: A Cross-Cultural Examination. *Journal of Business Research*, 63(12), 1342–1348.

Pearson, C. S. (1991). *Awakening the Heroes Within*. New York: HarperCollins.

Piacentini, M. and Mailer, G. (2004). Symbolic Consumption in Teenagers' Clothing Choices. *Journal of Consumer Behaviour*, 3(3), 251–262.

Rapaille, C. (2006). *The Culture Code: An Ingenious Way to Understand Why People Around the World Live and Buy as They Do*. New York: Broadway.

Richins, M. L. and Dawson, S. (1992). A Consumer Values Orientation for Materialism and Its Measurement: Scale Development and Validation. *Journal of Consumer Research*, 19(3), 303–316.

Roedder John, D. (1999). Consumer Socialization of Children: A Retrospective Look at Twenty-Five Years of Research. *Journal of Consumer Research*, 26(3), 183–213.

Rokeach, M. (1973). *The Nature of Human Values*. New York: Free Press.

Rose, G. M. (1999). Consumer Socialization, Parental Style, and Developmental Timetables in the United States and Japan. *Journal of Marketing*, 63(3), 105–119.

Rose, G. M., Bakir, A., and Gentina, E. (2016) Money Meanings among French and American Adolescents. *Journal of Consumer Marketing*, 33(5), 364–375.

Rose, G. M. and Orr, L. M. (2007). Measuring and Exploring Symbolic Money Meanings. *Psychology & Marketing*, 24(9), 743–761.

Rose, G. M., Shoham, A., Kahle, L. R., and Batra, R. (1994). Social Values, Conformity, and Dress. *Journal of Applied Social Psychology*, 24, 501–519.

Schor, J. (1998). *The Overspent American: Upscaling, Downshifting, and the New Consumer*. New York: Basic Books.

Shank, R. C. (1999). *Dynamic Memory Revisited*. Cambridge, UK: Cambridge University.

Tang, T. (1992). The Meaning of Money Revisited. *Journal of Organizational Behavior*, 13(2), 197–202.

Tang, T. (1995). The Development Of A Short Money Ethic Scale: Attitudes Toward Money And Pay Satisfaction Revisited. *Personality and Individual Differences*, 19(6), 809–816.

Tang, T. (2016). Theory of Monetary Intelligence: Money Attitudes—Religious Values, Making Money, Making Ethical Decisions, and Making the Grade. *Journal of Business Ethics*, 133(3), 583–603.

Tang, T. and Liu, H. (2012). Love of Money and Unethical Behavior Intention: Does an Authentic Supervisor's Personal Integrity and Character (ASPIRE) Make a Difference? *Journal of Business Ethics*, 107(3), 295–312.

Tang, T., Tang, D., and Luna-Arocas, R. (2005). Money Profiles: The Love of Money, Attitudes, and Needs. *Personnel Review*, 34(5), 603–618, 623–624.

Thompson, C. J., Locander, W. B., and Pollio, H. R. (1989). Putting Consumer Experience Back into Consumer Research: The Philosophy and Method of Existential-Phenomenology. *Journal of Consumer Research*, 16(September), 133–146.

Tocqueville, A. (2000). *Democracy in America*. Chicago, IL: University of Chicago Press.

Ward, S. (1974). Consumer Socialization. *Journal of Consumer Research*, 1(2), 1–14.

Wernimont, P. F. and Fitzpatrick, S. (1972). The Meaning of Money. *Journal of Applied Psychology*, 56(3), 218–226.

Wilson, T. D. (2002). *Strangers to Ourselves: Discovering the Adaptive Unconscious*. Cambridge, MA: Belknap.

Yamauchi, K. T. and Templer, D. J. (1982). The Development of a Money Attitude Scale, *Journal of Personality Assessment*, 46(5), 522–528.

Zaltman, G. and Zaltman, L. (2008). *Marketing Metaphoria: What Deep Metaphors Reveal About the Minds of Consumers*. Boston, MA: Harvard Business School.

9

SOCIAL MEDIA AND VALUES

Christopher Lee and Lynn R. Kahle

Introduction

Musician Katy Perry, the most followed celebrity on Twitter, has over 102 million followers and has sent out over 8,000 tweets. To put that in perspective, 102 million is more than the population of all but 13 countries in the world (*The World Factbook*, 2016). Similarly, Real Madrid, one of the most followed sports organizations on social media, has 24.6 million followers and has sent out 57,700 tweets. The volume of followers is staggering as is the ability of individuals to communicate directly with other individuals on such a mass scale. Social media provides a platform to develop a brand (Kietzmann, Hermkens, McCarthy, & Silvestre, 2011; Kim & Ko, 2012), interact with sports fans (Mahan, 2011; Stavros, Meng, Westberg, & Farrelly, 2014), or simply engage with other individuals. Given an individual person is writing the tweets, social media provides a lens into the mind of the individual. What are they thinking? What are they feeling? How are they communicating their values?

Values

Values have received meaningful amounts of attention (Kahle & Guang-Xin, 2008; Suh & Kahle, 2017) since their introduction into the marketing literature (Beatty, Kahle, Homer, & Misra, 1985; Mitchell, 1983; Pitts & Woodside, 1984). Although several methods have been used, such as the Rokeach Value Survey (Rokeach, 1973), we have focused our energy on the List of Values (LOV). It utilizes nine values, including sense of belonging, excitement, warm relationships, self-fulfillment, being well-respected, fun and enjoyment in life, security, self-respect, and a sense of accomplishment (Kahle, 1996).

It has demonstrated reliability, validity, data analysis virtues, and ease of use in surveys (Kahle, Beatty, & Homer, 1986; Kahle & Valette-Florence, 2012). It has proven to have utility both in the business (Aiken, Sukhdial, Kahle, & Downing, 2015; Kahle, Duncan, Dalakas, & Aiken, 2001; Kurpis, Bozman, & Kahle, 2010; Sukhdial, Kahle, & Aiken, 2002) and in social media research (Lee & Kahle, 2016).

Research on the mean-end chains (Homer & Kahle, 1988; Reynolds & Olson, 2001) has demonstrated that consumers have a pattern of thinking about purchases. When asked about the reason for a purchase of a product or attribute, most consumers respond with a specific attribute of interest (e.g. I bought the car because it gets good gas mileage). When asked why that attribute matters, consumers usually answer with a consequence of the attribute or an attitude about it (e.g. it would save money). When researchers follow up with another question about why the consequence matters, consumers tend to reply with a core social value (e.g. I respect myself when I use my money responsibly). Thus, one could argue that the value → consequence or attitude → purchase sequence underlies most consumer behavior. The values link consumer identity with consumer action. Thus, understanding values is fundamental to understanding consumer behavior.

Social Media and Communication of Values

Given the instantaneous nature and the interpersonal discussions, social media represents a great mechanism to convey values. Social media has had explosive growth over the last decade or so and has been influential in everything from politics (Tumasjan, Sprenger, Sandner, & Welpe, 2010) to sports (Clavio & Walsh, 2013; Lee & Kahle, 2016) to health (Moorhead et al., 2013). Social media is embedded across a variety of industries and within the lives of millions of people. Given its broad reach and the ability to analyze the linguistic content, it represents a meaningful source to better understand the communication of values.

While people are exposed to traditional advertisements without their intention (Yoo, 2009), people often willingly communicate with companies on social media (de Vries, Gensler, & Leeflang, 2012). In other words, compared to a television commercial, advertisement on a street, or other forms of marketing, consumers often opt in to engage with companies on social networks. One study showed that consumers tend to visit stores more and produce positive word of mouth after being a fan of brand pages (Dholakia & Durham, 2010). As social media usage increases, academic research is expanding to further explore how customers and companies engage online. From creative strategies in social media marketing (Ashley & Tuten, 2015) to motivations for social media use (Witkemper, Lim, & Waldburger, 2012) to effects on sustainable marketing and behaviors (Lyon & Wren Montgomery, 2013; Minton, Lee, Orth, Kim, &

Kahle, 2012), academic research is increasingly using social media as a lens to study human behavior. While significant research has looked at values (Kahle et al., 1986; Kahle & Valette-Florence, 2012), only recently has research explored the value content of social media posts.

A Study of Values and Social Media Content of Professional Sports Organizations (Lee & Kahle, 2016)

A study by Lee and Kahle (2016) showed how emerging technologies such as the Linguistics Inquiry and Word Count (LIWC) software (Pennebaker, Chung, Ireland, Gonzales, & Booth, 2007; Pennebaker, Francis, & Booth, 2001; Tausczik & Pennebaker, 2009) can be used to computationally measure the linguistic differences in content. For example, past research has used this technology to show how positive political ads use more present and future tense compared to negative political ads, first-person plural pronoun usage is associated with higher status, and negative emotions are associated with lying (Tausczik & Pennebaker, 2009). Although LIWC is an automated linguistic analysis software, the results of the text analysis have been shown to be correlated with human evaluations of text (Alpers et al., 2005). Thus, LIWC and other similar computational linguistic technologies represent a very accurate method to better understand the linguistic, and value-laden, content of social media.

Lee and Kahle (2016) analyzed over 20,000 tweets across four Major League Baseball teams and four sports apparel companies. Tweets were collected from the Los Angeles Dodgers, San Francisco Giants, New York Yankees, and Boston Red Sox in Major League Baseball and Nike, Adidas, Reebok, and Under Armour in the apparel industry. Given the various business motivations in addition to the unique nature of sports (winning or losing, sponsorship, exciting plays, etc.), tweets from both sports teams and apparel companies were collected and analyzed using the LIWC software to explore values communication.

Based on a computational linguistics analysis, results showed significant differences in the communication of values (Kahle, 1983) in the content of tweets. Some brands, such as Under Armour and the New York Yankees, were able to stand out through strong communication of values, while others, such as Reebok, had no clear differentiation. The Yankees and Red Sox both emphasized the values of self-respect, while the Yankees also tweeted about being well-respected. The Dodgers and Red Sox, who were successful on the field during the time of data collection, tweeted more about fulfillment but, interestingly, not significantly more about accomplishment than other teams. The Giants differentiated their tweets, despite poor performance on the field, by emphasizing the value of fun and enjoyment in life.

Under Armour differentiated itself with tweets emphasizing both self-respect and being well-respected. Given their branding of "Protect This House" (Salter et al., 2005), their tweets are consistent with those efforts. Nike, with past slogans including "Just Do It" and "Find Your Greatness," tweeted about accomplishment more than any other brand which implies a coordinated branding effort. Adidas emphasized fun and enjoyment in life which falls in line with their lifestyle branding (Beer, 2017), while Reebok had no distinctive values associated with their tweets. Interestingly, despite the social nature and community aspects of sports, there was no significant difference between any apparel companies or teams on the sense of belonging value. The importance of this research is that your tweets may have meaningful, but subtle, influence acts on your brand.

A Study of Individual Values and Social Media Usage

A nationwide sample of individuals sheds some light on the relationship between values and social media usage. People who use social media for more than one hour a day are more likely to put more importance on the following values than people who use social media for less than one hour a day: a sense of belonging; being well-respected; excitement; and fun and enjoyment in life. These results suggest that social media is more than simply a communication or marketing tool but a tool for individuals to become part of a group (sense of belonging) while enjoying the conversation (fun and enjoyment in life). Building on this finding, people who put more importance on the values of sense of belonging, excitement, being well-respected, fun and enjoyment in life, self-respect, and a sense of accomplishment are more likely to use social media for longer periods of time in a day. In short, the more you value sense of belonging and fun and enjoyment, among other more external and interpersonal values, the more likely you are to use social media for longer periods of time. Social media networks, or brands on these platforms, could tap into this information by highlighting the sense of belonging and fun associated with the platform.

Beyond a look at individual values, the LOV (Beatty et al., 1985; Kahle et al., 1986) can be grouped in the following fashion:

Internal values: self-respect; a sense of accomplishment; self-fulfilling
External values: a sense of belonging; security; being well-respected
Interpersonal values: warm relationships with others; excitement; fun and enjoyment in life

Similar to the aforementioned results, people who use social media for more than one hour a day are more likely to put more importance on external and interpersonal values than people who use social media for less than one hour a day. In other words, social media users value the external and interpersonal natures of the communication rather than self-respect or self-fulfilling motivations. In addition, people who put more importance on external and interpersonal values are more likely to use social media for longer periods of time in a day.

While some networks, such as LinkedIn, often emphasize internal values such as accomplishment and fulfillment, the research shows that the external and interpersonal values drive social media behavior. Twitter, for example, is often described as a "water cooler" or "sports bar" which highlights the external and interpersonal values that drive usage of the platforms.

General Discussion and Future Research

Companies should be aware of the value-laden content of their social media posts and also how personal values are tied to social media usage. From an individual and business standpoint, the benefits of understanding personal values and lifestyle are well documented (Kahle & Valette-Florence, 2012). Given the use of social media as both a personal and business tool, it is critically important to have a strong understanding of how social media is used to communicate values.

Continued research into the linguistic and value makeup of social media posts represents a strong direction for future research. For example, given social media posts are made by individual employees, with their own set of personal values, it is important for companies to be aware that an individual employee's values may be inadvertently communicated through company channels. Two different employees may have different personal values (ex. value self-respect versus fun and enjoyment in life) but be responsible for the same corporate social media posts. Given the subtle linguistic and value differences discussed, there is the potential for brands to share inconsistent messaging. Language plays a critical role in branding given the text heavy nature of platforms such as Twitter and thus managers need to be aware of the value content and proposition of their social media campaigns.

The two primary studies discussed in this chapter looked at the social media content of companies and individual social media usage based on values but future research may look at the linguistic and value content of consumers' social media posts. For example, Adidas' post frequently contains text associated with the fun and enjoyment in life value. Does this translate to their followers on social media? In other words, does the content of Adidas' followers tweets contain more words associated with fun and enjoyment in life than followers of Under Armour or Nike? An exploration of follower tweets may further highlight the important nature of values and the value connection between a company and its followers. Future research could also look at the value-laden content between a wider array of companies. For example, does a high status company such as Tesla tweet different value content than a small company with a lower status? Is there a relationship between the value content of the tweets and other linguistic characteristics (such as pronouns)? In other words, do tweets that discuss fun and enjoyment in life, along with "we" resonate better with followers? Or do tweets that discuss fun and enjoyment in life in the present versus resonate more with people than those same tweets in the past tense? Social media offers a lens into the communication of values and thus a wealth of opportunity for additional research in the future.

References

Aiken, D., Sukhdial, A., Kahle, L., & Downing, J. A. (2015). Linking Fan Values and Sponsorship Effectiveness: The Case of Old School Values. *Sport Marketing Quarterly*, *24*(1), 56.

Alpers, G. W., Winzelberg, A. J., Classen, C., Roberts, H., Dev, P., Koopman, C., & Barr Taylor, C. (2005). Evaluation of Computerized Text Analysis in an Internet Breast Cancer Support Group. *Computers in Human Behavior*, *21*(2), 361–376.

Ashley, C., & Tuten, T. (2015). Creative Strategies in Social Media Marketing: An Exploratory Study of Branded Social Content and Consumer Engagement. *Psychology & Marketing*, *32*(1), 15–27.

Beatty, S. E., Kahle, L., Homer, P., & Misra, S. (1985). Alternative Measurement Approaches to Consumer Values: The List of Values and the Rokeach Value Survey. *Psychology and Marketing*, *2*(3), 181–200.

Beer, J. (2017). Why Adidas Is Going Beyond Fitness With Its New "AllDay" Lifestyle App | Fast Company. Retrieved October 25, 2017, from www.fastcompany.com/40438927/why-adidas-is-going-beyond-fitness-with-its-new-all-day-lifestyle-app.

Central Intelligence Agency (2016). *The World Factbook*. Washington, DC: Central Intelligence Agency.

Clavio, G., & Walsh, P. (2013). Dimensions of Social Media Utilization Among College Sport Fans. *Communication & Sport*, *2*(3), 261–281.

de Vries, L., Gensler, S., & Leeflang, P. S. H. (2012). Popularity of Brand Posts on Brand Fan Pages: An Investigation of the Effects of Social Media Marketing. *Journal of Interactive Marketing*, *26*(2), 83–91.

Dholakia, U. M., & Durham, E. (2010). One Café Chain's Facebook Experiment. *Harvard Business Review*, *88*(3), 26.

Homer, P. M., & Kahle, L. (1988). A Structural Equation Test of the Value-attitude-behavior Hierarchy. *Journal of Personality and Social Psychology*, *54*(4), 638–646.

Kahle, L. (1983). *Social Values and Social Change: Adaptation to Life in America*. New York, NY: Praeger.

Kahle, L. (1996). Social Values and Consumer Behavior: Research from the List of Values. In C. Seligman, J. M. Olson, & M. P. Zanna (Eds.), *The Ontario Symposium: Vol. 8. The Psychology of Values* (pp. 135–151). Mahwah, NJ: Lawrence Erlbaum.

Kahle, L., Beatty, S. E., & Homer, P. (1986). Alternative Measurement Approaches to Consumer Values: The List of Values (LOV) and Values and Life Style (VALS). *The Journal of Consumer Research*, *13*(3), 405–409.

Kahle, L., Duncan, M., Dalakas, V., & Aiken, D. (2001). The social values of fans for men's versus women's university basketball. *Sport Marketing Quarterly*, *10*(3), 156–163.

Kahle, L., & Guang-Xin, X. (2008). Social Values in Consumer Psychology. In C. P. Haugvedt, P. M. Herr, & F. R. Kardes (Eds.), *Handbook of Consumer Psychology* (pp. 275–285). New York, NY: Routledge.

Kahle, L., & Valette-Florence, P. (2012). *Marketplace Lifestyles in an Age of Social Media: Theory and Methods*. Armonk, NY: M.E. Sharpe.

Kietzmann, J. H., Hermkens, K., McCarthy, I. P., & Silvestre, B. S. (2011). Social Media? Get Serious! Understanding the Functional Building Blocks of Social Media. *Business Horizons*, *54*(3), 241–251.

Kim, A. J., & Ko, E. (2012). Do Social Media Marketing Activities Enhance Customer Equity? An Empirical Study of Luxury Fashion Brand. *Journal of Business Research*, *65*(10), 1480–1486.

Kurpis, L. H. V., Bozman, C. S., & Kahle, L. R. (2010). Distinguishing Between Amateur Sport Participants and Spectators: The List of Values Approach. *International Journal of Sport Management and Marketing, 7*(3–4), 190–201.

Lee, C., & Kahle, L. (2016). The Linguistics of Social Media: Communication of Emotions and Values in Sport. *Sport Marketing Quarterly; Morgantown, 25*(4), 201–211.

Lyon, T. P., & Wren Montgomery, A. (2013). Tweetjacked: The Impact of Social Media on Corporate Greenwash. *Journal of Business Ethics: JBE, 118*(4), 747–757.

Mahan, J. E. (2011). Examining the Predictors of Consumer Response to Sport Marketing via Digital Social Media. *International Journal of Sport Management and Marketing, 9*(3–4), 254–267.

Minton, E., Lee, C., Orth, U., Kim, C.-H., & Kahle, L. (2012). Sustainable Marketing and Social Media. *Journal of Advertising, 41*(4), 69–84.

Mitchell, A. (1983). *The Nine American Lifestyles.* New York, NY: Warner Books.

Moorhead, S. A., Hazlett, D. E., Harrison, L., Carroll, J. K., Irwin, A., & Hoving, C. (2013). A New Dimension of Health Care: Systematic Review of the Uses, Benefits, and Limitations of Social Media for Health Communication. *Journal of Medical Internet Research, 15*(4), e85.

Pennebaker, J. W., Chung, C. K., Ireland, M., Gonzales, A., & Booth, R. J. (2007). *The development and psychometric properties of LIWC2007* [software manual]. Austin, TX: LIWC.net.

Pennebaker, J. W., Francis, M. E., & Booth, R. J. (2001). *Linguistic inquiry and word count: LIWC 2001.* Mahwah, NJ: Lawrence Erlbaum Associates, 71.

Pitts, R. E., & Woodside, A. G. (1984). Personal values and consumer psychology. Lexington, MA: Lexington Books.

Reynolds, T. J., & Olson, J. C. (2001). *Understanding Consumer Decision Making: The Means-end Approach to Marketing and Advertising Strategy.* Mahwah, NJ: Psychology Press.

Rokeach, M. (1973). *The Nature of Human Values.* New York, NY: Free Press.

Salter, C., Bellis, R., Ungerleider, N., Trebor, S., Mohan, P., Wilson, M., … Lawson, S. (2005). Protect This House. Retrieved October 7, 2015, from www.fastcompany.com/53752/protect-house.

Stavros, C., Meng, M. D., Westberg, K., & Farrelly, F. (2014). Understanding Fan Motivation for Interacting on Social Media. *Sport Management Review, 17*(4), 455–469.

Suh, W. S., & Kahle, L. (2017). Social Values in Consumer Psychology: Key Determinants of Human Behavior. In M. Solomon & T. Lowrey (Eds.), *The Routledge Companion to Consumer Behavior* (pp. 139–151). New York, NY: Routledge.

Sukhdial, A., Kahle, L., & Aiken, D. (2002). Are You Old School? A Scale for Measuring Sports Fans' Old-school Orientation. *Journal of Advertising Research, 42*(4), 71–81.

Tausczik, Y. R., & Pennebaker, J. W. (2009). The Psychological Meaning of Words: LIWC and Computerized Text Analysis Methods. *Journal of Language and Social Psychology, 29*(1), 24–54.

Tumasjan, A., Sprenger, T. O., Sandner, P. G., & Welpe, I. M. (2010). Predicting Elections with Twitter: What 140 Characters Reveal about Political Sentiment. *ICWSM, 10*, 178–185.

Witkemper, C., Lim, C. H., & Waldburger, A. (2012). Social Media and Sports Marketing: Examining the Motivations and Constraints of Twitter Users. *Sport Marketing Quarterly; Morgantown, 21*(3), 170–183.

Yoo, C. Y. (2009). Effects Beyond Click-through: Incidental Exposure to Web Advertising. *Journal of Marketing Communications, 15*(4), 227–246.

SECTION III
Spiritual Aspects of Values

Values are central to people's lives because they convey what is important to us. Accordingly, it is important to identify the influencers of core value development. Religious and other spiritual beliefs are considered among these influencers. Chapters in this section discuss how values are related to religion and meditation.

Tanskul and Patara suggest that meditation can be used to divert consumers' focus away from materialistic aspirations, which, then, improves consumer well-being. Based on an ethnographic study and personal interviews, the authors explore how meditation affects consumer values, well-being, and happiness. Specifically, their research suggests that meditation focuses people's attention on the awareness of self, leads to higher self-acceptance, and decreases the importance of social comparison of success and wealth.

Minton and Kahle suggest that religion may serve as a determinant of core values for many people. More specifically, they propose that religion provides additional insight as an individual difference variable above and beyond other individual difference variables (e.g. need for cognition). This chapter suggests that examining this religious individual difference variable will provide a more comprehensive understanding of value differences among consumers.

10

MEDITATION AND CONSUMPTION

Nicha Tanskul and Yupin Patarapongsant[*]

This chapter aims to stimulate the discussion of how mindfulness meditation can help mitigate the impact of the consumer economy, experience of sadness, and powerlessness. By looking at the psychological mechanism derived from the mindfulness practice, the framework of how the mindfulness practice can alleviate the reliance on the coping mechanisms derived from consumption has been proposed.

Motivation

In everyday life, it is difficult to avoid a situation where we encounter feelings of sadness or powerlessness. Furthermore, the competitive environment around us also creates a circumstance where, according to Fromm (1976), the emergence of the consumer economy has created the rise of a personality type called the marketing character: "Marketing characters are always in complete adaptation—I am as you desire me." Because marketing characters try to become what the society has imposed upon them, they actually abandon their core and are unable to maintain their strong sense of self. This lack of a sense of self creates a problem because the marketing characters are faced with emptiness. To cope with this emptiness, one of the strategies is to consume, possess, and achieve (Belk, 1989; Levy, 1959). The more marketing that characters consume, possess, and achieve, the more open they become to the concept of materialistic value. The more marketing characters become open to the

* Corresponding author: Dr. Yupin Patarapongsant, E-mail: yupin.patara@sasin.edu. Yupin Patarapongsant currently works at the Behavioral Research and Informatics in Social Sciences Research Unit, SASIN School of Business, Chulalongkorn University, Bangkok, Thailand. These authors contributed equally to this work.

materialistic value, the lower their subjective well-being (Sirgy, 1997) and the more unsatisfied with their life they become (Richins & Dawson, 1992).

Meditation and Its Typology

Meditation is defined by Merriam-Webster as "A private religious devotion or mental exercise, in which techniques of concentration and contemplation are used to reach a heightened level of spiritual awareness." Despite this, the specific description of meditation can be categorized into many varieties such as concentrative meditation, mindfulness meditation, and guided meditation (Table 10.1).

Our attention is directed toward mindfulness meditation, which has its origin from Buddhist teachings. Mindfulness is embedded in the eightfold path called right mindfulness (samma sati). Right mindfulness involves contemplating body, feelings, mind and phenomena, clearly comprehending mindfulness, and removing covetousness and displeasure in regard to the world (Bodhi, 2013).

TABLE 10.1 Typology of Meditation

Meditation typology	Description	Origin	Psychological impact
Concentrative Meditation	Concentrative meditation involves focusing attention on a single object and disengaging from other mental processes (thought, emotions, actions, or other cognitions). This object can be a mantra, one's breathing, picture, or physical experience.	Hinduism	Produces calming effect.
Mindfulness Meditation	Mindfulness meditation focuses on staying in the present and does not allow one's mind to wander in the past nor in the future. This requires the meditator to maintain his/her alert and aware state in nonjudgmental ways.	Buddhism	Awareness of his/her thought patterns without experiencing it, which leads to emotional equanimity.
Guided Meditation	Guided meditation focuses on a chant or mandala or complex universal experiences such as compassion.	Tibetan Buddhism	Reduces stress and depressive thoughts.

Note. Adapted from "Impact of Meditation: A Meta-Analysis" by Sedlmeier et al., (2012), *Psychological Bulletin*, Vol. 138, No. 6, p. 1141; Copyright 2012 by the American Psychological Association.

Mindfulness Concept and Measurement

Mindfulness (sati) is the element of watchfulness, the lucid awareness of each event that presents itself on the successive occasions of experience. The cognitive factor is indicated by the word sampajano "clearly comprehending" and adjective related to the noun sampajanna "clear comprehension"... The expression "clearly comprehending" thus suggests that the meditator not only observes phenomena but interprets the presentational field in a way that set arisen phenomena in the meaningful context. As the practice advances, clear comprehension takes on an increasingly more important role, eventually evolving into direct insight (vipassana) and wisdom (panna).

The mindfulness concept was studied by various scholars. The measurements capture the essence of mindfulness, which comprises awareness, attention, and openness to a nonjudgmental acceptance of all the things that we observe both internally and externally (Table 10.2). Due to variations in the mindfulness concept, it has resulted in different mindfulness measurements. These measurements are:

- Mindfulness and the Attention Awareness Scale, which was introduced by Brown and Ryan (2003). This scale focuses on measuring the frequency of the mindfulness experience in daily life. The higher the score, the higher the frequency of self-reported mindfulness experiences.
- The Toronto Mindfulness Scale was introduced by Bishop et al. (2003). This scale measures the changes in the degree of mindfulness immediately after the consumers complete the meditation practice.
- The Kentucky Inventory of Mindfulness was introduced by Baer et al. (2004). This scale measures the four dimensions of mindfulness skills, which include observing, describing, acting with awareness, and accepting or allowing the present experience without judgment.
- The Freiburg Mindfulness Inventory was introduced by Walach et al. (2006), which outlines mindful presence, nonjudgmental acceptance, openness to experience, and insight. However, this measurement is limited to those with meditation experience.

Mindfulness Meditation Impact on Psychological Effect of Consumers

Mindfulness meditation has been suggested to influence the psychological effect in two paths. The first path involves attention control and the other the shift in perspectives (Sedlmeier et al., 2012). The *attention control* path leads to a significant decrease in emotional reactivity. This path was attained through the executive components of attention (Posner & Petersen, 1990) or executive control (Fan & Posner, 2004), whereby stimuli, thoughts, emotions, and actions are voluntarily selected despite habitual tendencies. Thus, this attention control path enables meditators to withhold a habitual or impulsive response

TABLE 10.2 Conceptualization of Mindfulness

Brown and Ryan (2003)	*Bishop et al. (2004)*
Mindfulness is a state of consciousness that includes two components: 1 Awareness: Monitoring inner and outer environment. 2 Attention: Process of focusing on conscious awareness and providing heightened sensitivity to a limited range of experience (Westen, 1999).	Bishop et al. (2004) suggested that there are components involved in the model of mindfulness: 1 Self-regulation of attention 2 Sustained attention 3 Attention switching 4 Inhibition of elaborative processing 5 Orientation to experience 6 Curiosity 7 Experiential openness 8 Acceptance 9 De-centered perspective 10 Subjectivity and transient nature
Baer et al. (2004) There are four mindfulness skills that have been suggested by the current literature from psychology and stress reduction: 1 Observing: Emphasis on the importance of the observing, noticing, or attending to a variety of stimuli including internal phenomena and external phenomena. 2 Describing: This is done in a nonjudgmental way by briefly labeling observed phenomena and attending to the present moment. 3 Acting with awareness: Engaging fully in one's current activity with undivided attention or focusing with awareness on one thing at a time. 4 Accepting or allowing without judgment by refraining from labeling good/bad, right/wrong, or worthwhile/worthless.	*Buchheld, Grossman, and Walach (2001)* There are namely four components: 1 Attention to the present moment without personal identification with the experience at hand. 2 Nonjudgmental and nonevaluative attitude toward self and others. 3 Openness to one's own negative and positive sensations, perceptions, mood states, emotions, and thoughts. 4 A process-oriented, insightful understanding of experience at a more general level than immediate experience.

Note: Adapted from the Mindfulness and Attention Awareness Scale (Brown & Ryan, 2003), Toroton Mindfulness Scale (Bishop et al., 2003), Kentucky Inventory Mindfulness Scale (Baer et al., 2004), and Freiburg Mindfulness Inventory (Walach et al., 2006).

voluntarily and successfully. Orientation to experience, change in perspective, or overall perception enable the meditator to step back and witness meditator's own thoughts and experiences instead of immersing in them. It involves observing one's cognitive processes, which is similar to cognitive therapy (Kaplan et al., 1993), where the goal is to identify and correct maladaptive cognition

(Beck, 1979). Eventually, meditators are able to face the negative emotional state because they realize that this emotional state is only temporary (Sahdra et al., 2011; Sedlmeier et al., 2012).

The Positive Impact of Mindfulness Meditation

- Through the practice of mindfulness meditation, mood and stress disturbance (Kaplan et al., 1993) can be reduced due to the mindfulness self-regulatory function (Brown & Ryan, 2003). Mindfulness helps consumers to act in ways that are congruent with their values and interests. These actions are also experienced in more enjoyable manners and enhance perpetual mindful behavior.
- Mindfulness meditation also enhances overall self-esteem feelings of worth, benevolence, and self-acceptance. It also reduces impulsivity and the ego-defense mechanism. The effects were postulated to arise from the fact that mindfulness meditation helps meditators recognize the nonself (anatta) concept. The adoption of the nonself concept provides the meditator a sense of liberation, increased self-control, and equanimity (Emavardhana & Tori, 1997).
- Through the path of attention control, mindfulness meditation enhances the ability to focus and detach awareness to all objects of attention while maintaining a nonjudgmental, self-accepting attitude, which results in the ability to cope with satiety cues through reduction of the binge eating appeal as an escape mechanism (Kristeller & Hallette, 1999).
- Through the path of orientation to experience, the self-devaluative or hopeless thoughts will be recognized as only thoughts and are unlikely to result in ruminative thinking (Bishop et al., 2004). Consequentially, this reduces the risk of experiencing depression (Teasdale et al., 2000) and vulnerability to anxiety disorder (Roemer & Orsillo, 2002).
- The mindfulness meditation practice improves the self-regulation of the response inhibition task. This also influences the positive changes in the adaptive socioemotional functioning, which is a basis for emotional well-being (Sahdra et al., 2011).
- Brief mindfulness meditation has been suggested to enhance the ability to self-regulate emotions, which results in the improvement in cognitive tasks. Studies show improvement in visuospatial processing, working memory, and executive functioning (Zeidan et al., 2010).
- The study by Hollis-Walker and Colosimo (2011) found that mindfulness can create happiness through the path of self-compassion. The research suggested that self-compassion, which generally coexists with the mindfulness traits, enhances psychological well-being.
- Mindfulness meditation has an impact on how its effects have been evaluated according to the Affect Valuation Theory (AVT). In this case, meditators would value a calm effect more than others, while they may or may not experience the calmness arising from meditation (Koopmann-Holm et al., 2013).

- Mindfulness meditation also enhances the sense of coherence, self-esteem, and purpose in life because of its ability to promote relaxation, alleviate stress, and increase self-respect (Oshita, et al., 2013)
- Mindfulness meditation also causes us to focus on the present and move away from the future and past, which reduces the negative effects from the sunk cost bias that generally arises when ruminating on an action from the past (Hafenbrack, et al., 2014).

Consumer and Consumption

When reflecting on reasons for consumption, despite the fact that consumers like to consume to satisfy their basics needs, consumption is also a tool to cope with various situations.

Affective Experience of Sadness

When consumers experience sadness from a sense of irrevocable loss, they encounter a sense of helplessness. This experience of helplessness will stimulate more consumption. This consumption occurs in order to regain a sense of control (Garg & Learner, 2013).

Self-deficit that Arises from Social Comparison or Self-evaluation

Consumers tend to compare themselves automatically and unintentionally to others outside their own awareness (Festinger, 1954). This comparison is usually made with consumers in the same prototypical or target group. It can be made either upward or downward. When consumers find that they underperform others on a dimension that is important to their self-concept, they may experience a self-deficit situation (Gao et al., 2009) where someone's self-view is in doubt. In another situation, consumers may face a circumstance that causes them to doubt themselves when they feel that there are discrepancies between the desired self-view and the actual self-view (Gao et al., 2009; Kim & Gal, 2014).

Powerlessness

This is a situation where consumers experience the lack of power or capacity to control their own or another's resources and outcome (Magee & Galinsky, 2008; Rucker & Galinsky, 2008). One method to restore a sense of power is through conspicuous consumption that signals a person's status to others. This tendency to participate in conspicuous consumption depends on consumers' self-monitoring behavior (Snyder, 1974). People with high self-monitors prefer products advertised via the soft-sell approach, which focuses on building a positive image associated with using the product, emphasizing the benefits

TABLE 10.3 Situation and Consumption Strategy

Situation	Consumption Strategy
Effective experience of sadness	Hedonic consumption
	Impulsive consumption
Self-deficit	Compensatory consumption
Powerlessness	Conspicuous consumption

that consumers would receive from gaining respect in the eyes of others, and answering to the motive of seeking status and approval from other. On the other hand, the hard-sell approach focuses on creating utility and functionality benefits for the consumers rather than creating consumers images when using the product (Fox, 1984; Rucker & Galinsky, 2008) (Table 10.3).

The aforementioned situations have increased the tendency for consumers to participate in the following consumption strategies in response to the situations:

- Research also established that consumption, particularly *hedonic consumption*, enhances happiness. Hedonic consumption involves enjoyment, fun, and pleasure (Alba & Williams, 2013; Burroughs & Rindfleisch, 2002; Dhar & Wertenbroch, 2000; Guevarra & Howell, 2015). It is worth noting that this type of hedonic consumption yields different life satisfactions based on whether these consumptions are material or experiential. Recent research has established that the consumption of experiential product and life experience consumption yield a higher well-being than material items. Furthermore, experiential products and consumption overall provide a venue for identity expression. Yet, life experience consumption offers higher relatedness satisfaction (Caprariello & Ries, 2013) and experiential product offers higher competence satisfaction (Schmitt & Zarantonello, 2013).
- *Impulsive consumption* arises when the desire to consume overcomes the willpower to resist it (Hoch & Loewenstein, 1991). Willpower has been defined as the determination, strength of will, or self-control to resist the particular impulse. Depending on how consumers construe themselves, if they see themselves as more interdependent (i.e. value connectedness, conformity and group harmony, and place high value on security and safety), then they will be less impulsive in consumption, especially when their peers are present (Zhang & Shrum, 2008).
- *Compensatory consumption* can be defined as the consumption that aims to offset a self-threat or an experience of self-discrepancy (Kim & Rucker, 2012), which is an inconsistency between the desired self-view and the actual self-view (Higgins, 1987). Furthermore, compensatory consumption can be classified into two categories: proactive compensatory consumption

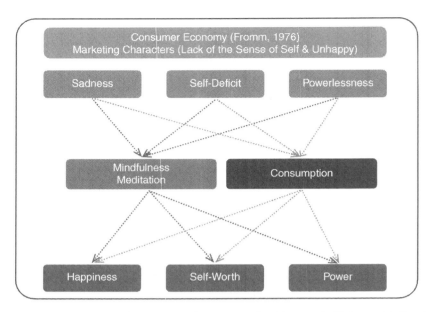

FIGURE 10.1 Proposed Theoretical Framework: How Mindfulness Meditation Alleviates Reliance on Consumption as Coping Strategies.

and reactive compensatory consumption. Proactive compensatory consumption refers to consumer behavior that is motivated by a precautious mindset to protect or guard the self in an effort to prevent a discrepancy from arising in the future. Yet, reactive compensatory consumption focuses on the need to reconcile an activated self-discrepancy by distracting oneself from such threats (Kim & Rucker, 2012).

- *Conspicuous consumption* refers to the act of acquiring goods, not for their inherent objective or subjective value but to signal a social status (Banerjee & Duflo, 2007; Veblen, 1899, 1994, Figure 10.1).

Mindfulness Meditation and Consumption

In the previous section, mindfulness meditation has been shown to have an impact on consumer psychological factors, i.e. reducing mood and stress disturbance (Kaplan et al., 1993), enhancing self-acceptance (Emavardhana & Tori, 1997), enhancing the ability to cope with satiety cues (Kristeller & Halette, 1999), reducing ruminative negative thinking of self-devaluation (Bishop et al., 2004), enhancing ability to self-regulate emotion (Zeidan et al., 2010), improving self-regulation (Sahdra et al., 2011), inducing happiness (Hollis-Walker & Colosimo, 2011), shifting the effective preference to calmness (Koopmann-Holm et al., 2013), enhancing self-esteem and a sense of coherence and purpose in life (Oshita, et al., 2013), and reducing the negative effect from the sunk cost bias (Hafenbrack, et al., 2013).

When consumers are mindful, they become more aware of their thought patterns and are less likely to immerse themselves in their thoughts, emotions, and feelings. They are also more open and willing to accept difficult circumstances because they know that the encountered situation is only temporary. Therefore, when they have encountered sadness or any other effects, they are less likely to immerse themselves in those effects because they are experiencing them with awareness and are able to regulate their emotions (Kaplan et al., 1993; Zeidan et al., 2010). As a result, feeling sadness and helplessness is no longer prominent in their minds. Hence, they do not need to participate in hedonic consumption to improve their mood. Also, they do not need to participate in impulsive consumption in order to reduce feelings of helplessness or to regain a sense of control.

In the case of experiencing self-deficit, mindfulness meditation also helps practitioners gain self-acceptance (Emavardhana & Tori, 1997) through the path of orientation to experience, change in perspective, or reperceiving. The self-acceptance was proven to be the fundamental component of self-worth (Crowne & Stephens, 1961; Kim & Gal, 2014). Hence, when consumers are more self-accepting, they are less susceptible to self-deficit information and are less likely to be influenced by the information from social information (Ellis & Dryden, 1997) because they evaluate themselves more objectively (Ellis & Dryden, 1997; Hayes, 1995; Kim & Gal, 2014). This application also applies to the case of powerlessness. In this case, they do not need to rely on conspicuous consumption to signal their status because they objectively evaluate who they are in the power dimension and are able to accept their position.

In conclusion, by practicing mindfulness meditation, consumers are less reliant on consumption as a coping strategy because, by being mindful, this helps them cope with the difficult situations they face in life.

Methodological Issues

First-person Experience and Inner Experience

Recent research has suggested that it is important to study meditation using the first-person experience (Walach, 2014). This is what is called inner experience. The author argues that inner experience provides researchers a subjective knowledge of the first-person perspective. While meditating, we turn our consciousness to observe our own thoughts and reduce or limit the background noises, whether they are thoughts, impressions, experiences, or even anticipations for the future. The author has suggested that the sharing of inner experiences should help researchers compile all of these experiences from various studies to create a substantial case. Furthermore, documenting the experiences can measure the different stages reached through inner experience, which brings more structure to thoughts and feelings.

Ethnographic Research in Meditation

Ethnographic research was completed, and it indicated that there is a need for more ethnographic research in this particular subject of meditation. Pagis (2010) suggested viewing silence as a meaningful and constitutive environment by looking at the shared dimension of silence. According to linguists and conversational analysts, silence can be used to question, promise, deny, warn, threaten, insult, request, or command (Saville-Troike, 2012). Interestingly, Kurzon (2007) indicated the differences between situational silence and conversational silence. Kurzon (2007) described situational silence as a means to allow certain experiences to surface. This silence occurs when one pays attention to art, religious, or formal rituals. Intersubjectivity defined as a joint consciousness of interacting individuals (Scheff, 1990) has also been redefined as the process of requiring constant product and maintenance in which a constant dialectic between the self and the other takes place (Pagis, 2010). In this case, meditators share the same activity, but the object of their attention is not identical. Therefore, to regain a sense of understanding from each other, one can perceive the experiences of another through his or her body language expressions. When meditators are in the meditation hall, this provides them a community of time and space. Meditators may not be able to express their experience in words to others. However, they are able to share the understanding of their experience with the researcher, if the researcher is willing to follow the same procedure as them. In another words, researchers are able to share the intersubjectivity with meditators by following the same practice of meditation. Thus, once the intersubjectivity is established, personal time and space can turn into a community time and space without the need of sharing the same object of attention. Meditators can act and react by observing the silence and non-silence of others and by observing the movement and non-movement of others. Silent intersubjectivity allows for communal support, not by sharing specific details of the experience or content but through the sharing of the process and form or the process of self-reflection.

Our Ethnographic Pretest Study on Meditation and Consumption

Design

The qualitative method has been useful to reveal multiple different aspects of the subject of interest, and it provides researchers an opportunity to consider evidence from a different perspective (Atkinson & Hammersley, 1994; Perry, 2002). The two qualitative research methods, participant observation and active interviews, have been employed to investigate the consumers in a naturalistic environment and gain an in-depth understanding of the process and interactions. The fieldwork was conducted at a meditation center located in Evanston, Illinois by the first author to explore both Buddhist and non-Buddhist meditation practitioners.

The data were collected during the winter of 2012. The goal of this study was to explore the meditation practice and how it affects consumption. The field study conducted at the meditation center was completed through the consent of a meditation center administrator, meditation instructors, and meditation practitioners. It was conducted during Friday and Sunday meditation classes to allow the first author to explore the impact of the different types of meditation practices. The Friday class was structured into four different types of meditation practices that included body meditation, mind meditation (samatha practice), emotional meditation (Chod practice in Tibetan), and general meditation. The following hour was an open discussion on meditation and dharma in general. The Sunday meditation class included two practices that included chanting and mind meditation (samatha practice), and they combined both sitting and walking meditation.

Findings

1   Meditation in order to free the self from suffering: The reasons for practicing meditation may differ across individuals; however, they all share a common theme, which is "suffering." Suffering has been defined as the pain that is caused by injury, illness, loss, etc. This can be physical, mental, or emotional pain. Suffering can be caused by the loss of self (Charmaz, 1983). Furthermore, suffering can arise from the political, economic, and institutional impacts on consumers. This type of suffering is called social suffering (Kleinman et al., 1997).

2   There is an interconnection between self, meditation, and consumption. Our interview with the informant has suggested that meditation helps the meditator regain a sense of self and reduce the need for consumption.

The following transcript includes the personal communication with Meditation Practitioner A, who is a non-Buddhist:

FIRST AUTHOR: Do you think there is a shift in perspective towards consumption? Like we were discussing about craving in the class?

PRACTITIONER A: Yes, I certainly do. If we practice meditation properly, meditation can direct you towards the right action. You are approaching your life from a different perspective. You know what I mean. It is not like I need to have this. I want to have this.

FIRST AUTHOR: So what is your meditation approach and goals?

PRACTITIONER A: I do not need it to be happy. It is nice that I can have it but I don't really need it to make me happy. You know, like it is not what is important. It is not important to have a new car. What is important is do I care for other people? But whether somebody will come to that conclusion, I am not so sure about it. When I was a kid, my mother would buy me clothes. My mother is a good shopper but I could not stand shopping. She would bring home a cute gown or nice clothes and I felt very happy now, but then after a while, I felt somewhat empty.

FIRST AUTHOR: Because it was not sustained?

PRACTITIONER A: Yeah… and that's what happens when people just concentrate on craving. When you are acquiring, you keep on acquiring more and more and more because you were happy for that moment and, like you say, it is not sustained. Getting things cannot make you happy. Do you know what can make you happy?

FIRST AUTHOR: Yourself?

PRACTITIONER A: Yeah… it sounds kind of cliché but … you know, I think the practice of Buddhism can reduce the desire.

(A. B. Interviewee, personal communication, Month, Day, Year)

The following transcript includes the personal communication with Meditation Practitioner B, who is a Buddhist:

FIRST AUTHOR: Do you think that after you do meditation, you have made any changes in your lifestyle?

PRACTITIONER B: Yes, I think I am much more aware. And things don't mean as much. I want to have fewer things, and I notice a difference in my response towards my mother. That's when I see the difference, in how I respond to my mother.

FIRST AUTHOR: You've mentioned that you don't want things anymore…

PRACTITIONER B: Yes, I mean I have a lot of things. It doesn't mean that now I want to live in a tent, because I wouldn't do well in the tent. But I don't need to accumulate so many things. It doesn't seem necessary.

FIRST AUTHOR: And why is that?

PRACTITIONER B: It just doesn't seem necessary or, you know, attachment. I don't need to be attached to the things, so it is easier to say, but I am not using this just to let somebody else use it.

FIRST AUTHOR: Have you ever doubted before why we feel so attached to things?

PRACTITIONER B: Well, I think I never thought that I was really attached to things. I am not a really materialistic person. You know, I like nice things and have a nice chair and nice couch, but there is some other awareness that having things is not what it is about. That's what it is. It is more of a spiritual awareness that having millions of things isn't going to make you happy. What's going to make you happy is going to be you from the inside.

FIRST AUTHOR: And how can our internal self-make ourselves happy?

PRACTITIONER B: We have to feel compassion for ourselves. That is a good start, but it takes a lot of practice.

(A. B. Interviewee, personal communication, Month, Day, Year)

Having compassion toward self and a focus on the present can shift a person's perspective toward consumption. This conclusion has been supported by the definition of happiness with two positive emotions: excitement and calmness (Mogilner et al., 2012). The preference toward either excitement or calmness depends on the temporal focus. Hence, when consumers focus on the present, they prefer the calmness happiness. Yet, when consumers focus on the future, they prefer the excitement happiness. The underlying explanation is the alignment between consumer temporal focus and emotions. Meditation practitioners experience a shift in their temporal focus to the present and, therefore, the calmness emotional happiness is exercised over the excitement emotional happiness. Richins (2013) revealed that high-materialism consumers consistently showed hedonic elevation in product-evoked emotions before purchase, followed by a hedonic decline after purchase. This hedonic elevation appears to be due to the expectation among high-materialism consumers that the purchase of a desired product will transform their lives in significant and meaningful ways. Furthermore, the state of anticipating and desiring a product may be inherently more pleasurable than the product ownership itself.

Conclusion and Future Research

Suffering intertwines with the concepts of self, whether it is a self-concept, self-identity, self-appraisal, shaken self, lack of self-efficacy, self-confidence, self-deficit, and self-acceptance. The forces of suffering related to the self have made us feel uneasy and unhappy. The need for evaluation urges us to conduct a social comparison or an internal comparison with our aspired self. Once we perform the self-appraisal, we may encounter a situation where we feel inadequate with our self-identity, lose our self-confidence, or experience self-deficit. Furthermore, interactions with people around us, or the expectations that have been set upon us by the relativism in our society, lead to insecurity as a shaken self. Despite a strong urge of self-appraisal, and to learn how to deal with the emotions that arise from interactions with others, meditation can help us reorganize ourselves. Mindfulness meditation focuses our thoughts on the awareness of our senses and our feelings, thus acting as an observer of self. Furthermore, meditation allows us to have compassion toward ourselves and others. It creates higher self-acceptance of who we are rather than focusing on self-deficit and the social comparison of success.

The relationship between meditation, temporal focus, and materialism can be explored in the future study. Materialists are future-oriented and have a stronger preference toward excitement happiness and excitement consumption. On the contrary, those who practice meditation are more present-focused and have a stronger preference toward calm happiness and calm consumption. Thus, meditation practice may induce calmness happiness over excitement happiness.

References

Alba, J. W., & Williams, E. F. (2013). Pleasure principles: A review of research on hedonic consumption. *Journal of Consumer Psychology*, **23**(1), 2–18.

Atkinson, P., & Hammersley, M. (1994). Ethnography and participant observation. In N. K. Denzin & Y. S. Lincoln (Eds.). *Handbook of Qualitative Research* (pp. 248–260). Thousand Oaks, CA: SAGE.

Baer, R. A., Smith, G. T., & Allen, K. B. (2004). Assessment of mindfulness by self-report: The Kentucky Inventory of Mindfulness Skills. *Assessment*, **11**, 191–206.

Banerjee, A. V., & Duflo, E. (2007). The economic lives of the poor. *Journal of Economic Perspectives*, **21**(1), 141–168.

Beck, A. T. (Ed.). (1979). *Cognitive Therapy of Depression*. New York: Guilford press.

Belk, R. W. (1989). Extended self and extending paradigmatic perspective. *Journal of Consumer Research*, **16**(1), 129–132.

Bishop, S. R., Lau, M., Segal, Z., Anderson, N., Abbey, S., & Devins, G., et al. (2003). Development and validation of the Toronto Mindfulness Scale. Unpublished Work.

Bishop, S. R., Lau, M., Shapiro, S., Carlson, L., Anderson, N. D., Carmody, J., Segal, Z. V. & Devins, G. (2004). Mindfulness: A proposed operational definition. *Clinical Psychology: Science and Practice*, **11**(3), 230–241.

Bodhi, B. (2013). Arahants, Buddhas and Bodhisattvas. In *The Bodhisattva Ideal, Essays on the Emergence of Mahāyāna, Kandy, Sri Lanka*, 1–30.

Brown, K. W., & Ryan, R. M. (2003). The benefits of being present: mindfulness and its role in psychological well-being. *Journal of Personality and Social Psychology*, **84**(4), 822.

Burroughs, J. E., & Rindfleisch, A. (2002). Materialism and well-being: A conflicting values perspective. *Journal of Consumer Research*, **29**(3), 348–370.

Caprariello, P. A., & Reis, H. T. (2013). To do, to have, or to share? Valuing experiences over material possessions depends on the involvement of others. *Journal of Personality and Social Psychology*, **104**(2), 199.

Charmaz, K. (1983). Loss of self: A fundamental form of suffering in the chronically ill. *Sociology of Health & Illness*, **5**(2), 168–195.

Crowne, D. P., & Stephens, M. W. (1961). Self-acceptance and self-evaluative behavior: A critique of methodology. *Psychological Bulletin*, **58**(2), 104.

Dhar, R., & Wertenbroch, K. (2000). Consumer choice between hedonic and utilitarian goods. *Journal of Marketing Research*, **37**(1), 60–71.

Emavardhana, T., & Tori, C. D. (1997). Changes in self-concept, ego defense mechanisms, and religiosity following seven-day Vipassana meditation retreats. *Journal for the Scientific Study of Religion*, **36**(2), 194–206.

Ellis, A., & Dryden, W. (1997). *The Practice of Rational–Emotive Therapy* (2nd ed.). New York: Springer

Fan, J., & Posner, M. (2004). Human attentional networks. *Psychiatrische Praxis*, **31**(S 2), 210–214.

Festinger, L. (1954). A theory of social comparison processes. *Human Relations*, **7**(2), 117–140.

Fromm, E. (1976) *Man from Himself: An Inquiry into the Psychology of Ethics*. New York: Henry Holt and Company.

Fox, S. R. (1984). *The Mirror Makers: A History of American Advertising and Its Creators*. Chicago, IL: University of Illinois Press.

Garg, N., & Lerner, J. S. (2013). Sadness and consumption. *Journal of Consumer Psychology*, **23**(1), 106–113.

Gao, L., Wheeler, C., & Shiv, B. (2009). Products as compensation for self-confidence: subtle actions affect self-view confidence and product choice. In A. L. McGill & S. Shavitt (Eds.). *NA - Advances in Consumer Research*, Volume 36, (pp. 131–134). Duluth, MN: Association for Consumer Research.

Guevarra, D. A., & Howell, R. T. (2015). To have in order to do: Exploring the effects of consuming experiential products on well-being. *Journal of Consumer Psychology*, **25**(1), 28–41.

Hafenbrack, A. C., Kinias, Z., & Barsade, S. G. (2014). Debiasing the mind through meditation: Mindfulness and the sunk-cost bias. *Psychological Science*, **25**(2), 369–376.

Hayes, S. C. (1995). Knowing selves. *Behaviour Therapist*, **18**, 94–96.

Higgins, E. T. (1987). Self-discrepancy: A theory relating self and affect. *Psychological Review*, **94**(3), 319.

Hoch, S. J., & Loewenstein, G. F. (1991). Time-inconsistent preferences and consumer self-control. *Journal of Consumer Research*, **17**(4), 492–507.

Hollis-Walker, L., & Colosimo, K. (2011). Mindfulness, self-compassion, and happiness in non-meditators: A theoretical and empirical examination. *Personality and Individual Differences*, **50**(2), 222–227.

Kaplan, K. H., Goldenberg, D. L., & Galvin-Nadeau, M. (1993). The impact of a meditation-based stress reduction program on fibromyalgia. *General Hospital Psychiatry*, **15**(5), 284–289.

Kim, S., & Gal, D. (2014). From compensatory consumption to adaptive consumption: The role of self-acceptance in resolving self-deficits. *Journal of Consumer Research*, **41**(2), 526–542.

Kim, S., & Rucker, D. D. (2012). Bracing for the psychological storm: Proactive versus reactive compensatory consumption. *Journal of Consumer Research*, **39**(4), 815–830.

Kleinman, A., Das, V., Lock, M., & Lock, M. M. (Eds.). (1997). *Social Suffering*. Berkeley, CA: University of California Press.

Koopmann-Holm, B., Sze, J., Ochs, C., & Tsai, J. L. (2013). Buddhist-inspired meditation increases the value of calm. *Emotion*, **13**(3), 497.

Kristeller, J. L., & Hallett, C. B. (1999). An exploratory study of a meditation-based intervention for binge eating disorder. *Journal of Health Psychology*, **4**(3), 357–363.

Kurzon, D. (2007). Towards a typology of silence. *Journal of Pragmatics*, **39**(10), 1673–1688.

Leilei Gao, Christian Wheeler, and Baba Shiv (2009), Products As Compensation For Self-Confidence: Subtle Actions Affect Self-View Confidence and Product Choice, in NA - *Advances in Consumer Research* Volume 36, eds. Ann L. McGill and Sharon Shavitt, Duluth, MN: Association for Consumer Research, Pages: 131–134

Levy, Sidney J. (1959). Symbols for Sale. *Harvard Business Review*, **37** (July–August), 117–124

Magee, J. C., & Galinsky, A. D. (2008). 8 social hierarchy: The self-reinforcing nature of power and status. *Academy of Management Annals*, **2**(1), 351–398.

Mogilner, C., Aaker, J., & Kamvar, S. D. (2012). How happiness affects choice. *Journal of Consumer Research*, **39**(2), 429–443.

Oshita, D., Hattori, K., & Iwakuma, M. (2013). A Buddhist-based meditation practice for care and healing: An introduction and its application. *International Journal of Nursing Practice*, **19**, 15–23.

Pagis, M. (2010). From abstract concepts to experiential knowledge: Embodying enlightenment in a meditation center. *Qualitative Sociology*, **33**(4), 469–489.

Perry, N. E. (Ed.). (2002). Using Qualitative Methods to Enrich Understandings of Self-regulated Learning: A Special Issue of "Educational Psychologist". Mahwah, NJ: Lawrence Erlbaum Associates, Incorporated.

Posner, M. I., & Petersen, S. E. (1990). The attention system of the human brain. *Annual Review of Neuroscience*, **13**(1), 25–42.

Richins, M. L. (2013). When wanting is better than having: Materialism, transformation expectations, and product-evoked emotions in the purchase process. *Journal of Consumer Research*, **40** (June), 1–18.

Richins, M. L., & Dawson, S. (1992). A consumer values orientation for materialism and its measurement: Scale development and validation. *Journal of Consumer Research*, **19**(3), 303–316.

Roemer, L., & Orsillo, S. M. (2002). Expanding our conceptualization of and treatment for generalized anxiety disorder: Integrating mindfulness/acceptance-based approaches with existing cognitive-behavioral models. *Clinical Psychology: Science and Practice*, **9**(1), 54–68.

Rucker, D. D., & Galinsky, A. D. (2008). Desire to acquire: Powerlessness and compensatory consumption. *Journal of Consumer Research*, **35**(2), 257–267.

Sahdra, B. K., MacLean, K. A., Ferrer, E., Shaver, P. R., Rosenberg, E. L., Jacobs, T. L., … & Mangun, G. R. (2011). Enhanced response inhibition during intensive meditation training predicts improvements in self-reported adaptive socioemotional functioning. *Emotion*, **11**(2), 299.

Saville-Troike, M. (2012). *Introducing Second Language Acquisition*. Cambridge: Cambridge University Press.

Scheff, T. J. (1990). *Microsociology: Discourse, Emotion, and Social Structure*. Chicago: University of Chicago Press.

Schmitt, B., & Zarantonello, L. (2013). Consumer experience and experiential marketing: A critical review. *Review of marketing Research*, **10**, 25–61. Emerald Group Publishing Limited.

Sedlmeier, P., Eberth, J., Schwarz, M., Zimmermann, D., Haarig, F., Jaeger, S., & Kunze, S. (2012). The psychological effects of meditation: A meta-analysis. *Psychological Bulletin*, **138**(6), 1139.

Sirgy, M. J., Grewal, D., Mangleburg, T. F., Park, J. O., Chon, K. S., Claiborne, C. B., … & Berkman, H. (1997). Assessing the predictive validity of two methods of measuring self-image congruence. *Journal of the Academy of Marketing Science*, **25**(3), 229.

Snyder, M. (1974). Self-monitoring of expressive behavior. *Journal of Personality and Social Psychology*, **30**(4), 526.

Teasdale, J. D., Segal, Z. V., Williams, J. M. G., Ridgeway, V. A., Soulsby, J. M., & Lau, M. A. (2000). Prevention of relapse/recurrence in major depression by mindfulness-based cognitive therapy. *Journal of Consulting and Clinical Psychology*, **68**(4), 615.

Veblen, T. (1899). *The Theory of the Leisure Class: An Economic Study in the Evolution of Institutions*. New York, NY: Macmillan Company.

Veblen, T. (1994). *The Theory of the Leisure Class* (Dover Thrift Editions).

Walach, H., Buchheld, N., Buttenmüller, V., Kleinknecht, N., & Schmidt, S. (2006). Measuring mindfulness—the Freiburg mindfulness inventory (FMI). *Personality and Individual Differences*, **40**(8), 1543–1555.

Walach, H. (2014). Towards an epistemology of inner experience. In *Meditation–Neuroscientific Approaches and Philosophical Implications* (pp. 7–22). Cham, Switzerland: Springer.

Westen, D. (1999). *Psychology: Mind, brain, and culture* (2nd ed). New York: Wiley.

Zeidan, F., Johnson, S. K., Diamond, B. J., David, Z., & Goolkasian, P. (2010). Mindfulness meditation improves cognition: Evidence of brief mental training. *Consciousness and Cognition*, **19**(2), 597–605.

Zhang, Y., & Shrum, L. J. (2008). The influence of self-construal on impulsive consumption. *Journal of Consumer Research*, **35**(5), 838–850.

11

RELIGION

The New Individual Difference Variable and Its Relationship to Core Values

Elizabeth A. Minton and Lynn R. Kahle

Core values are repeatedly cited as being extremely important to our understanding of consumer behavior (Beatty, Kahle, Homer, & Misra, 1985; Homer & Kahle, 1988; Kahle, 1996; Sheth, 1983). However, there has been much less investigation exploring the influencers to core value development. Because of the importance of religion in many aspects of life (Bailey & Sood, 1993; Choi, Paulraj, & Shin, 2013; LaBarbera, 1987; Muhamad & Mizerski, 2007), religion serves as a determinant of core values for many (Minton & Kahle, 2013). Prior research on religion and consumer behavior has been examined mostly from a correlational standpoint (Mokhlis, 2009; Zaichkowsky & Sood, 1989); however, to maximize our understanding of religion's influence on consumer behavior, religion needs to be viewed as an individual difference variable (IDV).

Discussion of religion is found infrequently in the marketing literature, and more specifically in the consumer behavior literature, partly due to religion's presence as a taboo topic (Bailey & Sood, 1993) as well as being seen as an adjoining discipline but not part of the consumption process (MacInnis & Folkes, 2010). However, when religion is viewed as an IDV rather than just a correlational element or the marketization of religious goods, religion can be directly incorporated into a consumer's acquisition, consumption, and disposal of goods and services in the marketplace, which MacInnis and Folkes (2010) identify as being within the boundary region for consumer behavior.

Therefore, this conceptual paper and, more broadly, this program of research explore the prominent influence of religion on consumer behavior, specifically as religion serves as an IDV. We propose that religion provides additional insight as an IDV above and beyond prior IDVs (e.g. advertising skepticism, need for cognition, and risk aversion). For example, a person that is highly religious would be more likely to hold to the core tenants of their faith and thereby should be more moral and caring for others. Although other IDVs may touch on these traits, the religious IDV will provide a more core and comprehensive understanding of differences among consumers that should be taken into consideration in any research on consumer behavior.

Individual Difference Variables

An IDV is just that; it represents a measure where individual consumers have varying levels of response, performance, or identification with the measure. More precisely, Zelenski (2006) describes that an IDV "is something internal to people, is generally stable over time, is consistent across situations, and allows us to make distinctions among individuals" (p. 206). IDVs are common in the marketing literature with such IDVs ranging from need for cognition (Cacioppo, Petty, & Kao, 1984) to advertising skepticism (Obermiller & Spangenberg, 1998) to self-monitoring (Snyder, 1974). Consumers' varying response to each of these IDVs provides insight into numerous consumption behaviors as well as assists companies in identifying target markets.

However, Haugtvedt, Petty, and Cacioppo (1992) caution that IDVs do not equate with theory. Just because a researcher measures several IDVs, this does not mean that they are guaranteed to influence consumer behavior, just as past researchers have found (Kassarjian & Sheffet, 1981). IDVs must be used in conjunction with a theoretical framework to provide meaningful insights into our understanding of consumer behavior (Haugtvedt et al., 1992). Too often, IDVs are included as control variables to account for additional variance and increase an effect size without adequate rational as to why the IDV performs as it does (Klockars, 2010). Klockars (2010) recommends that researchers and reviewers ensure that every IDV is connected to the research questions, hypotheses, theory, and conceptual development to ensure that the IDV provides quality contributions to the field.

We propose a new IDV that has been under-researched but builds on a strong foundation of theory to address the concern of prior researchers over the poor theoretical support for IDV use in research (Haugtvedt et al., 1992; Kassarjian & Sheffet, 1981; Klockars, 2010). The new IDV that we propose is religion, which contributes to a consumer's core value development (Minton & Kahle, 2013) among many other areas (Bailey & Sood, 1993; Choi et al., 2013; LaBarbera, 1987; Muhamad & Mizerski, 2007). In addition, one's religion is accompanied by core religious texts that contribute to theory development (Minton, 2013; Minton & Kahle, 2013; Putrevu & Swimberghek, 2013). Referring back to Zelenski's (2006) definition of an IDV, such a variable must include four attributes: (1) be internal to people, (2) be generally stable over time, (3) be consistent across situations, and (4) allows for distinctions to be made between individuals. Religion fills each of these four attributes with its inherent internal nature, its stability over time (especially after adulthood), its

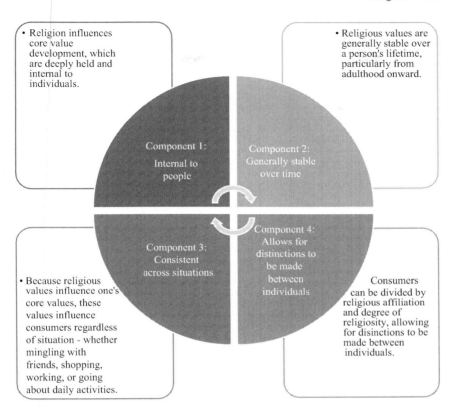

• Religion influences core value development, which are deeply held and internal to individuals.

• Religious values are generally stable over a person's lifetime, particularly from adulthood onward.

Component 1:
Internal to people

Component 2:
Generally stable over time

Component 3:
Consistent across situations

Component 4:
Allows for distinctions to be made between individuals

• Because religious values influence one's core values, these values influence consumers regardless of situation - whether mingling with friends, shopping, working, or going about daily activities.

Consumers can be divided by religious affiliation and degree of religiosity, allowing for disinctions to be made between individuals.

FIGURE 11.1   Components of an Individual Difference Variable (IDV) and Religion.

consistency in influencing consumer behavior across most situations, and the clear distinctions between individuals of different religious beliefs and varying degrees of devotion to such beliefs. See Figure 11.1 for an illustration of how religion fits the four qualities of an IDV.

Religion

Before delving into the many intricacies of religion and associated theories, it is important to define what religion is. Religion is composed of two main elements: (1) religious affiliation and (2) religiosity (Minton & Kahle, 2013). A consumer's religious affiliation provides an answer to *what* they believe, whereas a consumer's religiosity provides an answer to *how strongly* they believe. More specifically, Minton and Kahle (2013) define religious affiliation as "a commonly held set of beliefs and values that guide external behavior and an internal search for meaning" (p. 14). In comparison, these authors define religiosity as "the degree to which one holds religious beliefs and values both through an internal spiritual connection and external religious practices and behaviors" (pp. 12–13).

With these definitions established, we now turn to past research that has established a connection between religion and consumer behavior. In general, there has been little research examining the influence of religion on consumer behavior (Hirschman, 1983; Lindridge, 2005; Rindfleisch, Wong, & Burroughs, 2010). Some cite the taboo nature of the topic as a reason for the limited research on religion (Bailey & Sood, 1993; LaBarbera & Gurhan, 1997; Kahle, Kau, Tambyah, Tan, & Jung, 2005; Mokhlis, 2006), while others point to religion being perceived as not a component of consumer behavior (Hirschman, 1983). Regardless of the reason for the limited research, more research is needed examining religion as an IDV to provide a better understanding of how this core consumer trait influences consumption processes.

With that being said, there has been some research examining the influence of religion in marketing, although not explicitly referring to religion as an IDV. For example, Saroglou (2005) found that the more religious a consumer is, the more likely they are to be pro-social by showing less aggression, higher altruism, and higher empathy. Again, consumers have different levels of religiosity (hence the term individual *difference* variable), and therefore will exhibit different levels of pro-social behaviors. LaBarbera and Gurhan (1997) found that highly religious consumers have higher subjective well-being. Similar to well-being, Poulson et al. (1998) find that highly religious females are less likely to consume alcohol and participate in risky sexual behavior than less or nonreligious females.

In addition to religiosity's influence on a consumer's behaviors and views of their self, religiosity also influences more global viewpoints. For example, Vitell and Paolillo (2003) find that highly religious consumers are more supportive of ethical idealism in comparison to ethical relativism. Ethical idealism emphasizes that actions are either right or wrong universally, whereas ethical relativism suggests that actions are right or wrong in the eyes of the beholder. These differences in ethical idealism/relativism have wide reaching implications on views of others' behavior, decisions, and policies developed in the workplace, and the behaviors individual consumers participate in, among other ways.

In relation to branding and advertising, Choi (2010) finds that highly religious consumers are more brand loyal than less or nonreligious consumers. Possibly, a religious consumer's loyalty to his or her religious doctrine and divine being leads to loyalty in other aspects of life. Although there may be heightened brand loyalty among highly religious consumers, McDaniel and Burnett (1990) find that highly religious consumers are more critical of a store's efficiency in the shopping process, friendliness of sale's personnel, and product quality. Thus, religious consumers require a store to show signs of quality and good customer service before loyalty can be established. With regard to advertising,

Taylor, Halstead, and Haynes (2010) show that highly religious consumers are more supportive of the use of religious symbols in advertising; however, when a business performs poorly that uses a religious symbol in advertising, the highly religious consumer is more critical of the business than if no religious symbol was used. Using religion as an IDV can enable marketers to understand the loyalty of consumers, importance of various store aspects, and design of advertisements, as well as assist in marketing-related strategic decision-making.

In addition to level of religiosity, a consumer's religious affiliation is also a component of religion as an IDV. As previously stated, religious affiliation describes what consumers believe, whereas religiosity describes how strongly consumers believe. Kahle et al. (2005) found that consumers of different religious affiliations differ in what values are most important to them with Christians most valuing self-respect and warm relationships, Muslims and Hindus most valuing self-respect and security, Buddhists most valuing warm relationships and being respected, and Taoists most valuing self-fulfillment and being respected. Following the IDV concept, a consumer that identifies more or less strongly with these religious affiliations would be more or less likely to exhibit these core values.

In addition to value differences, a consumer's family structure is influenced by their religion. Muslims are the most likely to have a traditional family (i.e. husband/wife household with husband working and wife raising the kids) in comparison to nonreligious consumers (Mokhlis, 2009). Christians, Hindus, and Buddhists are also more likely to have traditional families than nonreligious consumers, although not to the prominence of Muslims. Along a similar line of thinking with regard to family structure, Heiman, Just, McWilliams, & Zilberman (2004) found differences in food choice based on religious affiliation with Christians, Jews, and Muslims most likely to buy whole fresh chicken as opposed to cut or frozen chicken. Although this may seem trivial, these differences may be tied back to family structure with a parent having time at home to prepare fresh food. We should note, however, that just because more religious consumers have traditional families, this does not mean that religious families always have one parent staying at home. Family structure is changing, and the influence of religion as an IDV is likely to change as a result. Thus, future research that explores religion as an IDV needs to be routinely reviewed and replicated to ensure accuracy of the findings to current day traditions.

In a more holistic review of religion and marketing research, Minton and Kahle (2013) identified ways that religion influences a variety of marketing components including advertising, new product development, marketing strategy, and business interactions. Within each of these components, religion as an IDV assists in understanding consumer behavior and associated consumer attitudes in response to marketing actions. Table 11.1 presents a reproduction of their summary.

TABLE 11.1 Summary of How Religion Influences Marketing Components[a]

In advertising

- Religious individuals are more likely to view gender/sex-related products as controversial.
- Timing of controversial ads should be considered (e.g. after children's bedtimes).
- Muslims want more advertising regulation, Christians and Hindus feel that current regulation is good, and Buddhists and Taoists want less regulation.
- Religious consumers seek word-of-mouth recommendations from religious in-group.

In new product development
- Examine target market's religion and religiosity before prototype is developed.
- Takeoff times for new work-related products in highly religious countries are slower in comparison to less religious countries.
- Catholics perceive more risk in purchase decisions than Jews and thus advertising may need to address risk concerns.

In market strategy
- Religion is a necessity in determining overall market strategy.
- Ignoring religion can result in offending a consumer's core values, failing to create targeted advertisements, and potentially miss an entire market opportunity.
- Religious targeted products (e.g. *halal* or *kosher*) foods are purchased by nonreligious consumers as well.
- Religion helps to provide a more detailed understanding of target market wants and needs.

In business interactions
- Highly religious employees lay greater emphasis on moral behavior and are more likely to see behaviors as controversial.
- Allowing freedom to wear religious clothing (e.g. the Muslim's *hijab*) is essential to religious individuals feeling a sense of connection to a business.
- Frontline employees need to be trained in consumer's religious customs to not offend consumers during personal interactions.
- Business marketers need to be aware of client's religious values to create advertisements and offer products in conjunction with the client's values.

a Reproduced with permission from the authors, Minton and Kahle (2013), from their book *Belief Systems, Religion, and Behavioral Economics: Marketing in Multicultural Environments.*

To enhance the contribution that religion as an IDV can make to our understanding of consumer behavior and marketing, research in this area, as mentioned earlier, needs to be accompanied with strong theory (Haugtvedt et al., 1992; Kassarjian & Sheffet, 1981; Klockars, 2010; Minton & Kahle, 2013). We will provide a brief overview of several theories that could inform research on religion as an IDV, but we want to emphasize that this is not an exhaustive list. Theory should be selected as it applies to the topic being studied. The theories described herein provide a starting point for research in this area.

First, attribution theory posits that individuals describe the source of attitudes and actions as either internal to one's self or external to the environment (Kelley & Michela, 1980). In the context of religion, three sources of attributions become possible: (1) internal to one's self, (2) external to the physical environment, and (3) external to a God, divine being, or other spirit (Spilka & Schmidt, 1983; Spilka, Shaver, & Kirkpatrick, 1985). Consumer attributions are especially important for consideration in service failure or poor performance. Consider this example: a consumer goes to a grocery store near dinner time and experiences an extremely long wait in the checkout line. The consumer has the possibility of three types of attributions. First, the consumer could attribute the long wait to their self, reasoning that it was their fault for coming to the store at such a busy hour. Second, the consumer could attribute the long wait to the external environment, citing the business as needing to have more cashiers on duty or more check stands open. Finally, the consumer could attribute the long wait to a divine intervention in which a God or divine being is trying to teach the consumer patience. This may seem like an extreme example, but many other examples exist. For instance, a consumer may experience winning the lottery, the death of a friend due to a malfunctioning car, or the availability of a limited product and attribute this experience to an internal, physical external, or religious external source. Consumers with varying levels of the religion IDV are likely to attribute the source of a company's failure or poor performance differently to each of these three main sources with consumers scoring highly on the religion IDV most likely to make religious attributions.

Similar to attribution theory, self-determination theory posits differences between the internal and external environments, particularly with regard to motivation. More specifically, self-determination theory suggests that consumers have both controlled and autonomous motives for their behavior (Deci & Ryan, 2012; Moller, Ryan, & Deci, 2006; Ryan & Deci, 2000). Controlled motives are regulated by external regulations, in other words, actions of the external environment. In contrast, autonomous motives are governed by one's self and, therefore, are more a function of one's internal environment (Deci & Ryan, 2012). In the case of sustainable consumption, an autonomous motive would be one's desire to care for the planet, while a controlled motive would be a city's tax on any recyclable items placed in a general garbage bin. The religion IDV may be more likely to influence autonomous motives given their root in core values (e.g. sustainability, caring for the planet) rather than controlled motives given their root more in the physical political system (e.g. tax-based disincentives).

In understanding the development of marketplace behaviors, such as shopping habits, persuasion knowledge, or reliance on marketing communications, theories related to the social construction of information may come into play. Theories of social construction are important for understanding the religion IDV because religion is likely to influence how much a consumer interacts within a religious network (a social group), thereby influencing the integration of the views of the religious network into the consumer's own views (Kahle et al., 2005; Stark & Bainbridge, 1980; Weaver & Agle, 2002). Social learning theory helps to describe this process as people learn what behaviors and attitudes are culturally appropriate largely based on the behaviors and attitudes of people around them (Bandura, 1971). Other theories, such as information integration theory, are also pertinent to the study of marketplace behaviors in describing how attitudes are formed and then reformed based on new information from others or the environment (Anderson, 1981). Again, the religion IDV is likely to influence a consumer's reliance on religious social networks or other religious information sources, which will influence what is perceived as appropriate and inappropriate behaviors in the marketplace.

When examining how a consumer evaluates other people, such as in a sales environment, social relations theory could be used as the foundation for understanding judgments (Kenny, 1994; Kenny & La Voie, 1984). According to social relations theory, judgments of others are a social construction of the target (e.g. the sales person), the perceiver (e.g. the consumer), and any existing relationship between the target and the perceiver. Given that judgments are often a result of social construction, the religious affiliation and level of religiosity of both the target and the perceiver should interact to influence final judgment formation. For example, religious consumers (the perceiver) are generally more trusting of others (the target) that present religious cues (Taylor et al., 2010). In this example, the religion of both the perceiver and the target represents scores on an IDV that come together to influence final judgment formation.

Here, we have discussed how five theories, attribution theory, self-determination theory, social learning theory, information integration theory, and social relations theory, can be used to explain how the religion IDV influences consumers and the marketplace. Again, we want to emphasize that these are only a handful of theories that can contribute to our understanding of the religion IDV. Researchers should review the literature and identify the theory or theories that best explain the phenomenon being studied rather than conducting purely correlational research.

Research Questions Addressing Religion as an IDV

Given that part of the purpose of this chapter is to describe a stream of research, we provide a list of potential research questions utilizing religion as an IDV. These questions do not serve as an exhaustive list but rather a starting place for research exploring religion as an IDV that contributes to our holistic understanding of consumer behavior. We encourage researchers specializing in specific consumer behaviors to question how religion may influence such specific behavior. For example, researchers could examine how the religion IDV differentially influences views of the self, post-consumption activities, lifestyle choices, consumption constellation development, or online shopping behaviors. Again, each of these activities should be connected with theory to provide the greatest understanding of why the religion IDV is influencing consumer behavior.

We also encourage researchers in other fields, such as religion or psychology, to take their understanding of religion or IDVs into the context of consumption and marketing. Finally, we hope that researchers will partner together to tackle some of the most challenging questions surrounding religion as an IDV to bring religion into mainstream marketing research. With that being said, here is a list of several possible research questions:

1   How does the predictive power of the religion IDV compare to other prominently used IDVs in marketing?
2   What is the best measure to use to assess religion as an IDV? Are some measures better for some situations while other measures are better for other situations? If so, how does this influence the reliability of the religion IDV?
3   How can the religion IDV be used to benefit religious and nonreligious consumers alike rather than manipulating them for the benefit of business alone?
4   When should religion IDV measures be administered in order to increase the validity of results? In other words, IDVs are generally stable over time, but are there certain days, seasons, or times in a person's life when the validity of the religion IDV would be decreased? If so, what are those times, and why does the religion IDV differ during those times?
5   Why does the religion IDV influence consumer behavior? We have introduced several theories that relate to the religion IDV, but these reflect behavior in general. We encourage researchers to explore theory relating to the religion IDV as it relates to each research topic.
6   Where does the religion IDV most predict consumer behavior? Are there certain settings or geographic locations where the religion IDV is more predictive than others? Why? For example, the religion IDV may function differently in a country that is composed of a variety of religious influences in comparison to a country suppressing religion. The latter situation of suppressed religion also addresses research question 4 with the challenges of administering religion IDV measures.

Conclusion

Religion pervades society (Mittelstaedt, 2002), thereby influencing a consumer's core values (Minton & Kahle, 2013). Given this influence of religion in so many aspects of life and consumers' varying religious beliefs and devotion to these beliefs, religion needs to be viewed as an IDV. IDVs are identified by four characteristics: they (1) are internal to people, (2) are generally stable over time, (3) are consistent across situations, and (4) allow for distinctions to be made between individuals. Religion fits each of these characteristics and thus should be classified as a new IDV. We have proposed a stream of research that supports religion as an IDV along with theoretical support for why the religion IDV should influence consumer behavior. By fully understanding the religion IDV, our understanding of consumer behavior will be improved, thereby leading to improved market offerings and respectful awareness of religious and nonreligious consumers alike.

References

Anderson, N. H. (1981). *Foundations of information integration theory*. New York, NY: Academic Press.

Bailey, J. M., & Sood, J. (1993). The effects of religious affiliation on consumer behavior: A preliminary investigation. *Journal of Managerial Issues, 5*(3), 328–352.

Bandura, A. (1971). *Social learning theory*. New York, NY: General Learning Press.

Beatty, S. E., Kahle, L. R., Homer, P., & Misra, S. (1985). Alternative measurement approaches to consumer values: The list of values and the Rokeach value survey. *Psychology & Marketing, 2*(3), 181–200.

Cacioppo, J. T., Petty, R. E., & Kao, C. F. (1984). The efficient assessment of need for cognition. *Journal of Personality Assessment, 48*(3), 306–307.

Choi, Y. (2010). Religion, religiosity, and South Korean consumer switching behaviors. *Journal of Consumer Behaviour, 9*(3), 157–171.

Choi, Y., Paulraj, A., & Shin, J. (2013). Religion or religiosity: Which is the culprit for consumer switching behavior? *Journal of International Consumer Marketing, 25*(4), 262–280.

Deci, E., & Ryan, R. M. (2012). Self-determination theory. In P. A. M. Van Lange, A. W. Kruglanski & E. T. Higgins (Eds.), *Handbook of Theories of Social Psychology* (pp. 416–437). Thousand Oaks, CA: SAGE.

Haugtvedt, C. P., Petty, R. E., & Cacioppo, J. T. (1992). Need for cognition and advertising: Understanding the role of personality variables in consumer behavior. *Journal of Consumer Psychology, 1*(3), 239–260.

Heiman, A., Just, D., McWilliams, B., & Zilberman, D. (2004). Religion, religiosity, and food consumption. *Journal of Food Quality and Preferences, 8*, 9–11.

Hirschman, E. C. (1983). Religious affiliation and consumption processes: An initial paradigm. *Research in Marketing, 6*, 131–170.

Homer, P. M., & Kahle, L. R. (1988). A structural equation test of the value-attitude-behavior hierarchy. *Journal of Personality and Social Psychology, 54*(4), 638–646.

Kahle, L. R. (1996). Social values and consumer behavior: Research from the list of values. In C. Seligman, J. M. Olson & M. P. Zanna (Eds.), *The Psychology of Values: The Ontario Symposium* (Vol. 8, pp. 135–151). Mahwah, NJ: Lawrence Erlbaum Associates.

Kahle, L. R., Kau, A.-K., Tambyah, S.-K., Tan, S.-J., & Jung, K. (2005). *Religion, religiosity, and values: Implications for consumer behavior*. Paper presented at the Australian and New Zealand Marketing Academy Conference.

Kassarjian, H. H., & Sheffet, M. J. (1981). Personality and consumer behavior: An update. In H. H Kassarjian (Ed.), *Perspectives in Consumer Behavior* (pp. 160–180). Glenview, IL: Scott Foresman.

Kelley, H. H., & Michela, J. L. (1980). Attribution theory and research. *Annual Review of Psychology, 31*(1), 457–501.

Kenny, D. A. (1994). *Interpersonal perception: A social relations analysis.* New York, NY: Guilford Press.

Kenny, D. A., & La Voie, L. (1984). The social relations model. *Advances in Experimental Social Psychology, 18,* 142–182.

Klockars, A. J. (2010). Analysis of variance: Between-groups designs. In G. R. Hancock & R. O. Mueller (Eds.), *The Reviewer's Guide to Quantitative Methods in the Social Sciences* (pp. 1–14). New York, NY: Routledge.

LaBarbera, P. A. (1987). Consumer behavior and born again Christianity. *Research in Consumer Behavior, 2,* 193–222.

LaBarbera, P. A., & Gurhan, Z. (1997). The role of materialism, religiosity, and demographics in subjective well-being. *Psychology & Marketing, 14*(1), 71–97.

Lindridge, A. (2005). Religiosity and the construction of a cultural-consumption identity. *Journal of Consumer Marketing, 22*(3), 142–151.

MacInnis, D. J., & Folkes, V. S. (2010). The disciplinary status of consumer behavior: A sociology of science perspective on key controversies. *Journal of Consumer Research, 36*(6), 899–914.

McDaniel, S., & Burnett, J. (1990). Consumer religiosity and retail store evaluative criteria. *Journal of the Academy of Marketing Science, 18*(2), 101–112.

Minton, E. A. (2013). Religion and religiosity's influence on sustainable consumption behaviors. In L. R. Kahle & E. Gurel-Atay (Eds.), *Communicating Sustainability for the Green Economy* (pp. 73–87). Armonk, NY: M.E. Sharpe.

Minton, E. A., & Kahle, L. R. (2013). *Belief systems, religion, and behavioral economics: Marketing in multicultural environments.* New York, NY: Business Expert Press.

Mittelstaedt, J. (2002). A framework for understanding the relationships between religions and markets. *Journal of Macromarketing, 22*(1), 6–18.

Mokhlis, S. (2006). The effect of religiosity on shopping orientation: An exploratory study in Malaysia. *Journal of American Academy of Business, 9,* 64–74.

Mokhlis, S. (2009). Religious differences in some selected aspects of consumer behaviour: A Malaysian study. *Journal of International Management, 4*(1), 67–76.

Moller, A. C., Ryan, R. M., & Deci, E. L. (2006). Self-determination theory and public policy: Improving the quality of consumer decisions without using coercion. *Journal of Public Policy & Marketing, 25*(1), 104–116.

Muhamad, N., & Mizerski, D. (2007). Muslim religious commitment related to intention to purchase taboo products. *Journal of Business and Policy Research, 3,* 74–85.

Obermiller, C., & Spangenberg, E. R. (1998). Development of a scale to measure consumer skepticism toward advertising. *Journal of Consumer Psychology, 7*(2), 159–186.

Poulson, R. L., Eppler, M. A., Satterwhite, T. N., Wuensch, K. L., & Bass, L. A. (1998). Alcohol consumption, strength of religious beliefs, and risky sexual behavior in college students. *Journal of American College Health, 46*(5), 227–232.

Putrevu, S., & Swimberghek, K. (2013). The influence of religiosity on consumer ethical judgments and responses toward sexual appeals. *Journal of Business Ethics, 115*(2), 351–365.

Rindfleisch, A., Wong, N., & Burroughs, J. E. (2010). God & Mammon: The influence of religiosity on brand connections. In S. H. K. Wuyts, M. G. Dekimpe, E. Gijsbrecths & R. Pieters (Eds.), *The Connected Customer: The Changing Nature of Consumer and Business Markets* (pp. 163–201). Mahwah, NJ: Lawrence-Erlbaum.

Ryan, R. M., & Deci, E. L. (2000). Self-determination theory and the facilitation of intrinsic motivation, social development, and well-being. *American Psychologist, 55*(1), 68–78.

Saroglou, V., Pichon, I., Trompette, L., Verschueren, M., & Dernelle, R. (2005). Prosocial behavior and religion: New evidence based on projective measures and peer ratings. *Journal for the Scientific Study of Religion, 44*(3), 323–348.

Sheth, J. N. (1983). An integrative theory of patronage preference and behavior. In W. R. Darden & R. F. Lusch (Eds.), *Patronage Behavior and Retail Management* (pp. 9–28). New York, NY: North-Holland.

Snyder, M. (1974). Self-monitoring of expressive behavior. *Journal of Personality and Social Psychology, 30*(4), 526–537.

Spilka, B., & Schmidt, G. (1983). General attribution theory for the psychology of religion: The influence of event-character on attributions to God. *Journal for the Scientific Study of Religion, 22*(4), 326–339.

Spilka, B., Shaver, P., & Kirkpatrick, L. A. (1985). A general attribution theory for the psychology of religion. *Journal for the Scientific Study of Religion, 24*(1), 1–20.

Stark, R., & Bainbridge, W. S. (1980). Networks of faith: Interpersonal bonds and recruitment to cults and sects. *The American Journal of Sociology, 85*(6), 1376–1395.

Taylor, V., Halstead, D., & Haynes, P. (2010). Consumer responses to Christian religious symbols in advertising. *Journal of Advertising, 39*(2), 79–92.

Vitell, S. J., & Paolillo, J. G. P. (2003). Consumer ethics: The role of religiosity. *Journal of Business Ethics, 46*(2), 151–162.

Weaver, G. R., & Agle, B. R. (2002). Religiosity and ethical behavior in organizations: A symbolic interactionist perspective. *Academy of Management Review, 27*(1), 77–97.

Zaichkowsky, J., & Sood, J. (1989). A global look at consumer involvement and use of products. *International Marketing Review, 6*(1), 20–34.

Zelenski, J. M. (2006). Experimental approaches to individual differences and change. In A. D. Ong & M. H. M. van Dulmen (Eds.), *Oxford Handbook of Methods in Positive Psychology* (Vol. 13, pp. 205–219). New York, NY: Oxford University Press.

SECTION IV

Methodological Approaches

Values have important and central influence on people's lives. Accordingly, it is important to study values with objective, meaningful, reliable, and valid instruments. The chapters in this section offer different methodological approaches to examine values.

Alfano, Higgins, and Levernier (by linking means-end theory, laddering, and virtue theory) introduce a novel approach to study values and try to understand, or "map," virtue and value through obituaries. The first study included the analyses of obituaries from four local newspapers from four different cities, whereas the second study focused on obituaries from The New York Times. Both studies employed manual reading, coding, and analyzing over 1,000 obituaries. Study 3 introduced a semiautomated data mining process and tested this new method on several thousand obituaries. Study 4 aimed to test if the values described in obituaries are shared with the living obituary writers and their intended readers in the community.

Wu, by using the "Seven Dimensions of Religion" as a theoretical framework, examines the religion-brand relations through a two-part study, an online survey, and an electroencephalography (EEG) experiment. The results revealed that Apple devotees did not have transcendent feelings. More specifically, the results of EEG showed that when exposed to the Catholic visual stimuli, Catholic devotees triggered higher Alpha waves than their Apple counterparts did; however, when exposed to the Apple visual stimuli, Apple devotees did not trigger high Alpha waves than their Catholic counterparts did. Still, averaged Alpha waves found with the EEG study suggest that Apple taps into some of the same dimensions as religion, especially in the Material, Ritual, and Emotional aspects.

Martin, Palakshappa, and Woodside introduce a new method called zoomorphic forced metaphor-elicitation technique (FMET) to map Consumer DNA (C-DNA). In this research method, research participants identify an animal for a specific country and explain how the animal's attributes fit the specific country and the country's products or brands. By combining a research participant's FMET data from multiple countries, Martin, Palakshappa, and Woodside create that person's C-DNA. These authors suggest that these C-DNA maps can help researchers and marketing practitioners to understand how country and brand images compare and contrast from the perspective of consumers.

Gurel-Atay, Kahle, Lengler, and Kim provide a comparison and contrast of the two most popular value scales in psychology, marketing, communication, and other relevant disciplines: (1) the List of Values (LOV), developed by Kahle based on the Social Adaptation Theory, and (2) the Schwartz Value Scale (SVS), developed by Schwartz based on the Theory of Basic Human Values. Based on their results, the authors discuss several advantages of using the LOV over using the SVS in consumer research.

12

MAPPING HUMAN VALUES

Enhancing Social Marketing through Obituary Data Mining

Mark Alfano, Andrew Higgins, and Jacob Levernier

Preliminaries

Traditionally, marketers have sought to influence behavior and choice with the ultimate end of promoting the interests of employers or clients. The domain of marketing was convincing individuals and groups to purchase certain products over others, to spend rather than save, and to upgrade after deciding to buy. Starting in the 1970s, marketing researchers began to recognize that these persuasive techniques could be harnessed for other purposes as well. This was already obvious in the case of political advertising, in which platforms and policies could be linked with consumers' interests and self-concepts; relatedly, Kotler and Zaltman (1971) argued that marketing techniques could be used to promote the social good, with marketers' own material interests taking a back seat. In this approach, Kotler and Zaltman stated that ideas, ideals, and causes can be "sold" just like "cigarettes, soap, and steel." Andreason and Kotler (2008) later defined this type of "social" marketing as indistinguishable from traditional marketing except insofar as social marketers seek, as an ultimate end, to benefit their target audience and society more generally.

In this paper, we approach this social goal by linking two concepts from the field of marketing (*means-end theory* and *laddering*) with one from the philosophical field (*virtue theory*). Means-end theory has precedents in Aristotle's *Nicomachean Ethics* (2000) and John Stuart Mill's *Utilitarianism* (1861/1998) but has been developed in richer empirical detail by Reynolds and Olson (2001). According to this view, individuals' desires, goals, and values are organized in a relatively stable hierarchy with more specific, concrete, local, and instrumental preferences (e.g. wanting sports team A to prevail over sports team B) at the bottom and more general, abstract, global, and intrinsic values (e.g. pride in one's community) at the top. Between the maximally abstract and the maximally concrete are various mixed states that might be valued both instrumentally and intrinsically (e.g. the vicarious feeling of triumph).

Laddering is a technique for exploring individuals' value-hierarchies. In a common interview-based version of laddering (Reynolds & Olson 2001), the marketer asks a consumer why she, for instance, purchased a product. Typically, the answer to this question identifies some concrete feature of the product at one end of the hierarchy, such as its ingredients or immediate effects on the consumer. The interviewer then iterates the "why"-question until a fundamental, intrinsic value is identified. Repeated further, this process generates a chain of increasingly global values. To the extent that the interviewed consumer is typical of the group the marketer wants to target, her value-hierarchy can be used as a model of the group's values. Once the model is formed, it can be harnessed as a rhetorical tool. One standard way of doing this is to point to the features of a product that can be expected to engage people's mid-level values, explicitly or implicitly draw the connection to such values, and then point in the direction of the relevant intrinsic values. For instance, the marketer of a chocolate product draws the target audience's attention to the fact that the ingredients are from Brazil and Ethiopia. This concrete feature is then connected with the mid-level value of exoticism. Exoticism is, in turn, connected with the intrinsic value of originality. The basic idea behind this strategy is that persuasive messages are likely to fall flat if they are (perceived as) irrelevant to what consumers care about. Though it may be possible, to some extent, to change what people care about, it is easier and more effective to establish the relevance of one's product or service to what they already value.

As we have described it thus far, laddering seems to generate only linear networks between local preferences and global values. Common sense, reflection, and empirical research all suggest otherwise. For instance, in the Schwartz Values circumplex model (1992), the degree to which individuals value benevolence is positively correlated with the degree to which they value universalism and tradition but negatively correlated with the degree to which they value achievement, power, and pleasure. This suggests that values are embodied in complex, nonlinear networks, and that marketing messages will be more effective to the extent that they utilize more routes toward the same higher-level value.

For this reason, we believe that it is worthwhile to pursue means-end research not just through linear laddering but also with explicitly network-theoretic methods. One way to employ this method would be to data-mine existing corpora that may be rich in expressions of both communal and individual values. It remains an open question how to most accurately measure the distribution of values in a population. Several approaches have been developed, including the Schwartz circumplex mentioned earlier, as well as the models of Kahle et al. (1986), Rokeach (1973), and Graham et al. (2011). Graham et al. (2009) counted the number of value-laden words in sermons from politically liberal and conservative churches in order to make inferences about relative value structures within liberal and conservative groups more generally (while sermons from liberal churches focused relatively more on issues of group loyalty and concerns about harm and caring, sermons from conservative churches focused relatively more on issues of spiritual or physical purity and obedience to authority). Graham et al. (2009) thus utilized a lexical approach to understanding evaluative language, according to which everyday language reflects folk conceptions about the nature of morals and values more generally. This approach predicts that ideas that are particularly important to a community will naturally gain expression in that community's language, often as discrete descriptors (e.g. "loyal," "authoritarian," "nature-loving," etc.—see Christen et al., 2014). This type of lexical approach has a well-established history in the study of personality traits, a field that is also beginning to reintroduce evaluative terms (e.g. "wicked") to what it considers descriptors of traits (Saucier, 2009). Graham et al. (2009) focused specifically on popular words in religio-political discourse, and actively filtered out words unrelated to Moral Foundations Theory (Haidt & Joseph, 2004). With a similar lexical approach, we sought to examine the extent to which virtues, values, and constituents of well-being are carried in the language of different communities in the general (theory-agnostic) person-descriptors they use. Thus, unlike Haidt and Joseph, we planned to only filter out non-person-descriptors rather than applying a predetermined value framework.

This brings us to our perhaps surprising choice of corpora: we believe that obituaries are an especially rich resource for identifying people's values. Because obituaries are succinct and explicitly intended to summarize their subjects' lives, they may be expected to include only the features that the author or authors find most salient, not only for themselves as relatives or friends of the deceased, but also to signal to others in the community the socially recognized aspects of the deceased's character. Linda Zagzebski, a philosopher who specializes in virtue theory, proposed that "one way to express the depth required for a trait to be a virtue or a vice is to think of it as a quality we would ascribe to a person if asked to describe her *after her death*" (1996, emphasis ours). Such posthumous descriptions have a summative character to them, so positive or negative valence in them is presumably meant to evaluate the deceased's moral identity as a whole. In a similar vein, in Acceptance and Commitment Therapy (ACT), a popular form of clinical psychiatry, one of the primary interventions employed to help patients clarify and connect their values is to ask them to write their own obituary or eulogy (Hayes et al., 2011). Additionally, because social marketing typically aims to promote moral or social ends, the values relevant to social marketers are especially likely to crop up in these documents.

Beyond these essential connections, extracting values is also potentially useful to social marketers for several pragmatic reasons. First, obituaries, unlike other value-laden corpora such as sermons, diaries, and letters, are published in newspapers and readily available online. Second, it is fairly straightforward to use metadata to segment obituaries (and therefore markets) based on potentially moderating variables such as age, race, socioeconomic status, location, gender, and so on. Third, obituaries tend to focus primarily on moral values and virtues, which are typically the virtues and values social marketers wish to engage.

We expect the values expressed in these records to be diverse but also interconnected. Different communities and individuals are unlikely to unanimously agree on a single set of norms or ideals, but it would be equally surprising to find no significant overlap. Thus, the ideal approach to analyzing these texts will be sensitive to the typical (lack of) correlations between the various ways that we praise the dead. This sort of analysis could be conducted by developing an extensive list of positive and negative correlations between each term or phrase, but human observers have little to gain from a sprawling list of correlations between hundreds of variables. Thus, where we aim to present a holistic picture of the virtues expressed by each community, we will do so in the form of network graphs that represent hundreds or thousands of correlations in a single, easily digestible representation of the data.

In what follows, we begin by reviewing Studies 1 and 2, in which obituaries were carefully read and labeled. We then report Study 3, which further develops these results with a semiautomated, large-scale semantic analysis of several thousand obituaries. Next, we turn to Study 4, in which participants wrote prospective obituaries. We conclude with a general discussion and suggestions for further research.

Study 1: Local Obituaries

Given our goal of using obituaries to further our understanding of ordinary people's values, it was important to select sets of obituaries that are representative of the general public's values, insofar as this is possible. To this end, we selected local newspapers with obituaries of people from all walks of life instead of targeting obituaries of larger newspapers that selectively write about famous individuals. We anticipated that obituaries from newspapers such as

The New York Times would be both more selective (only covering a few famous or infamous individuals) and more comprehensive (written with the goal of telling a rich and captivating story of those few individuals whose lives were deemed worthy of note). We also found that, while *Times* obituaries are authored by professional writers, the obituaries of ordinary folks in local newspapers are typically composed by laypeople. The stories of (in)famous individuals in the *Times*, while more interesting, include a full range of virtues, vices, and value-neutral descriptions. Our initial goal, though, was to target obituaries as a means of developing a better understanding of *positively* (or at worst neutrally) valenced terms and phrases (see Study 2 for a brief discussion of obituaries from *The New York Times*).

Methods

Obituaries published between November 2013 and January 2014 were collected from newspapers in four cities: *The Register Guard* (Eugene, Oregon), *The Mat-Su Valley Frontiersman* (Wasilla, Alaska), *The Flint Journal* (Flint, Michigan), and *The Hampshire Gazette* (Amherst, Massachusetts).[1] These were read with an eye to agent-level descriptions of the deceased (e.g. "hard-working," "honest," "generous"). General categories of traits were developed inductively as obituaries were read, with additional categories added as new types of descriptions were found that did not match previously added labels.

Results

We collected and analyzed 928 obituaries (52% female) in total across the four cities, with 708 containing agent-level descriptions of the deceased (51% female) as summarized in Table 12.1.

We were particularly interested in investigating trends in the co-occurrence of descriptions of the deceased within obituaries. To see this, the co-occurrence

TABLE 12.1 Total Number of Obituaries Collected from Four Newspapers, Broken Down by Gender; Number in Parentheses Reports How Many Obituaries Contained Agent-Level Descriptions of the Deceased

City	Male	Female	Total
Amherst, MA	266 (215)	299 (240)	565 (455)
Eugene, OR	91 (75)	76 (43)	167 (118)
Flint, MI	66 (44)	81 (59)	147 (103)
Wasilla, AK	21 (13)	28 (19)	49 (32)
Total	444 (347)	484 (361)	928 (708)

of traits X and Y was treated as an undirected edge in a network, with the weight of each edge equal to the total number of obituaries in which the deceased was described as both X and Y. The resulting networks for each city and the combined network of traits are represented visually below. The graphs below were generated with *Gephi*, using a standard ForceAtlas layout with heightened stabilization, attraction distribution, and label adjust.

Figure 12.1 displays the traits ascribed to the deceased in Eugene. This graph depicts trait frequency with size (e.g. obituary writers highlighted volunteering more often than integrity, represented by the fact that "volunteer"

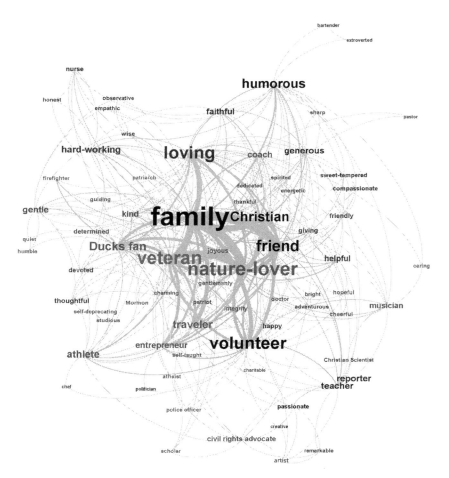

FIGURE 12.1 Co-occurrence of Traits in Eugene Obituaries. Label Size Was Determined by Total Occurrences, Edge Width by Total Co-occurrences, and Label Color by Gender Differences (Black = More Female, Light Gray = More Male, Dark Gray = Mixed, Continuous Scale).

is larger than "integrity" in the graph). Gender differences are represented with label coloring on a continuous scale between black and light gray, with terms colored black to the extent that they tended to be ascribed to women, light gray to the extent that they tended to be ascribed to men, and dark gray for terms that were roughly equal in frequency after adjusting for total word count of male and female obituaries. Finally, line thickness represents the frequency of co-occurrence of traits, with thick lines indicating pairs of terms that were frequently ascribed to the same individual. A label's position is not meaningful on its own, but positions carry meaning in relation to the positions of every other node. In graphs such as these, node positions are determined by an iterated application of three forces: (1) gravity, pulling all nodes to the center, (2) attraction, pulling nodes together if they are connected by an edge, with the strength of the attraction determined by the weight of the edge, and (3) repulsion, whereby all nodes are pushed away from all other nodes.[2]

Similar analyses were conducted using the trait-terms gathered from obituaries from Wasilla, Alaska (Figure 12.2), Amherst, Massachusetts (Figure 12.3), and Flint, Michigan (Figure 12.4).

In addition, we combined the data for all four towns, and then split it to create maps of the values and virtues associated with women (Figure 12.5) and with men (Figure 12.6).

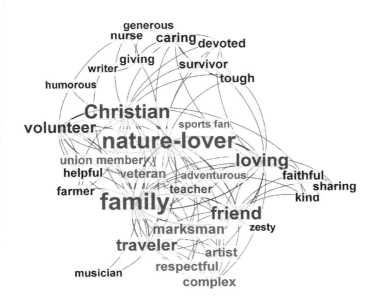

FIGURE 12.2   Co-occurrence of Traits in Wasilla Obituaries. See Figure 12.1 for Details on Graph Layout.

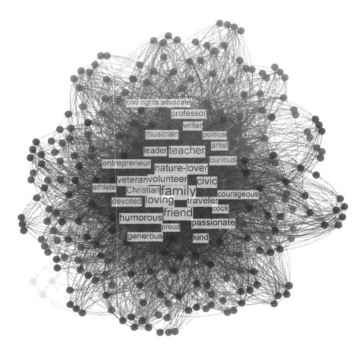

FIGURE 12.3 Co-occurrence of Traits in Amherst Obituaries; To Reduce Clutter, Only the Most Prominent Traits are Labeled (As Measured by PageRank). See Figure 12.1 for Details on Graph Layout.

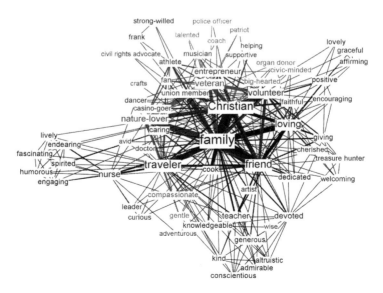

FIGURE 12.4 Co-occurrence of Traits in Flint Obituaries. See Figure 12.1 for Details on

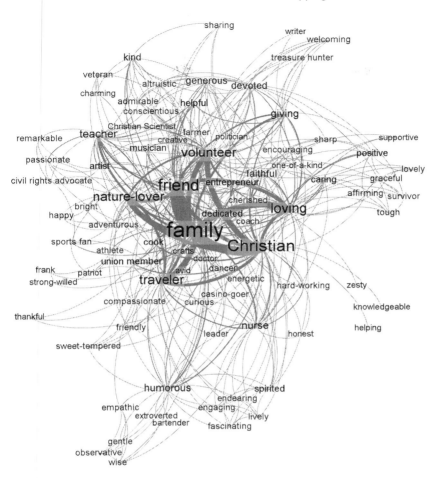

FIGURE 12.5 Co-occurrence of Traits in Female Obituaries in Amherst, Eugene, Flint, and Wasilla. See Figure 12.1 for Details on Graph Layout.

Discussion

Naturally, these maps are only one perspective on the value-networks of the communities they represent. We believe, though, that they point to underutilized approaches to social marketing. For instance, suppose the Sierra Club, a nonprofit public interest organization, were designing a social marketing campaign. They would, of course, want to connect with people whose identity is of a nature-lover. One straightforward way to do this would be to call attention to the direct environmental impacts of the Sierra Club, connect those with mid-level values, and then connect those to the valued identity of being a nature-lover. In addition, however, a social marketer might try to connect

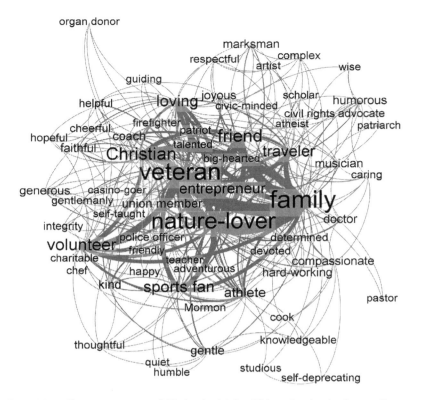

FIGURE 12.6 Co-occurrence of Traits in Male Obituaries in Amherst, Eugene, Flint, and Wasilla. See Figure 12.1 for Details on Graph Layout.

through closely related identities, such as being athletic or being a veteran. Instead of or in addition to saying, "Support the Sierra Club! We help save the coastal redwoods, a unique forest that any nature-lover would hold dear," they could say, "Support the Sierra Club! We maintain trails through the coastal redwoods, a beautiful hiking trail that any athlete would want to traverse," or "Support the Sierra Club! We help save the coastal redwoods, a national landmark dear to any patriot."

Study 2: *New York Times* Obituaries

We anticipated that local newspapers would be a useful place to look for variability in expressions of commonly shared values. However, we also wished to investigate the obituaries of significant figures because these might give us a better picture of the character traits of people who are commonly seen as great and noteworthy. It might be that people generally take certain traits to be virtuous for friends and loved ones, such as honesty and dedication, while evaluating famous individuals in a different light, perhaps differentially valuing traits such as leadership and decisiveness. To explore this possibility, we read and coded obituaries from *The New York Times*, following a similar set of methods as in Study 1.

Methods

All obituaries published by *The New York Times* from 1 October 2013 to 1 February 2014 were read and analyzed. As with Study 1, information was gathered at the age at death, gender, and traits of the deceased.

Results

A total of 74 obituaries (13% female, an eye-popping statistic) from *The New York Times* were read and labeled based on trait-ascriptions found in the obituaries. Three-hundred thirty-seven trait types were included in the sample, with an average of 8.5 traits per obituary. As in Study 1, the resulting sets of traits were analyzed from a network perspective. Where someone was described as both X and Y, an undirected edge was created linking X to Y, with edge weight based on the total number of people described as both X and Y, resulting in 3,939 edges. This network is displayed in Figure 12.7.

Discussion

Value-maps like the one in Figure 12.7 represent a complex social structure of valuation. They show what ordinary or somewhat-well-placed people consider important about praiseworthy and noteworthy individuals—not necessarily what those individuals were really like, nor what they aspired to be like. Nevertheless, since people, especially famous people, tend to be extremely concerned with how they're perceived, even such maps of second-order values can be useful. For instance, suppose a lobbyist for the Nuclear Age Peace Foundation, an NGO committed to the abolition of nuclear weapons, was appealing to heads of state in hopes of persuading them to support nuclear disarmament. They would, of course, want to connect with the desire to be seen as good leaders. One straightforward way to do this would be to call attention to the direct societal impacts of disarmament, connect those with mid-level values, and then connect those to the valued identity of being a good leader. In addition, however, a social marketer might try to connect through closely related identities, such as being honored. Instead of or in addition to saying, "Support disarmament! It protects innocent lives, an intrinsically valuable resource that any leader would hold dear," they could say, "Support disarmament! It will lead citizens and foreigners alike to honor and esteem you."

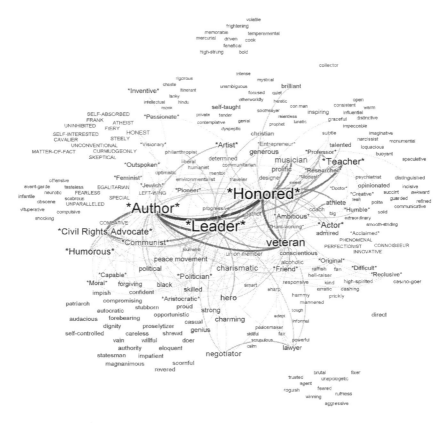

FIGURE 12.7 Character Traits Ascribed in *New York Times* Obituaries. Trait are Labeled Based on the Gender of the Deceased (Male Only = Low-ercase; Female Only = UPPERCASE; Both Male and Female = Proper). Label Sizes Reflect PageRank, and Edge Width Reflects Edge Weight. Edges with Edge Weight <2 and Nodes with Weighted Degree <10 were Hidden to Reduce Clutter.

Study 3: Large-Scale Data Mining of Local Obituaries

After manually reading, coding, and analyzing over 1,000 obituaries in Studies 1 and 2, we were interested in developing methods for automatically encoding the traits ascribed in obituaries on a significantly larger scale. Hand-coding has clear advantages, especially with regard to our confidence that sampled obituaries are correctly parsed as ascribing traits to the deceased (rather than, say, commending caretakers for their devotion to the deceased). However, if an automated or semiautomated process should turn out to give similar results to the results of manual reading, we could be reasonably confident that the automated processes are not too compromised by misapplications of terms to the deceased (false positives) or missing content (false negatives) to render their results suspect. To gather more data and to test general reliability of a semiautomated data mining process, we sought to test new methods on a batch of several thousand obituaries.

Methods

Obituaries were collected from *ObituaryData.com* in collaboration with the Alumni Office of the University of Oregon. *ObituaryData.com* is a data-warehousing company that maintains a subscription to the United States' Social Security Death Master File, allowing a wide and nearly complete sample of deaths and respective obituaries within the US.[3] The University Alumni Office's account included permission to search the full text of all archived obituaries for keywords including the university's name and most common abbreviation, U. of Oregon. We conducted automated acquisition of the entire collection of obituaries matching these terms, totaling 13,209 records from March 2000 to May 2014 and containing over 3.9 million words.

Gathered records comprised the following information about the deceased: name, city and state of residence, date of birth, date of death (or, lacking this, date of obituary publication), and full-text obituary content. Age in years at death was calculated from date of birth and date of death. In addition, forenames of the deceased were used to guess gender (Female, Male, or Unknown). To accomplish this, we compiled the most popular 4,275 female and 1,219 male names in the US as of 2005, based on 1990 US Census Bureau Data and other sources in 2005.[4] The female and male name-lists were each ordered by decreasing popularity of name. The forename of the deceased in each gathered obituary record was then compared with both lists and assigned the gender of whichever list in which it appeared higher (e.g. if the name of the deceased was given as "Bobby" in the obituary record, the record was listed as "Male," because "Bobby" was listed as a more popular male than female name in the Census Bureau name lists).

Using *ConText*, a program developed for semantic network analysis, we performed the following manipulations of the text: (1) changed all letters to lowercase, (2) applied a generic stoplist to the texts, (3) identified bigrams, and (4) merged near-synonyms.[5] After steps (1) and (2), the resulting text, comprising two million words, was used to generate a full list of terms used in all obituaries; two of the three authors then independently read through this full word list and selected each unigram or bigram that could serve as a description of the deceased. The remaining author then reviewed all terms in cases where the first two authors disagreed. Terms selected by at least two of the three authors were retained; all other words from the original texts were deleted. We then reviewed the list of terms again and identified cases of synonyms or near-synonyms. Synonyms were retained based on the following general rules:

1   Adjectives (e.g. "Honorable") were preferable to past participles (e.g. "Honored"), which were preferable to Gerunds (e.g. "Honoring"), which were preferable to nouns (e.g. "Honor").
2   Words (e.g. "Adventist") were preferable to phrases (e.g. "Adventist Church").
3   Singular nouns (e.g. "Airplane," to describe a theme of a pilot's life) were preferable to plural nouns (e.g. "Airplanes").
4   Person-descriptors (e.g. "Pilot") were preferable to "themes" (e.g. "Airplane").

After two members of the research team had made independent judgments on conflicting terms, the *openNLP (open Natural Language Processing)* package in R was used to automatically tag each judgment suggestion by Part of Speech (POS), including its singular vs. plural status for count nouns. Conflicting judgments were then automatically resolved using the rules mentioned earlier. Conflicts unresolved in this automated way were then resolved manually by the remaining research team members. Through this process, for example, "accomplish," "accomplished," "accomplishing," "accomplishment," and "accomplishments" were all replaced with "accomplishment." In doing so, we ran the risk of conflating semantically distinct terms in some contexts; however, this approach was preferable to not identifying the semantic similarity of these terms in the majority of contexts where they might be used more or less interchangeably.

With the texts filtered and cleaned, we then constructed a semantic map of the obituaries, treating co-occurrence of terms X and Y within the same obituary as an undirected edge in a network. This resulted in a network of 910 nodes and 19,034 edges. Given the scale of this network, it would not be informative to present a visual representation of it in its entirety; thus, we developed a summary visualization. This visualization, shown in Figure 12.8, simplified the network by collapsing closely connected nodes into a single group node. Using *Gephi's* modularity measure (resolution = 1.0), nodes were assigned to groups based on which terms tended to be clustered together. Groups of nodes were then treated as individual nodes.

Results

In Figure 12.8, nodes represent large sets of trait-terms.

Labels were assigned manually based on the common theme we identified in each cluster. Node size was determined by the number of terms subsumed within each group. Edge width was determined by edge weight between nodes, which, in turn, was based on the co-occurrence of traits in each group. Node positions were determined by an iterated application of the ForceAtlas algorithm with heightened attraction distribution and repulsion strength.

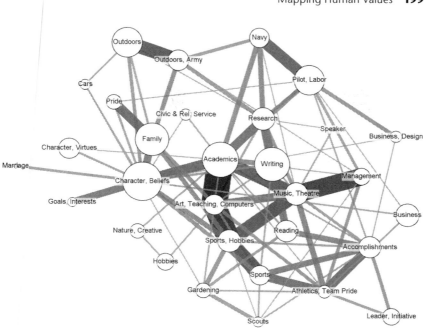

FIGURE 12.8 Groups of Traits Ascribed to 13,209 Deceased University of Oregon Alumni. Trait Terms were Grouped Based on Modularity Measure and Groups were Labeled Manually Based on the Judged Common Theme among the Traits in Each Group. Node Circle Size Indicates the Number of Traits Subsumed in Each Group, and Edge Width and Color Reflect the Number of Between-group Connections.

Discussion

Before we initiated this semiautomated analysis, it was an open question whether this process would produce results similar to those of manual reading. The results suggest that semiautomated data processing results in a network of trait-terms similar to those identified by the authors in carefully reading individual obituaries, but the results diverge from the results of Study 1 in some important respects.

First, we observed a substantially higher frequency of scholarly traits. Far more people were described as writers, scientists, researchers, students, teachers, etc. In the obituaries analyzed in Study 1, family, friendship, and faith were consistently at the core of the network; in the current study, these traits were still frequently mentioned but were less central to the network than academic attributes. This difference is naturally explained by differences in the original data. The obituaries used for Study 1 came from local newspapers where friends or relatives of any deceased person may write about the deceased, but for the present study, obituaries were filtered to include only those mentioning

University of Oregon. Thus, most people described in these obituaries were either students or university employees, and obituary writers took their university affiliation to be sufficiently important to the deceased to include this in their obituary, so it is no surprise that they tend to be described with more academic language.

Second, we observed higher modularity and more distinct patterns in the clustering of traits in the present study. This is best explained by the larger sample size. With over 13,000 obituaries to draw from, we could more easily identify the real patterns of connections and disregard less frequent or accidental connections.

Third, in addition to virtues and values, which were explicitly coded for in the manual studies, this automated study turned up many constituents of well-being. While it does not seem correct to say that accomplishments, athletics, gardening, or hobbies are *virtues* or *values*, they do seem to be part of what makes some lives enjoyable or worthwhile. If this is on the right track, it suggests that obituaries may be especially good resources for positive psychologists and marketers who are interested in what people enjoy for its own sake.

In the wake of federal and state divestment, public universities face serious budget problems that they've attempted to solve by, among other things, soliciting donations from alumni. We believe that the kind of network we've developed for the University of Oregon could be used to guide their outreach to alumni. In addition to connecting with former students' commitment to academics, social marketers working on behalf of the university could connect to closely related values, such as moral character, sports, music, theatre, and dance. Instead of or in addition to saying, "Support the University of Oregon! We educate students and perform valuable research," they could say, "Support the University of Oregon! We cultivate the moral character of our students, and we engage the community through extracurricular activities like sports, music, theatre, and dance."

Study 4: Prospective Obituary Writing

One limitation of using obituaries to inform social marketing is that this information concerns the values ascribed to the deceased, and it remains an open question whether, or to what extent, these values are shared by the living. It's not unreasonable to guess that these values are shared with the living obituary writers and their intended readers in the community, but it would be better if the method of extracting values from obituaries were calibrated with other measures of the values of individuals and communities. For example, while the gender discrepancies observed in professional and lay-written obituaries probably reflect sexist attitudes in our society, these gender-based differences may have been more or less pronounced in the lives of the deceased. By calibrating obituary data with other sources, we can identify relevant cohort effects, and social marketers targeting specific age groups may better understand the unique constellation of values embraced by each cohort in a community.

The present study considers prospective obituaries written by study participants instead of actual obituaries. We aimed to test the following hypotheses:

1   Prospective obituaries written by younger participants will have less pronounced gender-based differences.
2   In writing obituaries for themselves, older participants will focus more on career, organizational affiliation, family, and character traits related to hard work and loyalty, while younger participants will focus more on friends and social personality traits such as being humorous, kind, or fun.
3   Prospective obituaries concerning friends will focus more on personality traits related to benevolence and generosity while those for family members will focus more on loyalty and commitment.
4   Descriptions that participants *hope* will be in their obituary will be more uniformly positive than those that they *expect* will be in their obituary.
5   Prospective obituaries will only rarely include hobbies, personal preferences, and facts regarding their life history.
6   All four types of hypothetical obituaries will be more similar to obituaries written by and for laypeople than those written about famous individuals by professional authors.

Methods

One thousand twenty-two participant workers were recruited using Amazon Mechanical Turk and compensated with $0.50. The mean age was 33.5, with ages ranging from 18 to 75, and 56% were male. Participants were randomly assigned to one of four conditions: Self-Hoped (259), Self-Expected (252), Close Friend (247), or Family Member (252).[6] In each condition, participants were asked to provide five words or phrases that will appear in a hypothetical obituary. For example, in Self-Hoped, participants read:

> We'd now like to ask you to reflect for a few moments on your own values and life, then answer the following question:
>   Which five words or phrases do you hope will be used to describe you in your own obituary?

In Self-Expected, "hope" was replaced with "expected," and in Close Friend and Family Member, "your own values and life" was replaced with "the values and life of one of your close friends / a close living family member." Participants also provided demographic information (age, gender, and location).

Results

In each condition, participants identified sets of values highly similar to those identified in actual obituaries, as seen in Table 12.2.

TABLE 12.2 Most Frequent Traits Ascribed across All Four Conditions

Term	Frequency	Term	Frequency	Term	Frequency
Loving	396	Intelligent	82	Fun	55
Caring	377	Good	81	Father	52
Kind	321	Giving	75	Compassionate	51
Funny	175	Mother	73	Selfless	51
Loyal	123	Hard	71	Thoughtful	51
Honest	116	Friendly	64	Creative	48
Friend	101	Strong	61	Life	48
Generous	99	Helpful	60	Working	46
Loved	93	Family	57	Wife	43
Smart	92	Happy	57	Great	40

In general, the traits highlighted in these hypothetical obituaries mirror those of actual obituaries. "Loving," "caring," and "kind" are central virtues in both, and both sets emphasize a range of familial, friendship, and personal virtues. Some notable differences were found, however. Local obituaries frequently mention being a veteran, nature-lover, volunteer, traveler, and adherent of a particular religion, and obituaries from the *New York Times* most frequently emphasized being honored, an author, a leader, or a veteran. These words rarely appear in this set of prospective obituaries, even after combining nearby terms (e.g. treating "honor," "honorable," and "respected" as "honored"), with the following frequencies: religious (49), nature-lover (34), honored (22), volunteer (28), sports fan (8), leader (6), author (4), traveler (3), and veteran (1).

Some of these differences have natural explanations. Since the Mturk workers were limited to just five words or phrases, we would expect them to pass over life activities such as hiking or traveling and instead focus on paradigmatic virtues such as honesty and generosity. The decreased emphasis on religiosity may be due to younger people being less religious, but it may also be explained by the salience of religion, God, and the afterlife while writing an actual obituary. The most common virtues ascribed to notable, famous individuals are almost entirely absent in the prospective obituaries, perhaps suggesting that what we deem virtuous for ourselves and our loved ones more closely approximates the virtues ascribed to the dead in local death notices. Veteran status, however, is frequently highlighted in both types of actual obituaries while being virtually nonexistent in those written by these Mturk workers. This may be due to the demographics of the Mturk workforce; however, even if Mturk workers are less likely to be veterans, this would not explain why only one participant in the Family or Friend conditions characterized their loved one as a veteran. This may be due to their friend or family member status being most salient; or perhaps military service, like other careers, was not as noteworthy as other traits when participants were limited to just five descriptions.

We anticipated significant age-based differences in these hypothetical obituaries. Specifically, we hypothesized that older participants would more frequently highlight career, organizational affiliation, family, hard work, and loyalty, while younger participants would identify the virtues of being fun, humorous, and kind. We also expected more gender-based differences in the traits identified by older participants. Results were divided into three roughly equal groups based on age: Young (18–27), Middle (28–35), and Old (36–75). In comparing these groups, we did not find strong support for our predictions. Young and old alike frequently mentioned "fun," "kind," and "humorous," with young participants doing so only slightly more frequently. Career and organizational affiliations were rarely mentioned by any group. While each age group identified important familial relations, older participants identified these relations slightly more. The virtues of loyalty and working hard were frequently mentioned by each age group. The hypothetical obituaries of older participants differed more along gender lines than those of younger participants, but the difference was very small (only 4% higher in Old) after replacing gendered terms with gender-neutral variants (e.g. "mother" and "father" each changed to "parent").[7]

Two unexpected patterns were identified, however. First, as should have been expected, older participants mentioned God and religion more frequently than younger people. Second, younger participants more frequently identified a constellation of affective traits, including Nice, Warm, and Passionate. Overall, though, the results in each age group were strikingly similar. This suggests that information provided by actual obituaries may be highly valuable for social marketing insofar as the values and virtues ascribed to the deceased are recognized as values and virtues by many adults of all ages.

We next compared traits provided in the Self-Expected and Self-Hoped conditions. Generally, the most prominent traits expected to appear in the obituary were also those traits participants hoped to see, except that the core values of being honest, loving, humorous, and generous were emphasized more by those imagining their ideal obituary while social relations like being a friend, mother, or husband were identified more frequently by participants imagining their expected obituaries. Combining the results from these two conditions, a list of 5,090 undirected edges between 438 nodes was generated identifying the most prominent patterns of co-occurrence. Traits tended to cluster into three major groups within this network. The ten most cited traits in each group are noted below in order of PageRank in the network.

Cluster #1: friend, loved, family, mother, father, wife, husband, missed, dedicated, daughter

Cluster #2: caring, loving, humorous, honest, loyal, hard worker, helpful, smart, friendly, happy

Cluster #3: kind, intelligent, generous, creative, quiet, thoughtful, curious, nice, good, wise

The first group stands out as focusing on social relations, while the second highlights social virtues, and the third group generally focuses more on personal virtues, including not only paradigmatic moral virtues (e.g. kindness and generosity) but also epistemic virtues (e.g. intelligence, creativity, curiosity, and wisdom).

Prospective obituaries for friends and family members were compared with an eye to the virtues of benevolence and loyalty. Terms such as "compassionate," "generous," "giving," and "loving" were coded as benevolence traits, while terms such as "dedicated," "loyal," and "thoughtful" were coded as loyalty traits. Our expectations were wrong. Loyalty was highlighted slightly more in descriptions of friends (13% vs. 11% of all words used in each condition), and benevolence was highlighted significantly more in describing family members (40% vs. 33%).

Finally, we compared responses in the Self-Expected and Self-Hoped conditions with the anticipation of finding that hopeful hypothetical obituaries would be more uniformly positive. Terms were categorized as virtues, vices, affiliations, or neutral. Traits were categorized as virtues or vices just in case they would be judged as virtues or vices almost unanimously. "Affiliation" terms included social roles (e.g. friend, mother), hobbies (e.g. artist, writer), and affiliations (e.g. Christian). All of these terms were probably viewed positively by our participants, but they were separated from the virtues to give a more impartial analysis. Neutral terms (e.g. decent, silent, stubborn) may have been intended by their authors as virtues but were categorized as neutral because, we believe, one could reasonably see these as vices. The results do not show any marked difference between hopeful and expected hypothetical obituaries. In each condition, less than 1% of terms were neutral or vices. However, expected obituaries did include more affiliation or hobby-related traits (15% in expected vs. 11% in hopeful), perhaps suggesting that idealized obituaries focus more on paradigmatic virtues. The lesson to learn is that the contents of obituaries are expected to be uniformly positive, and that our participants share the norm of only speaking well of the dead.

Discussion

An advantage of drawing from actual obituaries is that we avoid the possibility of obituary writers being influenced by researcher expectations and the distorting influence of survey participants' apathy, carelessness, or desire to give witty responses. While a small number of our Mturk responders included (presumably) insincere virtues such as "shaman," "pirate," and "blah," almost all participants seemed to take their work seriously. From this study, we learn that the traits typically identified in actual obituaries mirror the constellation of virtues provided by living participants to describe themselves and their loved ones, and that what we hope people will say about us postmortem resembles what we expect them to say. Both observations provide further support for relying on obituaries as a measure of individual and communal values, and that the virtues ascribed to the recently deceased are also treated as virtues of the living, both young and old.

General Discussion and Future Directions

The methods used in the present studies could easily be extended to consider other public records of value. Using online tools such as *Lexis Advance*, one could scour newspapers or court opinions for specific terms. One could then visualize a term's position in the larger semantic network, and, using sentiment analysis, identify the relative positive or negative valence surrounding the term. Alternatively, researchers could analyze large collections of text from social media sites such as Twitter and Facebook to identify general trends in positive or negative trait-ascriptions, though "#RIP" and related Twitter searches did not produce useful results. Unlike obituaries, these data will certainly include large proportions of negative judgments, but tools such as sentiment analysis could help in distinguishing positive, negative, and neutral descriptions.[8]

Obituaries aim to broadcast to readers facts about the deceased and to convey intimate, summative portraits. Nonetheless, it is worth consideration that, especially for obituaries authored by friends and family with the intent to publish in a local newspaper, the work of "morality mining" (Christen et al. 2013) could be interpreted as intrusive. Such concerns are especially salient when researchers are neither members of authors' local communities (as in the non-Eugene samples in Study 1) nor manually reading and interpreting each obituary as a document of a once-living person (as in Study 3). Aggregating public records that were likely originally intended by their authors to be read singly, while *legally* unproblematic, could be ethically suspect if authors feel that their words are being taken out of context or used for purposes that they did not intend and to which they were not afforded an opportunity to consent.[9]

The potential for this type of emotional reaction reveals an ethical weight associated with this class of data, and also points to the value of intent in interacting with these records. This ethical weight indicates the value of these data for research and marketing undertaken with the intent of promoting the social good. It is striking, for example, that religion, personal relations, and community service are emphasized in four geographically and culturally distinct cities. For professionally commissioned obituaries such as many in *The New York Times* (Study 2), we saw a very different set of values expressed, with virtues such as being a loving father taking a back seat to leadership qualities such as charisma and entrepreneurial ambition.[10] Although this type of research could be undertaken to manipulate a ritual of public grieving into an abstract data-generating mechanism divorced from its original context, those wishing to understand the moral language of local communities, especially to perform value-relevant work within or translating across those author communities, may find valuable insight into this approach.

There are several enticing prospects for applying this research beyond straightforward social marketing. First, if researchers could acquire a comprehensive dataset of obituaries from the Anglophone world, they could compare and contrast values across international geographic lines (e.g. the United States vs. Scotland vs. Singapore vs. New Zealand). Such research could be useful to international negotiators. Second, software developers could team up with clinical psychologists and psychiatrists to develop a smartphone or tablet app that guided someone through the ACT obituary intervention mentioned earlier. This could help to partially automate psychological therapy. Finally, software developers could team up with geographers to develop a map of the Anglophone world's values that could be used by people deciding where to live, somewhat like the www.walkscore.com mapping software.

Notes

1 Eugene was chosen as a representative of the Pacific Northwest that is less influenced by in-migration than Portland and Seattle. Wasilla was chosen for potential cultural differences between Eugene—a somewhat large, left-leaning university town—and Wasilla—a small, right-leaning suburb adjacent to a major military base. Flint represents a rust belt city with a substantially lower median income. Finally, we chose Amherst as it is one of the most liberal, highly educated cities in the United States.
2 The spatial proximity of two nodes may indicate an important connection between the two, but this need not be the case. If there is an edge with high edge weight connecting the two, this will pull them closer together. However, the position of any two given nodes is also the product of the aggregated movement and forces of every other node in the network. Node positions only perfectly reflect edge weights in an N-dimensional graphical representation where N = the total number of nodes.
3 *ObituaryData.com's* "About" page claims that their records are 95%+ complete.
4 These name lists were compiled by *MongaBay*, who made them available at http://names.mongabay.com/male_names.htm and http://names.mongabay.com/female_names.htm.
5 A stoplist is a list of generic words that carry little semantic content (e.g. "the," "and," "or," "an," etc.) and are typically removed when analyzing large corpora of texts. Bigrams are pairs of words (e.g. "Eagle Scout").
6 Twelve participants were removed from our analysis for failing to complete the study.
7 Gendered titles were made gender-neutral to more clearly focus on gender differences indicating real differences in social norms, values, or expectations.
8 The work of Diesner et al. (2014) in analyzing the impact of social justice documentaries is especially useful for seeing how the tools of web data mining and network analysis could be used for social marketing.
9 For a recent study that caused the kind of uproar we envision, see Kramer et al. (2014).
10 The NYT obituary for Yvonne Brill is a good case study for this difference between local and big paper obituaries. Brill's obituary originally began with this sentence: "She made a mean beef stroganoff, followed her husband from job to job and took eight years off from work to raise three children." The author was criticized for leading with family values rather than professional accomplishments. The obituary was quickly changed to begin with "She was a brilliant rocket scientist," and no later mention of beef Stroganoff.

References

Andreason, A. & Kotler, P. (2008). *Strategic Marketing for Non-profit Organizations*, 7th edition. Upper Saddle River, NJ: Prentice Hall.

Aristotle, R. C. (2000). *Nicomachean Ethics*. Trans. R. Crisp. Cambridge, UK; New York, NY: Cambridge University Press.

Christen, M., Alfano, M., Bangerter, E., & Lapsley, D. (2013). Ethical issues of 'morality mining': When the moral identity of individuals becomes a focus of data-mining. In H. Rahman & I. Ramos (eds.), *Ethical Data Mining Applications for Socio-Economic Development*. 1–21. Hershey, PA: IGI Global.

Christen, M., Robinson, B., & Alfano, M. (2014). The semantic neighborhood of intellectual humility. In A. Herzig & E. Lorini (eds.), *Proceedings of the European Conference on Social Intelligence*, 40–9, CEUR-WS.org.

Diesner, J., Pak, S., Kim, J., Soltani, K., & Aleyasen, A. (2014). Computational assessment of the impact of social justice documentaries. In *iConference 2014 Proceedings*. 462–483. iSchools, doi: 10.9776/14125.

Graham, J., Haidt, J., & Nosek, B. (2009). Liberals and conservatives rely on different sets of moral foundations. *Journal of Personality and Social Psychology*, 96(5): 1029–46.

Graham, J., Nosek, B., Haidt, J., Iyer, R., Koleva, S., & Ditto, P. (2011). Mapping the moral domain. *Journal of Personality and Social Psychology*, 101(2): 366–85.

Haidt, J., & Joseph, C. (2004). Intuitive ethics: How innately prepared intuitions generate culturally variable virtues. *Daedalus*, 133(4): 55–66.

Hayes, S., Strosahl, K., Wilson, K. (2011). *Acceptance and Commitment Therapy: The Process and Practice of Mindful Change*. New York, NY: Guilford Press.

Kahle, L., Beatty, S., & Homer, P. (1986). Alternative measurement approaches to consumer values: The list of values (LOV) and values and life style (VALS). *Journal of Consumer Research*, 12(1): 405–9.

Kotler, P. & Zaltman, G. (1971). Social marketing: An approach to planned social change. *Journal of Marketing*, 35(3): 3–12.

Kramer, A., Guillory, J., & Hancock, J. (2014). Experimental evidence of massive-scale emotional contagion through social networks. *Proceedings of the National Academy of Sciences*, 111(24): 8788–90.

Mill, J. S. (1861/1998). *Utilitarianism*, edited with an introduction by Roger Crisp. New York, NY: Oxford University Press.

Reynolds, T. & Olson, J. (2001). *Understanding Consumer Decision Making: The Means-End Approach to Marketing and Advertising Strategy*. Mahwah, NJ: Lawrence Erlbaum Associates.

Rokeach, M. (1973). *The Nature of Human Values*. New York, NY: The Free Press.

Saucier, G. (2009). Recurrent personality dimensions in inclusive lexical studies: Indications for a big six structure. *Journal of Personality*, 77(5): 1577–614.

Schwartz, S. (1992). Universals in the content and structure of values: Theoretical advances and empirical tests in 20 countries. In M. Zanna (ed.), *Advances in Experimental Social Psychology*. Vol. 25, 1–65. New York, NY: Academic Press.

Zagzebski, L. (1996). *Virtues of the Mind*. Cambridge: Cambridge University Press.

13

APPLE'S RELIGIOUS VALUE

A Consumer Neuroscience Perspective

Yi-Chia Wu

Introduction

Researchers have been comparing the cultlike phenomenon of Apple, Inc. (hereafter "Apple") to a religion for over a decade (Belk & Tumbat, 2005; Firmin et al., 2010; Lam, 2001); however, a larger examination of the religious, and sometimes cultish, phenomena that occur between individuals and businesses or institutions is under-researched. Boome et al. (2011), in their BBC documentary, *Secrets of the Superbrands*, state that the host Alex Riley interviews technology consumers to explore how and why some brands achieve quasi-religious status. Boome et al. document the parallels between religion or religious experiences and how the Apple cult narrative unfolds. Parts of this comparison in academia and the media may originate from the secretive nature of Apple operations, which were hidden not only from its competitors but also from employees and customers (Lashinsky, 2012). Additionally, Apple's outperformance of competitors has drawn much attention from academia and marketers trying to understand the successes of the "Cult of Apple." Other firms face difficulties replicating Apple's successful business model and cofounder and CEO Steve Jobs' unique pursuit of designed simplicity of use (Segall, 2012).

Apple's own appreciation of itself as a corporation and religious experience emerged early: at Apple's first annual party in 1977, Steve Jobs dressed as Jesus Christ to represent himself as the savior of Apple (Young, 1988). The worshipful respect paid to Jobs was not enjoyed by other leaders in the company. According to Adam Lashinsky, author of *Inside Apple* (2012), whenever a request came directly from Jobs, everyone in the company had to finish that particular task, regardless of what else he or she was working on at that moment. No one would refuse Jobs' requests (Lashinsky, 2012). This was not only the case within Apple. Jobs' charm was irresistible to his fans and Apple's partners, and it still continues after his death in 2011. The former CEO of Apple, John Sculley, once said, "It was almost as if there were magnetic fields, some spiritual force, mesmerizing people. Their eyes were dazed. Excitement showed on everyone's face. It was nearly a cult environment" (Levy, 1994, p. 142).

Outside of Apple, the media has portrayed Jobs in a similar fashion. The cover of the January 2010 edition of *The Economist* presented Jobs as Moses, introducing the iPad on his hand as if it were an object of religious veneration. *The Economist* cover powerfully showed that the cult of Apple had spread virally, exerting influence on consumers both virtually and physically.

Beyond media coverage, Apple itself has used multiple mechanisms and marketing techniques to appeal to its customers. The cultlike success of this computer firm deserves examination, particularly when its technology allows one to access and connect to others at will. Reaching out to another individual is not limited to time, space, or physical locations. Researching Apple's cult-like phenomenon at this point in time allows us to understand the impact of brand worship in a comparative way, now and in the future. The focus of this research was to determine whether Apple, Inc. is similar to a religion in that it triggers in its devotees reactions similar to those of religious devotees. The description of Apple's cultlike following is based on the observation of Apple online community activities and Apple devotees' behavior. When a brand can be described as a religion, it is reasonable to explore the psychophysical effects that Apple has on its devotees.

Definitions of Religion

There are several definitions of religion (Argyle & Beit-Hallahmi, 1975; Batson et al., 1993; Bellah, 1991; Clark, 1958; Delener, 1990; Dollahite, 1998; James, 1961; O'Collins & Farrugia, 2013; Peteet, 1994). Among all of the definitions, they commonly address the infrastructure of the symbolic, religious system.

One definition of *religion* is "a unified system of beliefs and practices relative to the sacred things" (Delener, 1990, p. 27). Focusing more on individual practices, *religiosity* may be defined as "the degree to which a person adheres to his or her religious values, beliefs and practices and uses them in daily life" (Shukor & Jamal, 2013, p. 69). Religion is associated with the infrastructure, system, and organizational form of the belief organization. A religious practice relies on personal beliefs and one's commitment to a relationship with God as well as the organization.

Smart (1989) defines *religion* as "some system of worship or other practice recognizing a transcendent Being or goal" (p. 11). Stark and Bainbridge's (1996) definition of religion excludes the recognition of cults. They explain, "Cults are excluded because they represent an unconventional tradition" (p. 16). This definition is different from the common usage of the meaning of "cult" in marketing literature. More importantly, Stark and Bainbridge's definition also posits that "humans have a persistent desire for rewards only the gods can grant, unless humans become gods" (1996, p. 23).

As apparent by the differences in these descriptions, there is no one conclusive definition of religion (Hood et al., 2009). The definition used typically varies depending on the purpose and needs of the study (Wilkes et al., 1986). The definition of religion that provides the most precise description for this study is from James (1961): "The feelings, acts, and experiences of individual mean in their solitude, so far as they apprehend themselves to stand in relation to whatever they may consider the divine" (p. 42). After all, an individual's reaction or perception boils down to how one sees oneself responding and relating to the divine, including one's relationship to God, religious objects, rituals, or experiences. This description therefore focuses on the individual level.

On the individual level, Nelson (2006) defines *spirituality* as "the more experiential component of that relationship [with some ultimate being or reality], or more broadly to one's core values or search for meanings" (p. 407). In the 16th century, two denoted understandings of *religion* were widely accepted: "a particular system of faith and worship" and "the human reverential recognition of a higher or unseen power" (Paloutzian & Park, 2013, p. 26). The twenty-first-century academic redefines religion restrictedly as "individual and corporate beliefs and practices dealing with our relationships with some ultimate being or reality and is distinguished from *spirituality*" (Nelson, 2006). In other words, the word *religion* is now not only used within the spiritual context but also in non-spiritual contexts.

In *American Heritage Roget's Thesaurus* (2013), a *devotee* is equivalent to "a person who is ardently devoted to a particular subject or activity." Arruda-Filho et al. (2010) use devotee, or Apple Acolytes, to describe loyal Apple users. Fanatics and cultists are typically related to religious activities, whereas zealots, enthusiasts, and devotees are less associated with religion and politics; however, the latter group displays an unexplainable attraction toward what they are passionate about.

This study uses "devotees" for Apple and Catholics to represent those who adore and devote themselves to an organization that is considered worthy of investing their time and effort in, regardless of space, distance, negative image, or crisis occurring within Apple or their religious organizations.

Brands and Their Relationship to Religion

It is commonly known that loyal customers—individuals—bring profits to a company. However, it is important to realize that corporate evangelizing is far more critical than a focus on consumer attitudes because of the potential found in "conversion experiences, unquestioning faith, dedication, sacrifice, and the search for salvation" (Belk & Tumbat, 2005). The concept of "corporate evangelizing" is derived from protestant minister Billy Graham's School of Evangelism and was developed by Kawasaki, who was hired by Apple in the mid-1980s, to promote Mac hardware for software developers (Kawasaki, 1992).

Other brand literature examines how brands become iconic (Holt, 2004; Jenkins, 2008). Jenkins focuses on the image of a corporation that hides its pursuit of profits behind a transformed image. This positive image, repackaged as the corporate icon, in turn, is used to lure the respect of its consumers. More importantly, Jenkins points out a transition stage of users and viewers continuously participating in rituals and practices. According to Jenkins (2008), "Only if the iPod becomes my iCon" can the cult phenomenon emerge (p. 481).

Jenkins (2008) explains how a corporation becomes an icon as an indication of symbolic realism through a cultural context. The abstract representation of an iconic meaning is conveyed through the image that is merged with the message and through the development of consistent marketing campaigns. The text in the ads and personalized characteristics behind the big corporation also affect a brand's iconic status.

On the other hand, Jenkins (2008) claims that the impact of these images and messages, conveyed through different media, also induces a tendency toward fear with respect to the ideology presented by Apple. This ideology as explained by the author expresses the power of a corporation. Furthermore, if the ideology has a spiritual quality, respect arises spontaneously along with fear because of the recognized power communicated through the representative meaning of an icon that the ideology intends to portray.

Ample research has demonstrated that some Apple users develop zeal toward the Apple brand and its products. The connection between religion and Apple has been discussed in the literature from the perceptive of a brand community, specifically the Apple community, and neuroscience. Academic research focuses on the following: brand community (Arora, 2009; Felix, 2012; Muñiz & O'Guinn, 2001; Muñiz & Schau, 2005; Schau & Muñiz, 2006); brand influence on motivating behavior: Apple vs. PC users (Fitzsimons et al., 2008); brand image as ideology: iPod and iCon (Jenkins, 2008); life satisfaction with the iPod (Cockrill, 2012); symbolic realism of the iPod (Jenkins, 2008); brains and brands (Perrachione & Perrachione, 2008); social influences between PC and Apple users (Firmin et al., 2010); the cult of consumerism (Muñiz & Schau, 2005); the strategic competitive advantage of Apple products (Tariq et al., 2011); and iReligion: the Bible app (Torma & Teusner, 2011). Anthropologists view religion as a powerful tool for social bonding, which is also a way to sustain religion itself for survival advantages (Aamodt & Wang, 2008). These survival advantages extend to those who believe in it to preserve rituals and traditions. Allen (2011) suggests that "Apple, and likewise HBO, has figured out how to develop a cult, not just in a business sense but in a sort of spiritual one."

Technological Belief

Markets involve the participation of sellers and consumers and the exchange of products. The possession of products helps consumers to form values through daily consumption (Bickle, 2010). What Steve Jobs did beyond his competitors was combine spirituality and technology in business consumption into an inseparable ideology (Robinson, 2013) that helped form one's values, identity, and religion to provide evidence of one's existence.

In the marketing context, a company brand may be able to develop an iconic influence over its users. The iconic influences of Apple have impacted its followers and cultivated a following of devotees. For Apple devotees, an Apple device is not simply a machine that enables them to connect to the world, but a machine that creates values and meanings that seem unexplainable. Lam (2001) suggests that human beings recognize the power of the computer and therefore extend their attachment and relationship to computers.

Steve Jobs maximized this relationship. As Robinson (2013) describes:

> Jobs' Zen master Kobun Chino told him that he 'could keep in touch with his spiritual side while running a business.' So in true Zen fashion, Jobs avoided thinking of technology and spirituality in dualistic terms. But what really set him apart was his ability to educate the public about personal computing in both practical and mythic ways…The iconography of the Apple computer company, the advertisements, and the device screens of the Macintosh, iPod, iPhone, and iPad are visual expressions of Jobs' imaginative marriage of spiritual science and modern technology.
>
> *(Wired, n.p.)*

Accordingly, Lam (2001) describes the relationship between humans and computers as a mythical process that may result in a fervor akin to that of fervent believers in a religion.

Brand Community

According to Muñiz and O'Guinn (2001), the definition of brand community is "a specialized, non-geographically bound community, based on a structured set of social relationships among admirers of a brand" (p. 412). Also, brand community can be characterized as "complex entities with their own cultures, rituals, traditions, and codes of behavior" (Schau & Muñiz, 2002, p. 344).

Previous studies have explored the phenomenon of the Apple brand community as marginalized groups of consumers who helped solve issues among other consumers. For example, Muñiz and O'Guinn (2001) studied the Apple Newton community and how the evangelists in this community promoted the usage of the Newton PDA after it was discontinued in 1998. The community offered instructions for each other, even though Apple provided no technical support for Newton products, and it operated similarly to preserve rituals and a subculture that was not understood by the mainstream technology world.

On the same note, but from a different standpoint, Felix (2012) advocates the need to dissect consumers' motivations, attitudes, and decision-making processes on two levels: product and brand. At the product level, it is crucial to understand consumer barriers and conflicts that lead to choosing certain categories of products.

Religion and Personality

From the functional value of products (Sheth et al., 1991), consumers search for product traits that fit their needs. Consumption habits impact how and what consumers evaluate before they make purchasing decisions. Four types of iPhone users were identified: innovative users, techno-social users (Katz & Sugiyama, 2006), utilitarian users, and Apple Acolytes (*c.f.* Arruda-Filho et al., 2010). These types were based on two dynamics: the hedonistic appeal of, and devotion to, the iPhone. Apple Acolytes are devoted consumers whose intense loyalty to the brand can help it survive through "poor product performance, scandal, bad publicity, high prices, and absence of promotional efforts" (*c.f.* Arruda-Filho et al., 2010, p. 475). A devotee, not simply a user, is more likely to form a religious-like attachment (Arruda-Filho et al., 2010). As a dynamic and evolutionary categorization, iPhone users' preferences for new technology and devotion can change over time. The authors find that innovative users, defined as previously non-Apple users, can evolve their devotion to Apple to a level equal to that of the techno-social users. Moreover, techno-social users can possibly become Apple Acolytes. Yet, utilitarian users who can find alternatives become substitution users because their devotion to, and the hedonistic appeal of, the iPhone is low (Arruda-Filho et al., 2010).

Neuroscience and Religion

Each brain is wired slightly differently (Medina, 2008). Those whose neural mechanisms demonstrate a propensity to the formation of religious beliefs are more likely to also prefer organizational structures and ways of practicing rituals in other forms, such as political events and Apple fan clubs (Aamodt & Wang, 2008).

In order to understand how human brains comprehend religion, first we should be aware of the biological structure of our three and one-half pound brain. Neurons, the functional cell of the basic human nervous systems, carry sensory impulses through neural pathways to the brain (Newberg & D'Aquili, 2008). The nervous system is organized into two parts: the central nervous system (CNS) and peripheral nervous system (PNS), the latter of which includes the autonomic nervous system and the somatic nervous system. The CNS consists of the brain and spinal cord and PNS includes nerves linking all the body's parts. The mind's mystical experience is relevant to four areas: the visual association area, the orientation association area, the attention association area, and the verbal conceptual association area (Newberg & D'Aquili, 2008).

The visual association area consists of the occipital and temporal lobes. The former receives and processes visual information, and the latter helps us to perform complex visual tasks such as using a candle or a cross to formalize mediation or prayer. The orientation association area includes the posterior section of the parietal lobe, which processes sensory information such as hearing, touch, and vision from all over the body as well as overseeing spatial distinctions. This area is believed to be associated with spiritual experience because of its shaping of perception of "space and time, self and ego" (Newberg & D'Aquili, 2008, p. 29). The attention association area is located in the prefrontal cortex of the brain, which deals with complex decision-making processes. This area is triggered in various religious states, especially among Zen meditators during electroencephalography (EEG) measurement (Newberg & D'Aquili, 2008). Finally, the verbal conceptual association area is located at the junction of the temporal, parietal, and occipital lobes; it processes abstract concepts and then transforms them into words (Newberg & D'Aquili, 2008). This area directs important functions, such as causal relationships, that explain how we interpret myths and then describe them in the process of rituals.

Studies have demonstrated that the limbic system is associated with religious experiences because subjects experience dreamlike states, hallucinations, and out-of-body experiences while in an induced spiritual state (Newberg & D'Aquili, 2008). The hypothalamus controls the autonomic nervous system; the amygdala governs emotional functions; and the hippocampus generates emotions that are linked to memory, images, and learning. The limbic system integrates the nervous systems when reacting to stress.

Religion provides guidelines and rules for believers to follow, and religious beliefs help one to form the concepts of the moral values or judgments that formulate one's path to follow through one's cognitive development (Inzlicht et al., 2009). Neurologists explain the brain processes dealing with religion by explaining how human neurons process religion (Aamodt & Wang, 2008). Understanding how our brains process religion would not change believers' experiencing supernatural forces. These forces often function as guides to cognitive understanding of the supernatural.

Why is it important for us to know how human brains comprehend religion and other related concepts? The unique structure and function of the human brain allow humans to process information unlike any other creature. In order to form the construct of religion, two capabilities of the brain are required: the formation of and transmission of religious beliefs (Aamodt & Wang, 2008).

The latter capability enables humans to fabricate and shape social reasoning, which is highly developed in human beings and differentiated from other animals (Aamodt & Wang, 2008). The ability to decipher a complicated idea, make a reference, create an abstraction, and infer unseen forethought requires the evolution and sophistication of the human brain to make sense of one's life and existence.

One of the purposes of religion is to provide guidelines and moral boundaries to help individuals behave in a socially acceptable manner. If one is seeking understandable explanations about the events of one's life, then religion can perform this function (c.f. Inzlicht et al., 2009, p. 386). Therefore, religion can help to reduce insecurity and anxiety for a human being. Iyengar (2010) shows that people who follow a specific religion think more positively than those who are not religious. However, it is important to point out that atheists can behave positively, based on what they believe is the right action (Inzlicht et al., 2009). Inzlicht et al. (2009) used an EEG, a device measuring electrical activity in the brain, to identify two groups of people, religious and nonreligious, through examining their Anterior Cingulate Cortex (ACC) reactions. The ACC is the area in the brain that deals with anxiety. ACC enables one to reduce prediction error to avoid making mistakes. The authors developed a Religious Zeal scale, including "I aspire to live and act according to my religious beliefs"; "My religious beliefs are grounded in objective truth"; and "I would support a war that defended my religious beliefs" to evaluate subjects' attitude toward their own religion. They found that people who are religious activate less in the ACC than those who are not religious when working on an assigned task. Strong beliefs in religion bring a conviction that one can deal with unfamiliar circumstances.

The Alpha Wave and How It Was Discovered

History

There is a long history of the study of electrical activity in the body. The earliest known experiments were conducted in the 1780s by Luigi Galvani at the University of Bologna, where he studied electrical activity in the bodies of animals. A century later, the British physician Richard Caton was the first to discover that electrical activity existed in the brains of animals. In 1929, Hans Berger published the first EEG recordings of a human brain with wave patterns in sleeping and waking states. Berger's EEG recording showed long trains of regular waves with a frequency of 8–13 cycles per second (cps), and he called these waves Alpha rhythm. In later studies, additional waves at different frequencies were discovered, and they were given names from the Greek alphabet: beta, gamma, delta, theta, and less-studied waves such as mu and sensorimotor rhythm (Arroyo et al., 1993).

Herbert Krugman was the first to apply EEG to a marketing context. In his 1971 study, he examined the brain waves of a single subject, while the individual viewed print and TV advertisements. The Alpha wave is defined below, followed by the Beta wave and the Theta wave in *Mosby's Dictionary of Medicine, Nursing and Health Professions*:

Alpha Wave

One of several types of brain waves, characterized by a relatively high voltage or amplitude and a frequency of 8–13 Hz, Alpha waves are the "relaxed waves" of the brain and constitute the majority of waves recorded by electroencephalograms registering the activity of the parietal and the occipital lobes and the posterior parts of the temporal lobes when the individual is awake, relaxed, but not attentive, with the eyes closed. Opening and closing the eyes affect the patterns of the Alpha waves and the Beta waves. These are also called Alpha rhythms or Berger waves.

Beta Wave

One of several types of brain waves, characterized by relatively low voltage and a frequency of more than 13 Hz, Beta waves are the "busy waves" of the brain, recorded by electroencephalograph from the frontal and the central areas of the cerebrum when the patient is awake and alert with eyes open.

Theta Wave

One of several types of brain waves, characterized by a relatively low frequency of 4–7 Hz and a low amplitude of 10 μV, Theta waves are the "drowsy waves" of the temporal lobes of the brain and appear in electroencephalograms when the individual is awake but relaxed and sleepy.

Theoretical Foundation

This research used the Smart's seven dimensions of religion (1989)—which provides a view of comparative religions by observing the traits of the world's religions—as its theoretical foundation and as a basis for developing scales for Apple and Catholic devotees. The explanations and examples of the seven dimensions of religion (Smart, 1978, 1989, pp. 12–20; Smart, 1996) are:

1   The practical and ritual dimension: includes regular worship, praying, and marching. This dimension is relevant to patterns of behavior, considered practices rather than rituals, which are ways to develop spiritual awareness as well as ethical perspectives.

2   The experiential and emotional dimension: contains religious experience and feelings of being exposed to sacred awe, calmness and peace, the perception of emptiness, love, sensations of hope, and gratitude for favors being answered.

3   The narrative and mythic dimension: is the "storytelling" of a religion. Examples include written and oral forms of informal teachings, tales, adventures, alternative histories, and predictions about its founder, heroes, saints, the Evil One, and even the end of time.

4   The doctrinal and philosophical dimension: refers to the aspect of religion that describes relatively abstract and philosophical terms. For example, the doctrinal dimension in Buddhism is the philosophical projection of the world as an aid to salvation (Smart, 1998, p. 17) and impermanence. The "law of *karma*," or action, influences one's behavior because of reincarnation. An individual is reborn through many lives as a virtual traveler.

5   The ethical and legal dimension: includes the laws and moral and formal guidelines derived from the system. For instance, love is the main ethical attitude in the Christian faith; the Father, Son, and Holy Spirit were bonded through the connection of love.

6   The social and institutional dimension: the sixth and seventh dimensions require a physical form, whereas others are simply abstract. This dimension includes the study of a formal organization that involves a group of people and observations to see how it works among them, such as a church, the Indian caste system, or the variety of sacred persons or animals in the Hindu religion (Smart, 1998).

7   The material dimension: refers to buildings, architecture, art, images, icons, and instruments of ritual. These examples are in either simple or elegant presentations. Other examples also include the natural attributes of the Earth as well as sacred sites of human creation, which could be important to the system.

Methodology

This research recruited Apple (Catholic) devotees and indifferents to first evaluate their levels of devotion through a self-reporting survey. The purpose of using self-reporting as the first part of the study was to identify the levels of devotion of Apple (Catholic) devotees and indifferents. Each survey participant was categorized into one of four groups as to high vs. low levels of devotion in Apple and Catholicism. With participants' willingness to continue to the EEG study, each of them viewed Apple and Catholic visual stimuli while their Alpha waves were recorded. The researcher analyzed Alpha waves, which are commonly used for detecting the impact of religion on one's state of mind (Foster, 1990).

There were three stages in the EEG experiment (see Figure 13.1): expert panel, Apple (Catholic) visual stimuli, and the EEG experiment. The purpose

FIGURE 13.1 The EEG Experiment.

of the expert panel was to objectively select the visual stimuli that were used for the EEG experiment. In the EEG experiment, a set of Catholic and Apple visual-image stimuli were displayed on a computer screen, while participants' brain waves were recorded in another computer. Using visual stimuli helped clarify and measure, specifically and through the theoretical framework, devotees' reactions in Alpha waves to each dimension of Catholic and Apple stimuli. Once the visual-image stimuli were selected, the EEG experiment was conducted.

Samples

To increase the representativeness of the data, the survey was distributed in the Northeast, West, Midwest, and South regions of the U.S. Survey participants had to be Catholic and had to use Apple products to qualify for the survey. A total of 708 surveys were collected.

Considering that EEG participants for the experiment had to take the online survey first, it was necessary for EEG participants to be present. Therefore, at the end of the online survey, the following question appeared: "Are you interested in participating in the EEG study of the research, which includes an EEG reading while viewing religious and Apple pictures?" If participants chose "Yes," then they were asked to leave their name and e-mail. If participants chose "No," then the survey ended. After one week, the online survey participants were contacted by e-mail asking if they were willing to participate in the EEG study. A total of 60 qualified EEG participants (Male = 21, Female = 39, Average Age = 29.6, S.D. = 8.81) were analyzed.

EEG Recordings

This research used Infiniti 6.3 software in coordination with ProComp 2 manufactured by Thought Technology Inc. to record EEG data with a bipolar montage. Two active electrodes were placed at locations Fz and Pz with a linked-ear reference (A1-A2). Electrode placements on Fz-Cz-Pz will be introduced in the next section. Two channels were sampled at 256 samples per second and the notch filter was at 60 Hz. The Alpha, Beta, Gamma, and Theta waves were recorded and exported to a Word file. Since Catholic and Apple stimuli were counterbalanced and displayed from each EEG participant, the EEG recordings were first reorganized under the same stimuli.

Findings and Discussions

The analogy of Apple and religion depends on whether Apple influences its devotees in a similar way that Catholicism impacts its devotees. In order to examine this effect, this research also examined Apple devotees and Catholic devotees' reactions toward Apple and Catholic visual stimuli as a comparison.

One-way ANOVA was conducted to test the level of devotion in the EEG Alpha wave measurements. Table 13.1 presents the results of the two groups of devotees while they viewed Apple (left column) and Catholic (right column) visual stimuli in seven dimensions. In the Ritual Dimension, Catholic devotees' Alpha waves ($M = -4.63$, $SD = 6.20$) were much higher than Apple devotees' ($M = -9.1131$, $SD = 8.4456$). There was a statistically significant difference, $F (1, 58) = 5.494$, $p = .023$ at the 0.05 significance level, between Apple and Catholic devotees when they viewed Apple visual stimuli. On the contrary, when the two groups of devotees viewed Catholic visual stimuli, Catholic devotees' Alpha waves ($M = -3.24$, $SD = 8.39$) were higher than Apple devotees' ($M = -7.67$, $SD = 7.50$) in the Narrative Dimension, $F (1, 58) = 4.639$, $p = .035$. The difference is statistically significant at the 0.05 significance level. In the Legal Dimension, Alpha waves of Catholic devotees ($M = -3.38$, $SD = 6.76$) were higher than Apple devotees ($M = -7.45$; $SD = 9.15$), $F (1, 58) = 3.838$, $p = .055$), and the difference is marginally significant.

Figure 13.2 and Table 13.1 convey the same information, except Figure 13.2 which demonstrates the degree of reduction in Alpha waves between Catholic and Apple devotees. The blue bar represents Catholic devotees' Alpha wave changes, whereas the orange bar indicates Catholic devotees' Alpha wave changes, both compared to their recorded baseline. Figure 13.2 demonstrates that Apple devotees did not trigger the feeling of transcendence while viewing

TABLE 13.1 Statistically Significant Differences between Apple and Catholic Devotees

Dimensions	Apple Stimuli	Catholic Stimuli
	Apple Devotees/ Catholic Devotees	Apple Devotees/ Catholic Devotees
1 Ritual	✓	
2 Emotional		
3 Narrative		✓
4 Doctrinal		
5 Legal		✓
6 Institutional		
7 Material		

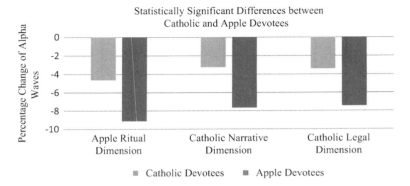

FIGURE 13.2 Statistically Significant Differences between Catholic and Apple Devotees in Alpha Wave Percentage Change.

Apple visual stimuli. Instead, Apple devotees processed the Ritual Dimension visual images much more than their counterparts.

The comparison between devotees demonstrates that Catholic devotees triggered higher Alpha waves than their Apple counterparts when viewing Catholic visual stimuli. Apple devotees did not trigger high Alpha waves compared with Catholic counterparts when they both viewed Apple visual stimuli. This pattern remained in all the dimensions, even though there are no statistically significant differences between devotees. The results show that Apple does not trigger in its devotees the spiritual feelings toward the visual stimuli.

Normally, the Alpha wave decreases when one is exposed to external stimuli. However, the amplitude recovers quickly afterward. This explains the negative value when the Alpha baseline is subtracted from the Alpha waves of each dimension. However, a religious individual was expected to reduce much less than a religious indifferent. Catholic visual stimuli in Study 2 had corresponding results in the dimensions. However, Apple visual stimuli did not result in the same expectation, but a reverse one.

In the EEG experiment, Catholic devotees had statistically significant higher Alpha waves when they viewed Catholic stimuli compared to Catholic indifferents, especially in the Material Dimensions when their devotion to Apple was low. In addition, Catholic devotees triggered higher Alpha waves compared to Catholic indifferents when they viewed Catholic stimuli in the Narrative, Legal, and the averaged seven dimensions when their devotion to Apple was low.

However, Apple devotees did not have a statistically significant increase of Alpha waves when they viewed Apple stimuli compared to Apple indifferents. Apple devotees did not trigger as high an Alpha wave when they viewed Apple stimuli as Catholic devotees did when they viewed Catholic stimuli. There was a statistically significant difference in the Material Dimension between Apple devotees and indifferents. Yet, the increased amplitude of Alpha waves was not as expected: Apple indifferents' Alpha waves were higher than devotees' when they viewed Apple stimuli. The same opposite results also occurred in the Ritual, Emotional, and the averaged seven dimensions in that Apple indifferents triggered higher Alpha waves than devotees when they viewed the Apple stimuli. That is, Apple devotees' Alpha waves reduced much less than Apple indifferents. This suggests that the Apple devotees did not have the subconscious transcendent feelings that the Catholic devotees did. The reduction of Alpha waves may suggest that Apple devotees processed the Apple visual stimuli more than indifferents. The Apple devotees' continuous processing of Apple stimuli could be the cause of the drastic decrease in Alpha waves. Apple indifferents' Alpha waves reduced slightly compared to their baseline. The outcome of Alpha waves in Catholic (Apple) devotees and indifferents demonstrates that it is feasible to examine the reactions toward a devotees' beloved brand subconsciously and objectively.

Conclusions

Religious connection is a private, personal, and emotional feeling. Previous research has focused on the impact of religion on consumer behavior (Mokhlis, 2009). Religious belief is very difficult to measure (Wilkes et al., 1986), particularly the spiritual experience that is rather personal and subjective, sometimes beyond description. Despite the difficulty in reaching a generalized measurement, religion could help to serve as the foundation of one's beliefs, attitudes, and behavior (Fishbein & Ajzen, 1975). If people are not satisfied with their religion for these purposes, they will find alternatives to fulfill portions of these needs such as an emotional bond, and more importantly, to make meaning of life through this alternative (Atkin, 2004). Whether Apple devotees have found an alternative to religion is a question this research intended to explore.

Theoretical Implications

The significance of this research lies in theoretical and methodological perspectives. Theoretically speaking, the Smart's seven dimensions of religion (1989) provide a framework to evaluate devotions in the developed seven classifications of devotion; these were measured with the same dimension in the EEG experiment.

The results of the online survey demonstrate that devotees and indifferents evaluate their level of devotion toward Apple and Catholicism from an individual's perspectives based on their self-reporting. Each individual executes their devotion to Apple and Catholicism in different ways, through combinations of items from several dimensions. The results represent a difference between an individual's experiences with Apple and Catholicism with what actually constitutes

Apple and Catholicism. The data from the self-reported psychometric question-naire are impeded by subjective measurements (Kuan et al., 2014).

Methodologically speaking, this research used self-reporting to provide a subjective evaluation in Catholic and Apple devotees' levels of devotion. The extent of devotion can be distinguished with ritual devotion, emotional devo-tion, etc. "It has been well established that patterns of brain activities are closely correlated with behavior and cognition" (Ohme et al., 2011). It is therefore appropriate to understand the cultlike following parallel to religion by using neuroscientific techniques—especially because the topic of religion can easily lead to biased answers with self-reporting. Therefore, the EEG experiment provided an objective measurement to examine whether Apple has the same impact as religion to its devotees.

The implementation of EEG in recording Alpha waves demonstrates un-conscious reactions toward seven dimensions of religion presented by visual stimuli. The EEG recording provides another measurement that the self-reporting survey was unable to accomplish (Wang & Minor, 2008). Hence, the seven dimensions of religion provide a theoretical framework for visual stimuli in the EEG experiment consistently throughout this research. The subjective self-reported data and neurological responses recorded by the EEG device enhance the understanding of subconscious feelings that are embed-ded in the level of devotion beyond one's recognition in the impact on one's awareness.

Practical Implications

In the EEG study, the Material, Ritual, and Emotional Dimensions of the Apple visual stimuli did show that Apple devotees processed Apple stimuli more than indifferents. Even though this research did not find transcendent feelings in the Apple devotees, the findings are worth exploring in terms of what businesses should give more focus to in their strategic development to appeal to devotees.

Interestingly, the Apple visual stimuli within the seven dimensions appealed to its devotees as shown in the averaged Alpha waves. This indicates that Apple devotees are involved and Apple taps into some of the same dimensions as re-ligion. Specifically, Apple devotees react strongly in the Material, Ritual, and Emotional aspects. The emotional appeal fits the description that "all decisions reference the emotional centers of the brain…Non-rational connections form the stickiest bonds" (Atkin, 2004, p. 199).

When comparing between Apple (Catholic) devotees and indifferents, both groups had statistically significant differences of Alpha waves reacting in the opposite direction in regards to the Material Dimension, which makes it an interesting aspect to discuss more deeply. Previous research emphasizes that

> Apple stores all embody the magic, fantasy, and mystery found in tradi-
> tional cathedrals of consumption but with the rise of technology and a
> more efficient means of consumption consumers are now more likely to
> visit treat (sic) these locations as an interactive advertisement—a play-
> ground for adults.
>
> *(Marshall, 2006, p. 10)*

It is implied in Marshall's (2006) study that the main purpose of Apple store
design is not the immediate purchase. Rather, the comparable design of Apple
stores as modern art museums provides a venue, a continuation of enchantment. Apple is aware that a majority of their customers shop online; yet, the
Apple store connects their customers with material goods through interactive
advertisements.

Customers also look for symbolic tools in a brand logo (Wang et al., 2012).
Logos functionalize daily tasks in which technology represents power that enables building ritualistic experiences with users. A business hoping to create a
cultlike following should create experiential relationships with customers in
these three dimensions, specifically buildings, symbols, and extraordinary experiences. This research provides a different perspective for examining Apple's
cultlike creation to influence its devotees at the neuroscientific level.

This research concludes that inconsistent statistical results from the self-
reporting survey and neuroscientific studies suggest that self-reporting cannot
predict neuroscientific responses. Rather than exploring how a religious person
behaves in a certain way, this research sought psychophysiological measures to
examine whether Apple is a religion as a number of marketing, sociology, and
neuromarketing studies have suggested. The survey and EEG measurements
contribute to efforts to capture the characteristics of Apple and Catholic devotees located in the Texas border region of the United States.

As Achrol and Kotler (2012) addressed in their seminal article, "to be a
skilled consumer researcher may mean one has to be half a neurophysiolo-
gist with expertise...marketing scholars will need educational backgrounds
in marketing on top of education in special fields of science such as neurophysiology" (p. 51). If this research had used only the self-reporting survey, the conclusion probably would have been "Apple has created a cult-like
following" because four factors were extracted from the operationalization
of the Apple scale. However, with the EEG Alpha wave measurement, this
research can conclude that while Apple may tap into some characteristics
of Catholicism, Apple does not garner the same transcendent reaction as
Catholicism on its devotees. Qualitative observations of cultlike following
can help explain how and why this phenomenon occurs. To claim Apple *is* a
religion is a strong statement that this research did not support with psychophysical measurements.

References

Aamodt, S. A., & Wang, S. (2008). *Welcome to your brain: Why you lose your car keys but never forget how to drive and other puzzles of everyday life.* New York, NY: Bloomsbury Publishing.

Achrol, R. S., & Kotler, P. (2012). Frontiers of the marketing paradigm in the third millennium. *Journal of the Academy of Marketing Science, 40(1),* 35–52.

Allen, F. E. (2011). The religion of Apple. *Forbes.* Retrieved from www.forbes.com/sites/frederickallen/2011/03/28/the-religion-of-apple/

Atkin, D. (2004). *The culting of brands: Turn your customers into true believers.* New York, NY: Penguin Group.

Argyle, M., & Beit-Hallahmi, B. (1975). *The social psychology of religion.* London: Routledge.

Arora, H. (2009). A conceptual study of brand communities. *ICFAI Journal of Brand Management, 6(2),* 7–21.

Arroyo, S., Lesser, R. P., Gordon, B., Uematsu, S., Jackson, D., & Webber, R. (1993). Functional significance of the mu rhythm of human cortex: An electrophysiologic study with subdural electrodes. *Electroencephalography and Clinical Neurophysiology, 87(3),* 76–87.

Arruda-Filho, E. J. M., Cabusas, J. A., & Dholakia, N. (2010). Social behavior and brand devotion among iphone innovators. *International Journal of Information Management, 30,* 475–80.

Atkin, D. (2004). *The culting of brands: When customers become true believers.* New York, NY: Portfolio.

Batson, C., Schoenrade, D. P., & Ventis, W. L. (1993). *Religion and the individual: A social-psychological perspective.* New York, NY: Oxford University Press.

Belk, R. W., & Tumbat, G. (2005). The cult of macintosh. *Consumption, Markets and Culture, 8(3),* 205–17.

Bellah, R. N. (1991). *Beyond belief: Essays on religion in a post-traditionalist world.* Berkeley: University of California Press.

Bickle, M. (2010). *Fashion marketing: Theory, principles and practice.* New York, NY: Fairchild Books.

Boome, A., Riley, A., Vale, J., & Dunn, L. (2011). *Secrets of the superbrands.* New York, NY: Films for the Humanities and Sciences.

Clark, W. H. (1958). How do social scientists define religion?. *The Journal of Social Psychology, 47(1),* 143–47.

Cockrill, A. (2012). Does an iPod make you happy? An exploration of the effects of ipod ownership on life satisfaction. *Journal of Consumer Behaviour, 11(5),* 406–14.

Delener, N. (1990). The effects of religious factors on perceived risk in durable goods purchase decisions. *Journal of Consumer Marketing, 7(3),* 27–38.

Devotee. (2013). *American heritage Roget's Thesaurus in Credo reference.* Boston, MA: Houghton Mifflin.

Dollahite, D. C. (1998). Fathering, faith, and spirituality. *Journal of Men's Studies, 7(1),* 3–15.

Felix, R. (2012). Brand communities for mainstream brands: The example of the yamaha r1 brand community. *Journal of Consumer Marketing, 29(3),* 225–32.

Firmin, M. W., Firmin, R. L., Wood, W. M., & Wood, J. C. (2010). Social influences related to college students' use of macintosh computers on an all-pc campus. *Computers and Education, 55(4),* 1542–51.

Fishbein, M., & Ajzen, I. (1975). *Belief, attitude, intention, and behavior: An introduction to theory and research.* Reading, MA: Addison-Wesley Pub. Co.

Fitzsimons, G. M., Chartrand, T. L., & Fitzsimons, G. J. (2008). Automatic effects of brand exposure on motivated behavior: How Apple makes you "think different". *Journal of Consumer Research, 35*, 21–35.

Foster, D. S. (1990). *EEG and subjective correlates of alpha frequency binaural beats stimulation combined with alpha biofeedback*: Memphis State University.

Holt, D. B. (2004). How brands become icons: The principles of cultural branding. Boston, MA: Harvard Business School Press.

Hood, R. W., Hill, P. C., & Spilka, B. (2009). *Psychology of religion, fourth edition: An empirical approach*. New York, NY: Guilford Publications.

Inzlicht, M., McGregor, I., Hirsh, J. B., & Nash, K. (2009). Neural markers of religious conviction. *Psychological Science (Wiley-Blackwell), 20(3)*, 385–92.

Iyengar, S. (2010). *The art of choosing*. New York, NY: Twelve.

James, W. (1961). *The varieties of religious experience*. New York, NY: Collier Books.

Jenkins, E. (2008). My ipod, my icon: How and why do images become icons?. *Critical Studies in Media Communication, 25(5)*, 466–89.

Katz, J. E., & Sugiyama S. (2006). Mobile phones as fashion statements: Evidence from student surveys in the us and Japan. *New Media and Society, 8(2)*, 321–37.

Kawasaki, G. (1992). *Selling the dream*. New York, NY: HarperCollins.

Krugman, H. E. (1971). Brain wave measures of media involvement. *Journal of Advertising Research, 11(1)*, 3–9.

Kuan, K. K. Y., Zhong, Y., & Chau, P. Y. K. (2014). Informational and normative social influence in group-buying: Evidence from self-reported and EEG data. *Journal of Management Information Systems, 30(4)*, 151–78.

Lam, P. (2001). May the force of the operating system be with you: Macintosh devotion as implicit religion. *Sociology of Religion, 62(2)*, 243–62.

Lashinsky, A. (2012). *Inside Apple: How America's most admired—and secretive—company really works*. New York, NY: Grand Central Publishing.

Levy, S. (1994). *Insanely great: The life and times of macintosh, the computer that changed everything*. New York, NY: Viking.

Marshall, J. (2006). Interactive window shopping: Enchantment in a rationalized world. *Electronic Journal of Sociology, 1*, 1–12.

Medina, J. J. (2008). Brain rules: 12 principles for surviving and thriving at work, home, and school. Seattle, WA: Pear Press.

Mokhlis, S. (2009). Relevancy and measurement of religiosity in consumer behavior research. *International Business Research, 2(3)*, 75–84.

Muñiz, A. M. Jr., & O'Guinn, T. C. (2001). Brand community. *Journal of Consumer Research, 27(4)*, 412–32.

Muñiz, A. M. Jr., & Schau, H. J. (2005). Religiosity in the abandoned Apple newton brand community. *Journal of Consumer Research, 31(4)*, 737–47.

Nelson, J. M. (2006). *Religion. Encyclopedia of multicultural psychology*. Thousand Oaks, CA: SAGE Publications, Inc.

Newberg, A., & D'Aquili, E. G. (2008). *Why God won't go away: Brain science and the biology of belief*. New York, NY: Random House Publishing Group.

O'Collins, G., & Farrugia, E. G. (2013). *A concise dictionary of theology*. Mahwah, NJ: Paulist Press.

Ohme, R., Matukin, M., & Pacula-Lesniak, B. (2011). Biometric measures for interactive advertising research. *Journal of Interactive Advertising, 11(2)*, 60–72.

Paloutzian, R. F., & Park, C. L. (2013). *Handbook of the psychology of religion and spirituality*, Second Edition. New York, NY: Guilford Publications.

Perrachione, T. K., & Perrachione, J. R. (2008). Brains and brands: Developing mutually informative research in neuroscience and marketing. *Journal of Consumer Behaviour, 7(4/5)*, 303–18.

Peteet, J. R. (1994). Approaching spiritual problems in psychotherapy: A conceptual framework. *Journal of Psychotherapy Practice and Research, 3(3)*, 237–45.

Robinson, B. T. (2013). How steve jobs turned technology—and Apple—into religion. *Wired.* Retrieved from www.wired.com/opinion/2013/08/how-jobs-turned-technology-and-media-into-religion/

Schau, H. J., & Muñiz, A. M. (2002). Brand communities and personal identities: Negotiations in cyberspace. *Advances in Consumer Research, 29(1)*, 344–49.

Schau, H. J., & Muñiz, A. (2006). A tale of tales: The Apple newton narratives. *Journal of Strategic Marketing, 14(1)*, 19–33.

Segall, K. (2012). *Insanely simple: The obsession that drives Apple's success.* New York, NY: Penguin Group US.

Sheth, J. N., Newman, B. I., & Gross, B. L. (1991). Why we buy what we buy: A theory of consumption values. *Journal of Business Research, 22*, 159–70.

Shukor, A. S., & Jamal, A. (2013). Developing scales for measuring religiosity in the context of consumer research. *Research in Contemporary Islamic Finance and Wealth Management, 13*, 69–74.

Smart, N. (1978), *The phenomenon of religion.* Oxford: Mowbrays.

——— (1989), *The world's religions: Old traditions and modern transformations.* New York, NY: Cambridge University Press.

——— (1996). *Dimensions of the sacred: An anatomy of the world's beliefs.* Berkeley: University of California Press.

——— (1998), *The world's religions.* Cambridge: Cambridge University Press.

Stark, R., & Bainbridge, W. S. (1996). *A theory of religion.* London: Rutgers University Press.

Tariq, M., Ishrat, R., & Khan, H. (2011). A case study of Apple's success with iconic ipod and iphone. *Interdisciplinary Journal of Contemporary Research in Business, 3(1)*, 158–68.

Torma, R., & Teusner, P. E. (2011). IReligion. *Studies in World Christianity, 17(2)*, 137–55.

Wang, Y. J., Hernandez, M. D., Minor, M. S, & Wei, J. (2012). Superstitious beliefs in consumer evaluation of brand logos. *European Journal of Marketing, 46(5)*, 712–32.

Wang, Y. J., & Minor, M. S. (2008). Validity, reliability, and applicability of psychophysiological techniques in marketing research. *Psychology and Marketing, 25(2)*, 197–232.

Wilkes, R. E., Burnett, J. J., & Howell, R. D. (1986). On the meaning and measurement of religiosity in consumer research. *Journal of the Academy of Marketing Science, 14(1)*, 47.

Young, J. S. (1988). *Steve jobs: The journey is the reward.* Glenview, IL, USA: Scott, Foresman.

14

COUNTRY-TO-ANIMAL-TO-BRAND-TO-CONSEQUENCES UNAIDED EVOCATIONS

Uncovering Consumer-brand DNA Using Zoomorphic Metaphor Elicitation

Drew Martin, Nitha Palakshappa, and Arch G. Woodside

Introduction

Most country image and country-of-origin studies adopt a narrow approach to explaining this dynamic relationship (cf. Shimp, Samiee, & Madden, 1993). A common approach to understanding consumer attitudes is asking respondents to choose from a small number of predetermined alternatives or rate attitudes on predetermined constructs using five- or seven-point rating scales. Woodside (2011, p. 154) argues that, "Direct questioning is insufficient for understanding and describing the actual thinking process." Structured surveys prevent people from explaining their feelings or actions. Considerable evidence suggests that most thinking occurs unconsciously (Bargh & Chartrand, 1999; Nisbett & Wilson, 1977), suggesting that structured survey instruments cannot measure information as stored in memories accurately.

Country image is a multidimensional construct including cognitive, affective, and conative components (Laroche, Papadopoulos, Heslop, & Mourali, 2005). Typically, country image studies focus on cognitive components (Roth & Diamantopoulos, 2009). Country image dimensions include innovation, design, prestige, and workmanship that vary by product category (Roth & Romeo, 1992) and build over time (Hong & Wyer, 1990). The literature suggests that a country's image as a producer is not too different from brand equity. While country equity and brand equity differ, the latter reinforces the former (Shimp, Samiee, & Madden, 1993).

The country-of-origin and country image literatures demonstrate the challenges with modeling human behavior. Generally, quantitative human behavior studies contribute to testing theories, but the results tend not to explain much data variation. For example, is regression analysis a better predictor than a simple tallying of data? Gigerenzer and Brighton (2009) demonstrate that regression fits the data better; however, a simple data tally's ability to predict is more accurate when testing empirical regression versus tally models on additional samples. Armstrong (2012) reports indexing rather than regression that finds causal condition/action statements neither attainable by regression nor prior experience. Adding more independent variables (e.g. n>10) to regression models increases the likelihood of multicollinearity and results in nonsignificant independent variables explaining high data variance (Woodside, 2013). The evidence suggests that data collection and analyses need to conform to how people think and store information. To assess country brand or product images, the study here asked informants to name brands or products that come to mind for the specific country. When a respondent does not buy branded goods from a given country, the general product category is requested. A follow-up question asks respondents to explain how the brands and products embody the animal previously mentioned.

Open-ended approaches allow respondents to interpret metal images and reduce distortion between images and thoughts. To understand this spontaneous cognitive processing requires accessing both conscious and unconscious memories. How can unconscious memories be accessed? Human thought processes primarily are metaphorical, suggesting more robust data if research works adapt to the respondents (see Lakoff & Johnson, 2008; Zaltman, 2003). Metaphors help people to structure their perceptions, thoughts, and activities. Metaphor elicitation helps to unlock memories filed away as stories or fragments. Asking respondents to self-interpret metaphors creates rich data. A domain structure within this experience conceptualizes an experiential gestalt. "Such gestalts are experientially basic because they characterize structured wholes within recurrent human experiences in terms of natural dimensions" (Lakoff & Johnson, 2008, p. 117). Interaction theory posits that a two-way transfer occurs between sources and target allowing for emic and etic interpretations (Black, 1962).

Images rather than words often shape thoughts (see Pinker, 1994). Combining nonverbal images and language helps consumers to convey richer representations and meanings (see Zaltman & Coulter, 1995). Animal metaphors often convey other meanings. Extending Woodside's (2010) zoomorphic forced-metaphor elicitation, respondents provide details about their perceptions of foreign countries and brands to provide a deeper understanding of what influences consumer thinking. Collecting these images for several countries helps to understand the variable relationships existing between individual consumers and their country and brand images. Essentially, these multiple country images create individual gestalt images or a person's Consumer DNA (C-DNA). This chapter demonstrates how using animal metaphors in interviews uncovers rich data about consumer behavior. Looking at how these relationships differ provides examples for how to construct C-DNA.

A Case of Complex Relationships: Product and Country Images

The country image literature demonstrates challenges understanding consumers' attitudes about a country's products. Studies exploring country image focus on country-of-origin, country-of-manufacture, country-of-brand, and country image issues. Typically, these studies collect data by asking respondents to rate their attitudes or feelings about foreign brands and products (d'Astous & Boujbel, 2007; Insch & McBride, 2004). Do self-reporting, five- and seven-point scales capture how people process information? Arguably, this data collection method insufficiently describes the actual thinking process (see Woodside, 2011). Reducing consumer attitudes to fixed categories fails to measure country-of-origin and country image complexities. For example, Shimp and Sharma's (1987) CETSCALE demonstrates consumers' preconceived ideas about foreign brands and products; however, six non-ethnocentric dimensions do not satisfy psychometric requirements. Why not ask respondents to describe products associating with specific countries?

Today's global markets create an additional wrinkle for identifying a product's home. Because a product's designing, sourcing, and manufacturing cross national borders, many products are hybrids. Prior studies suggest that consumers perceive country-of-design rather than country-of-assembly as more important in determining price (Chao, 1993), particularly for well-known brands. When the brand name is not known, country-of-manufacture becomes more important to consumers (Iyer & Kalita, 1997).

Exploring Unconsciousness

According to Zaltman (2003), up to 95% of consumers' thinking occurs unconsciously. Gigerenzer and Brighton (2009) suggest that the human cognitive system naturally creates a filtering system to reduce information that allows more efficient information processing. To process complex information, the best strategy is ignoring most of the information and following a rule of thumb. An environment of great uncertainty (e.g. buying an automobile) suggests that many variables need analyzing to determine the best solution. Gigerenzer (2007) recommends just the opposite and relies on a simple strategy rather than a complex one. Decision optimization becomes out of reach when too many variables are introduced into the decision-making model.

Why does the human cognitive system need heuristics to process information? According to Pierce (1962), a human cognitively processes information at no more than 40 bits per second; however, a high-quality music composition might specify a sequence of information at 300,000 bits per second (cf. Nørretranders 1991/1999). To increase the listening audience's ability to process the music, composers tend to sequence music in a musically grammatical order (e.g. recognizable chords, scales, themes, or ornaments). Typically, the listening audience appreciates listening to an orchestra when the sounds are somewhat predictable and repetitious. Listeners can process more by anticipating the repetition and the unconscious mind helps process the concert.

A person who has lost his car in a parking lot confirms this proposition. Previously, the driver navigated a large motor vehicle between and around both stationary and moving objects to position the car precisely between two white lines. Teaching someone to drive a car helps one to remember all the steps and maneuvers involved with parking. Experienced drivers allow the unconscious mind to process many of these steps to the point where the person does not recall where the car was parked.

Animals as Metaphors

Early evidence of animal imagery comes from ancient structures such as the Great Sphinx in Egypt. Describing vice as a multiform beast, Plato uses the terms lionlike and snakelike suggesting that animal metaphors existed in ancient Greece (Reeve, 2004). Animal metaphors offer an interesting study area because the animal word retains the original meaning (i.e. the animal) and the relationship between the animal and the transferred meaning is relevant to the informant. Advertisers recognize the usefulness of these associations and product brands incorporate positive animal metaphor imagery (Spears, Mowen, & Chakraborty, 1996). A few examples include Turtle Wax, Mustang automobiles, Tiger shoes, and Behr paint. Products even display national animal images on labeling to encourage buying products made in a specific country (Insch & Florek, 2009).

As animals lack language capacity, the animal is a metaphor and the metaphor and animal (Lippit, 1998). An animal word's semantic transfer also varies over time. For example, the word snake was introduced into the English language centuries before viper; however, snake acquired the same metaphorical meaning as viper (treachery) about the same time (Lehrer, 1985). All nations and cultures use animals to express cultural meanings that illustrate human characteristic dimensions (see Robin, 1977). While animal metaphors appear to be common in all languages, their meanings do not necessarily cross cultures (see Table 14.1). The evidence suggests that a human–animal cooperative and symbiotic relationship exists (Goatly, 2007; Levy, 1981).

TABLE 14.1 Figurative Meanings of Animal Terms

Animal	Country—Meaning
Cow	China—foolish
	Cyprus—dull (working too hard)
	Ethiopia—generous/innocent/naïve
	France—nasty
	Japan—slow, stupid
	Kenya—beautiful
Mouse	China—dirty
	France—girl (pejorative)
	Japan—nimble
	Malaysia—timid
	Palestine—small and weak
	Sweden—quiet, boring

Sources: Nesi, 1995; O'Donnell, 1990.

Mining Unconscious Memories

Gladwell's (2005) blink proposition suggests that people should trust their gut feelings (cf. Bargh, 2002). Unconscious memory directs gut; however, people lack insight into these memories. Allowing people to explain their feelings helps to release unconscious memories (see Wilson, 2002). Respondents tend to interpret their thoughts as stories rather than as lists and categories. Not surprisingly, these unconscious memories include episodic information about experiences, outcomes, and evaluations, including person-and-country and person-and-brand relationships (Fournier, 1998; Shank, 1990).

McCracken's long interview method (1988) serves as a guide for collecting data. Interviews come from a field study. Professional middle-class respondents in various countries agreed to participate in 60- to 90-minute interviews. Although a few questions were predetermined, researchers primarily focused on probing follow-up questions to ask respondents to elaborate on their feelings and attitudes. Using an open-structure approach allows respondents to interpret metal images reducing distortion between images and thoughts. Spontaneous cognitive processing requires accessing both conscious and unconscious memories to aide in the evaluation process. Figure 14.1 shows the general question progression.

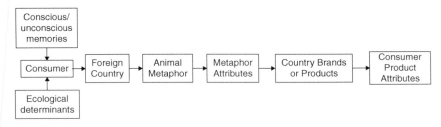

FIGURE 14.1 Zoomorphic FMET Model.

Country and Product/Brand Introspections

To demonstrate the procedure, interviews were conducted in India and the United States. The key interviewers have in-depth knowledge of the local cultural context and experience in qualitative methodologies. Audio-taped interviews were later transcribed for analysis. On-site interviews allow researchers to develop a more reflexive approach to the qualitative analysis (Hall, 2004; Hollinshead & Jamal, 2007). Respondents were prescreened to assure that they are middle-class, well-educated, and aware of foreign products and brands. While only a few cases are reported, purposeful samples should exceed Strauss and Corbin's recommendations (1998).

Woodside's (2010) zoomorphic forced metaphor-elicitation technique (FMET) is an indirect research method allowing both emic (self) and etic (researcher) interpretations uncover insights into consumer attitudes about country of origin, product, and brand image. First, the respondent is told the name of a foreign country and asked to name an animal that first comes to mind. Next, the respondent is asked to relate the animal's attributes or personality relating to the aforementioned country. Sometimes, this question is difficult to answer and probing follow-up questions helps respondents to explain the animal–country relationship. Occasionally, respondents realize that the animal and the country image are polar opposites in their minds. When an inverse relationship occurs, the animal named usually represents an ideal, positive image and the actual image is negative. This line of inquiry helps to understand the informant's conscious/unconscious country image.

Third, to assess brand or product images, informants are asked to name brands or products that come to mind for the specific country. Global brands are easier to recollect. When the respondent does not buy branded goods from a given country, the general product category is requested. Finally, respondents are asked to explain how the brands and products embody the animal previously mentioned.

Indian Consumers' Perspectives on New Zealand

The sheep and kiwi bird metaphors describe New Zealand as timid, docile, not aggressive, and innocent. While the animals are different, the metaphor attributes are similar. These nonaggressive metaphors translate to limited brand awareness as well. Respondents recalled only one New Zealand brand. Industries commonly mentioned include farming (dairy and wool products), tourism, and sports and they generally could not recall purchasing any products from New Zealand. One respondent recalls eating New Zealand Naturals ice cream. "[T]hey're [New Zealand Naturals] very soft and not a very aggressive kind of product, they don't go all out to sell it" (Santhosh). Figure 14.2 maps the consumer zoomorphic metaphor elicitation process of two Indian consumers about New Zealand products.

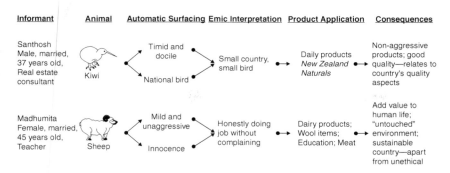

Informant	Animal	Automatic Surfacing	Emic Interpretation	Product Application	Consequences
Santhosh Male, married, 37 years old, Real estate consultant	Kiwi	Timid and docile / National bird	Small country, small bird	Daily products _New Zealand Naturals_	Non-aggressive products; good quality—relates to country's quality aspects
Madhumita Female, married, 45 years old, Teacher	Sheep	Mild and unaggressive / Innocence	Honestly doing job without complaining	Dairy products; Wool items; Education; Meat	Add value to human life; "untouched" environment; sustainable country—apart from unethical

FIGURE 14.2   Indian Consumers' Views of New Zealand.

Japanese Consumers' Perspectives on Germany

Japanese informants described Germany using falcon and wolf as metaphors. Misako described the hawk as a serious animal and a predator. The no–nonsense hawk appears to be a disciplined animal as well. As a bird of prey, the hawk needs to pay close attention to detail. The wolf shares these characteristics as a strict and serious animal as well as a predator. Wolves usually hunt larger animals as organized small groups.

Automobiles (Volkswagen and Mercedes-Benz), knives (Henkel), optics (Carl Zeiss), and ball bearings (Hans Haugg) are products describing Germany's precision manufacturing. Strict and serious fit an image of an uncompromising manufacturing process. Misako owns a set of Henkel knives and likes the quality. Previously, she bought German wine, but she cannot remember the brand name. "I bought the wine many years ago and liked the sweet taste" (Misako). Hideki's experience with Japanese products comes from his work as an engineer. "German companies make the finest optics" (Hideki). The only consumer product he could recollect was the Mercedes-Benz automobile. While Hideki aspires to own a Benz, he knows that this car is more aspirational than reality given his income and family needs. Figure 14.3 maps the consumer zoomorphic metaphor elicitation process of two consumers about German products.

United States Consumers' Perspectives on Japan

The crane and snow monkey describe perceptions of two US consumers about Japan. These images are a bit different, but the overall consequences appear to be similar. For Dave, the crane represents a majestic bird whose days are numbered. Rapid industrialization and a lack of environmental controls affected the crane's environment and the animal is rare in the wild. The crane metaphor suggests that restoring the animal's prominence will be difficult. Has Japan reached the tipping point? Dave owns two Japanese automobiles and he is very happy with

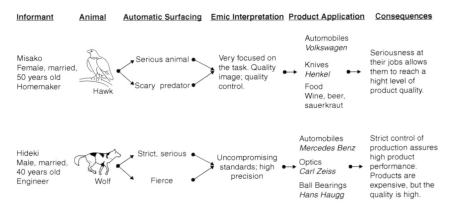

FIGURE 14.3 Japanese Consumers' Views of Germany.

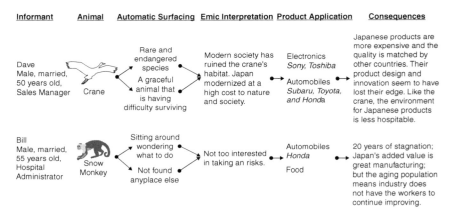

FIGURE 14.4 United States Consumers' Views of Japan.

them. Both cars are more than ten years old and he is not certain that his next automobile purchases will be from Japanese car manufacturers. "Japanese cars have really impressed me, but a Ford has as many bells and whistles" (Dave). Previously, he owned Sony televisions, but Dave now prefers Samsung.

Bill's snow monkey metaphor suggests that Japanese companies appear to be uncertain about how to restore their luster in the eyes of the consumer. Like the snow monkey, Japanese companies appear to be sitting around wondering what to do. "Japan's aging population seems to have affected their ability to continue innovating" (Bill). Japanese companies appear to be afraid to take risks. Although Bill owns two Honda automobiles and previously visited Japan, he could not recall any other Japanese brands. "Korean companies are doing to Japan what Japanese companies did to the US about 30 years ago" (Bill). Figure 14.4 maps the consumer zoomorphic metaphor elicitation process of two consumers about Japanese products.

Consumer DNA

The preceding section demonstrates that consumers' knowledge and attitudes about countries, brands, and products vary considerably suggesting that an ecological perspective helps to understand the context. Ecological systems move beyond dyads (e.g. consumer and product) and consider environmental influences on behavior, often at multiple different levels (see Bronfenbrenner, 1979). Environmental influences combined with conscious and unconscious memories form an individual profile of each consumer. These complex relationships are similar to an individual's DNA (deoxyribonucleic acid). Like genetic DNA, each person's C-DNA is unique. Figure 14.5 presents the double helix model of C-DNA showing the relationship between country and brand images.

In Figure 14.5, for each product category that a consumer purchases, both country and brand images create a strand that spans between each helix. The bifurcating vertical line is neutral. Any part of a helix or strand to the left suggests a positive image and to the right suggests a negative image. Several points are identified by letters in Figure 14.5. Position A shows neutrality for both country and brand images. Country image neutrality suggests limited exposure to a country and brand in a given category. Madhumita's C-DNA position for New Zealand appears neutral. Viewing New Zealand as mild and unaggressive at best is mildly positive. Madhumita could not name any New Zealand brands, so she cannot have either positive or negative brand images.

Position B shows negative country and brand images. Although the data do not demonstrate this position, global corporations based in the US experience concerns about economic nationalism by local people. For example, US fast food (e.g. McDonald's) entering foreign markets run into trouble when local people express concerns about economic nationalism and ruining the diet.

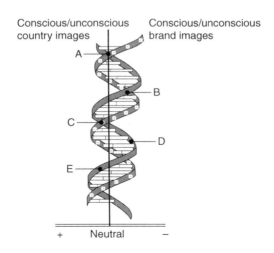

FIGURE 14.5   Consumer DNA.

While McDonald's success in France continues, the French people have not always embraced the golden arches (Rosenblum, 2004). Bill notes that Japanese manufacturing successfully penetrated the US market 30 years ago. Many US consumers embraced these less expensive alternatives that arguably performed better. Japan's success was not appreciated by all US consumers, particularly when the Japanese markets were more difficult for US businesses to enter. Trade issues are not the only factor influencing consumer product purchase decisions. A survey of 8,000 consumers in G8 countries found that 20% of foreign consumers would avoid buying US products due to the country's position on foreign affairs (Bruce, 2004). China has a similar country image problem in the US because some consumers express concerns about the country's human rights record. Most Chinese brands are unknown in the US and the products suffer from a poor quality image (Tian, 2013).

Position C shows both positive country and brand images. Sweden's Ikea reports the company's strongest growth in China (Ikea, 2014). This evidence suggests that the Ikea brand is popular among Chinese middle-class consumers. Some evidence supports Sweden's positive country image by Chinese consumers. In 1950, Sweden became the first Western country to establish diplomatic relations with China. From India, Santhosh appears to like both New Zealand and New Zealand Naturals (a premium ice cream). Both the country and the brand relate to positive images for him—a good product relating to New Zealand's quality aspects.

Position D shows a positive brand image and negative country image. In this case, a global brand appears detached from the country image. For example, the US image in the Middle East is bipolar; however, Apple's popularity with consumers is strong (Shuey, 2011). Ford automobiles are also gaining popularity in the Middle East. Ford reports 12% sales growth in the Middle East in 2013 with the Lincoln's sales doubling over the previous year (Varghese, 2014). Misako likes her Henkel knife set, but she uses a bird of prey to describe Germany as serious. While Misako does not express direct dislike for Germany, the hawk is described as a scary predator.

Finally, position E shows conflicting images with a positive country and negative brand images. Target's acquisition of Canada's Zellers received a cold shoulder by Canadians. Nostalgia and product quality issues turned Canadian consumers against Target (McGee, 2015). In China, a businessman destroyed his Mercedes-Benz to protest slow negotiations with the German automaker regarding his alleged warranty problems (August, 2002). In the US, consumer confidence in Toyota has been damaged by problems with the automobiles accelerating unintentionally. Toyota has recalled more than ten million vehicles and litigation due to wrongful-deaths has damaged the company's reputation (Seetharaman & Woodall, 2011). While this incident affects consumer confidence in Toyota, country image unlikely changes for most consumers. These examples appear to be aimed at the US retailer rather than country images.

Dave describes Japan as a graceful crane suggesting a positive country image. His mother owns a Toyota and she experienced an acceleration problem, so his impression of the Japanese carmaker is not positive.

A complete C-DNA for individual consumers would take considerable effort. A more realistic approach is using zoomorphic FMET to collect individual consumer data about a group of four to six countries. Data from these interviews would provide individual C-DNA profiles. Close matches likely exist among people with similar environmental influences, so individuals can be segmented into groups or sets. These profiles can be coded and compared using a fuzzy-set analysis (see Ragin, 2000).

Conclusion

Zoomorphic FMET offers a useful technique to examine the complexities of country and brand image on foreign products. As an indirect approach, zoomorphic FMET moves beyond the consumer-brand or consumer-country dyad to take a broader ecological perspective. Departing from a post-positivist methodology, loosely structured long interviews allow informants to express their impressions as stored in their memories. Getting informants to talk about their feelings, attitudes, and experiences allows interviewers to asking probing follow-up questions and encourage self-reflection by informants. These events trigger unconscious thoughts and allow deeper understanding of consumer behavior.

Sometimes, respondents find that the animals' anthropomorphic characteristics do not show clear relationships to their country image or product image. Usually, this mismatch occurs when an animal thought to exhibit positive anthropomorphism is matched with negative country or brand images. This seemingly counterintuitive finding reflects a gap between idea and actual. The evidence suggests a positive unconscious image and a negative conscious image. From a brand manager's perspective, this gap represents an opportunity to improve the brand's image abroad. Results also help managers to determine whether or not the country origin should be emphasized as well. A very negative country image suggests that the brand is better positioned as global rather than emphasizing country origin.

Asking respondents to identify animals for several countries allows researchers to create unique C-DNA profiles for each person. Purposeful sampling allows researchers to identify commonalities among study participants and to compare country and brand images longitudinally. Because many variables affect the consumer-country-brand triad, C-DNA is dynamic. This dynamism becomes a two-edged sword for brand managers. On the one hand, opportunity to reposition and win over consumers exists. However, country and brand images also deteriorate quickly. A customer arriving at her hotel room posts negative comments about the check-in process on social media (Martin & Isozaki, 2013). Consumers' negative feelings become part of the hotel's image at light speed. International events stirring nationalistic feelings potentially change consumers' attitudes about buying foreign products as well.

Zoomorphic FMET and C-DNA suggest new techniques for understanding consumer behavior in complex global markets. As country of origin becomes more difficult for consumers to determine brand and country images, they search for heuristics to simplify their decision-making process. Far more processing likely takes place at the unconscious level. Methods designed to access these unconscious memories become more essential.

References

Armstrong, J. S. (2012). Illusions in regression analysis. *International Journal of Forecasting*, 28, 689–694.

August, O. (2002). Mercedes bends as Chinese consumer exacts revenge on maker. *The Australian*, 8.

Bargh, J. A. (2002). Losing consciousness: Automatic influences on consumer judgment, behavior, and motivation. *Journal of Consumer Research*, 29(2), 280–285.

Bargh, J. A., & Chartrand, T. L. (1999). The unbearable automaticity of being. *American Psychologist*, 54(7), 462–479.

Black, M. (1962). Metaphor. In M. Black (Ed.), *Models and metaphors*. Ithaca, NY: Cornell University Press, 25–47.

Bronfenbrenner, U. (1979). *The Ecology of Human Development*. Cambridge, MA: Harvard Press.

Bruce, I. S. (2004). In the shadow of the east; as megabrands like Coke, Nike, and McDonald's appear to be losing the affection of consumers outside the US. *The Sunday Herald*, 5.

Chao, P. (1993). Partitioning country of origin effects: Consumer evaluations of a hybrid product. *Journal of International Business Studies*, 24(2), 291–306.

d'Astous, A., & Boujbel, L. (2007). Positioning countries on personality dimensions: Scale development and implications for country marketing. *Journal of Business Research*, 60(3), 231–239.

Fournier, S. (1998). Consumers and their brands: Developing relationship theory in consumer research. *Journal of Consumer Research*, 24(4), 343–373.

Gigerenzer, G. (2007). *Gut feelings*. New York: Penguin.

Gigerenzer, G., & Brighton, H. (2009). Homo heuristicus: Why biased minds make better inferences. *Topics in Cognitive Science*, 1(1), 107–143.

Gladwell, M. (2005). *Blink: The power of thinking without thinking*. New York: Little Brown.

Goatly, A. (2007). *Washing the brain: Metaphor and hidden ideology*. Amsterdam, NLD: John Benjamins Publishing Company.

Hall, C. M. (2004). Reflexivity and tourism research: Situating myself and/with others. In J. Phillimore & L. Goodson (Eds.), *Qualitative research in tourism: Ontologies, epistemologies and methodologies*. London: Routledge. 137–155.

Hollinshead, K., & Jamal, T. B. (2007). Tourism and "the third ear": Further prospects for qualitative inquiry. *Tourism Analysis*, 12, 85–129.

Hong, S. T., & Wyer, Jr, R. S. (1990). Determinants of product evaluation: Effects of the time interval between knowledge of a product's country of origin and information about its specific attributes. *Journal of Consumer Research*, 17(3), 277–288.

Ikea sales driven by strong Chinese demand. (2014). *The Irish Times*, 2.

Insch, A., & Florek, M. (2009). Prevalence of country of origin associations on the supermarket shelf. *International Journal of Retail & Distribution Management*, 37(5), 453–471.

Insch, G. S., & McBride, J. B. (2004). The impact of country-of-origin cues on consumer perceptions of product quality: A binational test of the decomposed country-of-origin construct. *Journal of Business Research*, 57(3), 256–265.

Iyer, G. R., & Kalita, J. K. (1997). The impact of country-of-origin and country-of-manufacture cues on consumer perceptions of quality and value. *Journal of Global Marketing*, 11(1), 7–28.

Lakoff, G., & Johnson, M. (2008). *Metaphors we live by*. Chicago, IL: University of Chicago Press.

Laroche, M., Papadopoulos, N., Heslop, L. A., & Mourali, M. (2005). The influence of country image structure on consumer evaluations of foreign products. *International Marketing Review*, 22(1), 96–115.

Lehrer, A. (1985). The influence of semantic fields on semantic change. In J. Fisiak (Ed.), *Historical semantics. Historical word-formation*. Berlin: Mouton, 283–296.

Levy, S. J. (1981). Interpreting consumer mythology: A structural approach to consumer behavior. *Journal of Marketing*, 45(3), 49–61.

Lippit, A. M. (1998). Magnetic animal: Derrida, wildlife, animetaphor. *Comparative Literature*, 113(5), 1111–1125.

Martin, D., & Isozaki, M. (2013). Path analysis of multinational strategic marketing decisions: Asia-Pacific hotel chain strategies in turbulent times. *Journal of Business Research*, 66(9), 1544–1549.

McCracken, G. (1988). *The long interview*. Newbury Park, CA: Sage.

McGee, S. (2015). Tim Hortons-Burger King merger serves big order of cross-border controversy. *The Guardian*.

Nisbett, R. E., & Wilson, T. D. (1977). Telling more than we can know: Verbal reports on mental processes. *Psychological Review*, 84, 231–259.

Nesi, H. (1995). A modern bestiary: A contrastive study of the figurative meanings of animal terms. *ELT Journal*, 49(3), 272–278.

Nørretranders, T. (1991/1999). *The user illusion* (J. Sydenham, Trans.). New York: Penguin. (Original work published 1991).

O'Donnell, P. E. (1990). Entre chien et loup: A study of French animal metaphors. *The French Review*, 63(3), 514–523.

Pierce, J. R. (1962). *Symbols, signals and noise*. London: Hutchinson.

Pinker, S. (1994). *The Language Instinct: How the Mind Creates Language*. Cambridge, MA: MIT Press.

Ragin, C. C. (2000). *Fuzzy-set social science*. Chicago, IL: University of Chicago Press.

Reeve, C. D. C. (2004). *Plato: Republic*. Translated From The New Standard Greek Text, With. Indianapolis, IN: Hackett.

Robin, P. A. (1977). *Animal lore in English literature*. Norwood, PA: Norwood Editions.

Rosenblum, M. (2004). Sacre bleu! McDonald's is a hug hit in France; after bombings and protests, the golden arches have found a place alongside the Arc de Triomphe. The Globe and Mail, L11.

Roth, K. P., & Diamantopoulos, A. (2009). Advancing the country image construct. *Journal of Business Research*, 62(7), 726–740.

Roth, M. S., & Romeo, J. B. (1992). Matching Product Category and Country Image Perceptions: A Framework for Managing Country-Of-Origin Effects. *Journal of International Business Studies*, 23(3), 477–497.

Seetharaman, D., & Woodall, B. (2011). Toyota seeks to settle acceleration case for $1.1 billion. www.chicagotribune.com/autos/ct-xpm-2012-12-26-sns-rt-us-usa-toyota-settlementbre8bp0g6-20121226-story.html

Shank, R. C. (2000). *Tell me a story.* Evanston, IL: Northwestern University Press.

Shimp, T. A., & Sharma, S. (1987). Consumer ethnocentrism: Construction and validation of the CETSCALE. *Journal of Marketing Research*, 24(3), 280–289.

Shimp, T. A., Samiee, S., & Madden, T. J. (1993). Countries and their products: A cognitive structure perspective. *Journal of the Academy of Marketing Science*, 21(4), 323–330.

Shuey, S. (2011). Apple shouldn't ignore Middle East customers. *Gulf News.*

Spears, N. E., Mowen, J. C., & Chakraborty, G. (1996). Symbolic role of animals in print advertising: Content analysis and conceptual development. *Journal of Business Research*, 37(2), 87–95.

Tian, K. (2013). Chinese companies endeavor to build up global brands. *China Daily*, 17.

Varghese, J. (2014). Ford motors registers 22% growth in Qatar. *Gulf Times.*

Wilson, T. D. (2002). *Strangers to ourselves: Discovering the adaptive unconscious.* Cambridge, MA: Harvard University Press.

Woodside, A. G. (2010). *Case study research.* Bingley, UK: Emerald.

Woodside, A. G. (2011). Responding to the severe limitations of cross-sectional surveys: Commenting on Rong and Wilkinson's perspectives. *Australasian Marketing Journal*, 19(3), 153–156.

Woodside, A. G. (2013). Moving beyond multiple regression analysis to algorithms: Calling for adoption of a paradigm shift from symmetric to asymmetric thinking in data analysis and crafting theory. *Journal of Business Research*, 66(4), 463–472.

Zaltman, G. (2003). *How customers think.* Boston, MA: Harvard Business School Press.

Zaltman, G., & Coulter, R. H. (1995). Seeing the voice of the customer: Metaphor-based advertising research. *Journal of Advertising Research*, 35(4), 35–51.

15

A COMPARISON AND CONTRASTING OF THE LIST OF VALUES AND THE SCHWARTZ VALUE SCALE

Eda Gurel-Atay, Lynn R. Kahle, Jorge Bertinetti Lengler, and Chung-Hyun Kim

Personal values, defined as "centrally held, enduring beliefs which guide actions and judgments across specific situations and beyond immediate goals to more ultimate end-states of existence" (Rokeach 1968/1969, 550), are standards to serve many purposes in daily life: they are central to people's lives (Kahle and Timmer 1983), are enduring and difficult to change (Rokeach 1973), and guide behaviors and judgments across specific situations (Kahle and Timmer 1983; Kahle and Valete-Florance 2012; Rokeach 1973), including political attitudes (Lee 2003), moral reasoning (Abdolmohammadi and Baker 2006), employee creative behavior (Rice 2006), healthy lifestyles (Divine and Lepisto 2005), and consumer behaviors (Limon, Kahle, and Orth 2009). Accordingly, it is important to measure values with objective, meaningful, reliable, and valid instruments. In consumer research, two measurements of values are used widely: the List of Values (LOV), developed by Kahle (1983), and the Schwartz Value Scale (SVS), developed by Schwartz (1992). The purpose of this chapter is to compare and contrast these two value measures. A third measure, the Rokeach (1973) Value Survey, has previously been compared and contrasted with the LOV (Beatty, Kahle, Homer, and Misra, 1985).

The List of Values

The LOV is based on the theories of values developed by Rokeach (1973), Maslow (1954), and Kahle (1983). Rokeach (1973) differentiated between instrumental (e.g. honesty, open-mindedness, and responsibility) and terminal values (e.g. a world at peace, equality, and inner harmony) and suggested that people use instrumental values to achieve their terminal values. Maslow (1954) used <u>values</u> and <u>needs</u> interchangeably and suggested that values/needs are hierarchically ordered. To attain a higher-order value/need, each lower-order levels of values/needs should be at least partially satisfied. Kahle (1983), in his Social Adaptation Theory, suggested that values influence the adaptation to life. More specifically, value development and value fulfillment affect the ways individuals adapt to various life roles. For instance, people who value warm relationships with others most may try hard to make friends and have good relationship with their friends, but people who value self-respect most may try to improve themselves continuously (Kahle, Boush, and Homer 1988; Kahle, Homer, O'Brien, and Boush 1997).

The LOV consists of nine values: a sense of belonging, excitement, warm relationships with others, self-fulfillment, being well-respected, fun and enjoyment in life, security, self-respect, and a sense of accomplishment (see Table 15.1). Some of these items are similar to the items included in Rokeach Value Scale (RVS) (Rokeach 1973). For instance, excitement is similar to RVS' exciting life, warm relationships with others are similar to RVS' true friendship, and being well-respected is similar to RVS' social recognition. Many of the values in the LOV can also be matched directly with a level in Maslow's Hierarchy of Needs. For instance, security from the LOV represents the safety level, a sense of belonging represents the belongingness level, and self-fulfillment represents the self-actualization level.

The values in the LOV can be considered in three dimensions (Homer and Kahle 1988): internal, external, and fun/excitement. Internal values reflect the belief that people can fulfill their values by themselves and include self-fulfilling, a sense of accomplishment, and self-respect. External values reflect the belief that people are dependent on others to fulfill their values. Being well-respected, sense of belonging, warm relationships with others, and security are included in this dimension. Fun/excitement values have an internal motivation to fulfill these values with other people and include excitement, and fun and enjoyment in life. The values in the LOV can also be organized into two groups based on the motivations for value endorsement. Excess values reflect the values

TABLE 15.1 The List of Values (LOV)

Sense of belonging (to be accepted and needed by our family, friends, and community)
Excitement (to experience stimulation and thrills)
Warm relationships with others (to have close companionships and intimate friendships)
Self-fulfillment (to find peace of mind and to make the best use of your talents)
Being well-respected (to be admired by others and to receive recognition)
Fun and enjoyment in life (to lead a pleasurable, happy life)
Security (to be safe and protected from misfortune and attack)
Self-respect (to be proud of yourself and confident with who you are)
A sense of accomplishment (to succeed at what you want to do)

people already attained (Piner 1983) and include all internal and fun/excitement values. Deficit values are values people lack and strive to attain (Drenan 1983); external values are also deficit values.

The Schwartz Value Scale

Schwartz (1994), based on Rokeach's conceptualization of values, defines values as desirable trans-situational goals that serve as guiding principles in life and suggests that the importance of values is different for each individual. As stated earlier, Rokeach (1973) organized values on two dimensions. Terminal values are ultimate goals of life, and they are considered as end-states of existence, such as happiness or social recognition. Instrumental values are the ways of life that lead to terminal values; in other words, they are the modes of conduct. Examples of instrumental values include honesty, open-mindedness, and responsibility.

The SVS is theoretically based on Rokeach's terminal values and consists of ten motivationally distinct types of values: power, achievement, hedonism, stimulation, self-direction, universalism, benevolence, tradition, conformity, and security (see Table 15.2). All these values are measured by multiple items, and many of these items are also included in the RVS. For instance, the SVS measures universalism through the following items: equality, social justice, wisdom, broadminded, protecting the environment, unity with nature, and a world of beauty. The RVS, on the other hand, includes equality, wisdom, and a world of beauty as terminal values.

The SVS assumes a structure of dynamic relations between ten values. More specifically, it is suggested that "actions expressive of any value have practical,

TABLE 15.2 Schwartz Value Scale (SVS)

Power: Social status and prestige, control or dominance over people and resources

Achievement: Personal success through demonstrating competence according to social standards

Hedonism: Pleasure or sensuous gratification for oneself

Stimulation: Excitement, novelty, and challenge in life

Self-direction: Independent thought and action—choosing, creating, exploring

Universalism: Understanding, appreciation, tolerance, and protection for the welfare of all people and for nature

Benevolence: Preservation and enhancement of the welfare of people with whom one is in frequent personal contact

Tradition: Respect, commitment, and acceptance of the customs and ideas that traditional culture or religion provide

Conformity: Restraint of actions, inclinations, and impulses likely to upset or harm others and violate social expectations or norms

Security: Safety, harmony, and stability of society, of relationships, and of self

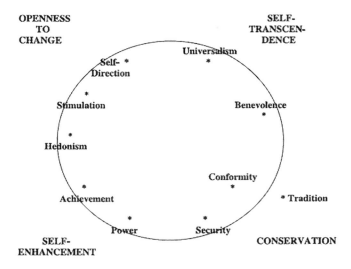

FIGURE 15.1 Quasi-Circumplex Model of the SVS.

psychological, and social consequences that may conflict or be compatible with the pursuit of other values" (Schwartz and Boehnke 2004, p. 231). For instance, hedonism values are compatible with achievement values and in conflict with conformity values. The pattern of value relations in terms of conflicts and incompatibility yields a circumplex structure (see Figure 15.1). In this circumplex structure, values that are adjacent to each other are more similar (i.e. compatible) and values that oppose each other are more different (i.e. in conflict). Moreover, this structure involves four dimensions of values: openness to change (self-direction and stimulation), conservation (tradition and conformity), self-enhancement (achievement and power), and self-transcendence (universalism and benevolence). Openness to change emphasizes independent thoughts, actions, and changes, whereas conservation emphasizes self-restriction, traditional practices, and stability. Similarly, self-enhancement emphasizes a person's own success and dominance over others, whereas self-transcendence emphasizes acceptance and welfare of others (Schwartz 1996).

LOV vs. SVS: A Comparison and Contrasting Study

Because both the LOV and the SVS are used extensively in consumer research, we wanted to compare and contrast these two value measures. Although these two popular instruments share similarities, they also have substantial differences (see Table 15.3). In terms of similarities, both the LOV and the SVS have their theoretical foundation from Rokeach's (1973) value conceptualization. Indeed, they both borrow values from the RVS (e.g. a sense of accomplishment/

TABLE 15.3 Comparison of the LOV and the SVS

	LOV	SVS
Number of Values	9	10
Number of Items	10	57
Scale Method	Rating 1: Important 9: Most Important	Rating (−1): Opposed to my principles (0): Not important (+7): Of supreme importance
Values Included	A sense of belonging, Excitement, Warm Relationships with Others, Self-Fulfillment, Being Well-Respected, Fun and Enjoyment in Life, Security, Self-Respect, and A Sense of Accomplishment	Power, Achievement, Hedonism, Stimulation, Self-Direction, Universalism, Benevolence, Tradition, Conformity, and Security

achievement; security; excitement/hedonism). Also, a nine-point importance rating scale is used for both measurements, but the end points are slightly different. The major difference between the LOV and the SVS is the number of items included in the scale. The LOV includes ten items; nine items are used to measure nine values and one item is used to select the most important value. The SVS consists of 57 items; these items are then combined together to form ten motivational values during data analyses.

In this chapter, we first examine the cross-cultural validity of the SVS' circumplex structure. In their article, Schwartz and Boehnke (2004) tested ten theoretical models regarding how values relate to each other. Model 1 considered each of the ten values as independent and tested how well a model of these ten orthogonal factors fits the data. Model 2 tested Schwartz's (1992) original quasi-circumplex model, in which the ten values were distributed at unequal intervals around a circle. Model 3 tested a modified quasi-circumplex model, a model that still ordered the values around a circle but also included central vs. peripheral positioning for tradition and conformity values. Model 4 combined tradition and conformity and tested a quasi-circumplex model with nine values. Model 5 tested another modified quasi-circumplex model where power and achievement values were located at the same polar angle in the circle and power was peripheral to achievement. Model 6 combined power and achievement values. Model 7 included four higher-order types of values: openness to change (combining stimulation and self-direction); conservation (combining security, conformity, and tradition); self-enhancement (combining power and achievement); and self-transcendence (combining universalism and benevolence). Model 8 freely estimated hedonism correlations to see if hedonism was closer to openness, to self-enhancement, or equally close to both. Model 9 included nature and social concern as subtypes within universalism. Model 10 tested personal security and group security as subtypes of security. In this study, we test three of the models explained earlier: Model 1 (because it was the starting point for the SVS), Model 2 (because it was the essence of the SVS), and Model 3 (because it was the modified, suggested, and mostly used version of the SVS). All other modifications suggested in Models 4–10 either did not fit the data well or were not adopted widely. Accordingly, and for the sake of simplicity, we decided to focus on the first three models in our chapter here.

After examining the validity of the circumplex structure of the SVS with our data, we assess the relations between the LOV values and the SVS values. Because both scales are used to assess basic human values, the values included in these scales are supposed to be related to each other in a meaningful way.

Method

A cross-cultural online study was conducted in three countries to compare the LOV and the SVS. Specifically, the survey was conducted in the United States (N=338), S. Korea (N=495), and Brazil (N=146). Our goal in collecting data from different countries and continents was not to conduct cross-cultural comparisons. Instead, we wanted to generate adequate variance in the constructs and to compare and contrast the LOV and SVS in different cultural settings as these two measures have been used cross-culturally extensively. Moreover, Schwartz and Boehnke (2004) combined data from many cultures in their analyses as their main purpose was to assess the theoretical models that would best fit "the basic pattern of value relations common to cultures, rather than to identify unique variants in particular cultures" (p. 234). Accordingly, in our analyses, we too combined data from the United States, Korea, and Brazil.

The survey questionnaire, which included the LOV and the SVS, was translated to local languages and then back-translated to English by bilingual speakers in each country. Experts resolved any apparent conflicts. We used quota samples in all three countries.

Results

First, we wanted to validate the quasi-circumplex model of the SVS described in Schwartz and Boehnke (2004). Then, we examined the correlations between values included in the LOV and values included in the SVS. LISREL 9.2 was used to assess the covariance matrices in the validation process, and SPSS 20 was used to examine the correlations between the LOV and the SVS.

Validity of the Quasi-Circumplex Model of SVS

In testing the three models specified earlier, we followed the same steps in writing the LISREL syntax as explained in Schwartz and Boehnke (2004). Table 15.4 shows the chi-square values as well as the two goodness-of-fit (GOF) statistics (RMSEA and SRMR) for the current study and two samples from the Schwartz and Boehnke (2004) paper.

First, we wanted to see that the ten values indeed are not independent of each other and a model of ten orthogonal factors would not fit the data well, as suggested by Schwartz and Boehnke (2004). As expected, and similar to what Schwartz and Boehnke (2004) found, the model did not fit the data well with a significant chi-square value and poor GOF statistics, suggesting that values are indeed related to each other.

A perfect circumplex model, in which the ten values were distributed at unequal intervals around a circle, was suggested and rejected by Schwartz (1992) earlier. In their 2004 paper, Schwartz and Boehnke tested this model again with their two samples and achieved an improvement over the first model. In our study, however, we did not experience the same improvement. On the contrary, RMSEA and SRMR values declined to worse when the quasi-circumplex model was applied.

Model 3 was a modified version of the original quasi-circumplex model. This modified model still includes ten values, and these ten values are still distributed around a circle. However, this time, tradition is located outside the conformity value but at the same polar angle in the circle. This modified model fits the data better than Model 2 for both samples in Schwartz and Boehnke (2004). In our study, however, neither of the GOF statistics changed, implying that no improvement over Model 2 was achieved.

As can be seen from Table 15.4, the results from our current study do not support the SVS' quasi-circumplex model (neither the original one nor the modified version). Moreover, Model 1 with ten independent factors provided a better fit than the quasi-circumplex model in our study. These results make the validity of SVS across different samples questionable.

Correlation between the LOV and the SVS

As we know, values are not independent of each other. Accordingly, values in the LOV and the SVS have statistically significant correlations with each other. Instead of examining and commenting on all these significant correlations, we focused on the relations with the highest correlation values to see if these relations make theoretical sense. For example, both scales include security; hence, security in LOV is expected to have the highest correlation with security in the SVS (instead of some other values from the SVS). Table 15.5 shows which values from the SVS have the highest correlations with the values from the LOV. Similarly, Table 15.6 shows which values from the LOV have the highest correlations from the LOV.

TABLE 15.4 Validity of the Quasi-Circumplex Model of SVS

	Results from Schwartz and Boehnke (2004): Sample 1			Results from Schwartz and Boehnke (2004): Sample 2			Results from the Current Study		
	χ^2 (df)	RMSEA	SRMR	χ^2 (df)	RMSEA	SRMR	χ^2 (df)	RMSEA	SRMR
Ten Correlated Factors (1)	391267 (989)	.083	.160	33538	.079	.150	6531 (815)	.099	.074
Quasi-Circumplex Model (2)	24048 (989)	.065	.088	19611 (989)	.060	.079	8711 (860)	.12	.30
Locating Tradition outside of Conformity at the Same Polar Angle in the Circle (3)	23356 (989)	.064	.081	19031 (989)	.059	.073	8942 (860)	.12	.30

TABLE 15.5 LOV and Correlations with SVS

LOV	SVS Value with the Highest Correlation
Sense of Belonging	Benevolence (r =.432, p <.001)
Excitement	Hedonism (r =.515, p <.001)
Warm Relationships with Others	Benevolence (r =.502, p <.001)
Self-Fulfillment	Self-Direction (r =.491, p <.001)
Being Well-Respected	Benevolence (r =.479, p <.001)
Fun and Enjoyment in Life	Hedonism (r =.576, p <.001)
Security	Security (r =.481, p <.001)
Self-Respect	Self-Direction (r =.444, p <.001)
Sense of Accomplishment	Achievement (r =.490, p <.001)

TABLE 15.6 SVS and Correlations with LOV

SVS	LOV Value with the Highest Correlation
Power	Excitement (r =.423, p <.001)
Achievement	A Sense of Accomplishment (r =.490, p <.001)
Hedonism	Fun and Enjoyment in Life (r =.576, p <.001)
Stimulation	Excitement (r =.449, p <.001)
Self-Direction	Warm Relationships with Others (r =.492, p <.001)
Universalism	Excitement (r =.396, p <.001)
	Warm Relationships with Others (r =.396, p <.001)
Benevolence	Warm Relationships with Others (r =.502, p <.001)
Tradition	Being Well-Respected (r =.422, p <.001)
Conformity	Being Well-Respected (r =.372, p <.001)
Security	Security (r =.481, p <.001)

Three of the LOV values have their highest correlations with benevolence (measured with four items: helpful, honest, forgiving, loyal, and responsible): a sense of belonging (to be accepted and needed by our family, friends, and community); warm relationships with others (to have close companionships and intimate friendships); and being well-respected (to be admired by others and to receive recognition). Benevolence, on the other hand, has its highest correlation with warm relationships with others. All these values refer to being involved with others and make sense to have high correlations with each other as social values. Interestingly, universalism (equality, social justice, wisdom, broadminded, protecting the environment, unity with nature, and a world of beauty), paired with benevolence under self-transcendence, has its highest correlation with two LOV values: warm relationships with others and excitement (to experience stimulation and thrills).

As can be expected, both excitement (to experience stimulation and thrills) and fun and enjoyment in life (to lead a pleasurable, happy life) have their highest correlation with hedonism (pleasure, enjoying life, self-indulgent). Hedonism, in turn, has its highest correlation with fun and enjoyment in life. Stimulation (daring, a varied life, an exciting life) from the SVS, on the other hand, has its highest correlation with excitement.

Two self-focused values from the LOV have their highest correlation with the self-focused value from the SVS. Specifically, self-fulfillment (to find peace of mind and to make the best use of your talents) and self-respect (to be proud of yourself and confident with who you are) are highly correlated with self-direction (creativity, freedom, independent, choosing own goals, curious). Interestingly, self-direction has its highest correlation with warm relationships with others, although it has relatively high correlations with self-fulfillment and with self-respect too.

A sense of accomplishment (to succeed at what you want to do) from the LOV has naturally its highest correlation with the achievement (ambitious, successful, capable, influential) value from the SVS. Similarly, achievement from the SVS has highly correlated with a sense of accomplishment from the LOV. A theoretically related value, power (authority, social power, wealth, preserving my public image) from the SVS, on the other hand, has its highest correlation with excitement.

Finally, security values from both the LOV (to be safe and protected from misfortune and attack) and the SVS (family security, national security, social order, clean, reciprocation of favors) have their highest correlations with each other. Tradition (devout, respect for tradition, humble, moderate) and conformity (self-discipline, politeness, honoring parents and elders, obedience), combined with security on the conservation corner of the quasi-circumplex model, on the other hand, have their highest correlations with being well-respected.

As the results show, nine values from the LOV have their highest correlations with five values (benevolence, hedonism, self-direction, achievement, security) from the SVS. In other words, five of the ten values (power, stimulation, universalism, tradition, and conformity) from the SVS did not have the highest correlations with any of the LOV values. Similarly, three of the LOV values (a sense of belonging, self-fulfillment, and self-respect) did not have the highest correlations with any of the SVS values.

Discussion

The purpose of this chapter is to compare and contrast two of the most widely used values scales in marketing: the LOV and the SVS. Specifically, we examined the validity of the SVS' circumplex model and assessed the relations between the LOV and the SVS values.

The comparison of the two scales suggests several advantages of using the LOV over using the SVS in consumer research. First of all, although the circumplex structure of the SVS was assessed "in over 200 samples in more than 60 countries from every inhabited continent (representative national samples, school teachers, university students, adolescents, samples of workers in specific occupations)" (Schwartz and Boehnke 2004, p. 232), this structure did not fit our data from three countries (i.e. the USA, Brazil, and Korea). This result made the validity of the circumplex structure of the SVS questionable. Circumplex validity may well depend on contextual and situational considerations.

Second, our correlational analyses revealed meaningful relations between most of the values included in the LOV and the SVS. In other words, the LOV and the SVS values are correlated with each other in a meaningful way. This finding provides convergent validity for both scales.

The LOV is simpler and shorter to administer, and it provides an easier task for the researchers and respondents as it includes only ten items in contrast to the 57 items of the SVS. Moreover, many of these 57 values in the SVS are not always directly related to consumer behaviors (e.g. honoring parents and elders, social justice, a world of beauty, and social order). Including items that are less relevant to consumers in their daily lives makes the scale unnecessarily long and demanding, and it reduces the potential validity. Also, including these less relevant items may hinder discovering the relations between values and consumer behaviors. The nine values included in the LOV, on the other hand, provide more relevancy to consumers' purchasing and consumption behaviors (see Beatty et al. 1985).

Conclusion

In this chapter, we only examined the validity of the circumplex model of the SVS and the relation between the LOV and the SVS values. Future research should examine the nomological validity of the LOV and the SVS in different cultural settings. Because values are considered as guiding principles of life, it is important to show for these two value scales how they can be effectively used to predict human behaviors, including consumer behaviors.

References

Abdolmohammadi, Mohammad J., and C. Richard Baker (2006), "Accountants' Value Preferences and Moral Reasoning," *Journal of Business Ethics*, 69 (1), 11–25.

Beatty, Sharon E., Lynn R. Kahle, Pamela Homer, and Shekhar Misra (1985), "Alternative Measurement Approaches to Consumer Values: The List of Values and the Rokeach Value Survey," *Psychology & Marketing*, 2 (Fall), 181–200.

Divine, Richard L., and Lawrence Lepisto (2005), "Analysis of the Healthy Lifestyle Consumer," *Journal of Consumer Marketing*, 22 (5), 275–83.

Drenan, Sarah (1983), "Values and Psychological Adaptation: Personality Factors," in *Social Values and Social Change: Adaptation to Life in America*, Ed. Lynn R. Kahle, New York: Praeger, 227–57.

Homer, Pamela M., and Lynn R. Kahle (1988), "A Structural Equation Test of the Value-Attitude-Behavior Hierarchy," *Journal of Personality and Social Psychology*, 54 (April), 638–46.

Kahle, Lynn R., Ed. (1983), *Social Values and Social Change: Adaptation to Life in America*, New York: Praeger.

Kahle, Lynn R., David Boush, and Pamela Homer (1988), "Broken Rungs in Abraham's Ladder: Is Maslow's Hierarchy Hierarchical?," in David Schumann, Ed., *Proceedings of the Society for Consumer Psychology*, Knoxville, TN: The University of Tennessee, 11–16.

Kahle, Lynn R., Pamela M. Homer, Robert M. O'Brien, and David M. Boush (1997), "Maslow's Hierarchy and Social Adaptation as Alternative Accounts of Value Structures," in Lynn R. Kahle and Larry Chiagouris, Eds., *Values, Lifestyles, and Psychographics*, Mahwah, NJ: Lawrence Erlbaum Associates, 111–37.

Kahle, Lynn R., and Susan G. Timmer (1983), "Perspectives on Social Values: A Theory and a Method for Studying Values," in Lynn R. Kahle, Ed., *Social Values and Social Change: Adaptation to Life in America*, New York: Praeger, 43–70.

Kahle, Lynn R., and Pierre Valette-Florence (2012), *Marketplace Lifestyles in an Age of Social Media: Theory and Method*, Armonk, NY: M. E. Sharpe.

Lee, Aie-Rie (2003), "Stability and Change in Korean Values," *Social Indicators Research*, 62–63 (1–3), 93–117.

Limon, Yonca, Lynn R. Kahle, and Ulrich R. Orth (2009), "Package Design as a Communications Vehicle in Cross-Cultural Values Shopping," *Journal of International Marketing*, 17 (1), 30–57.

Maslow, A. H. (1954), *Motivation and Personality.* New York: Harper.

Piner, Kelly E. (1983), "Individual Differences Associated with Value Selection," in Lynn R. Kahle, Ed., *Social Values and Social Change: Adaptation to Life in America*, New York: Praeger, 261–74.

Rice, Gillian (2006), "Individual Values, Organizational Context, and Self-Perceptions of Employee Creativity: Evidence from Egyptian Organizations," *Journal of Business Research*, 59 (2), 233–41.

Rokeach, Milton (1968/1969), "The Role of Values in Public Opinion Research," *Public Opinion Quarterly*, 32 (4), 547–59.

Rokeach, Milton (1973), *The Nature of Human Values*, New York: Free Press.

Schwartz, Shalom H. (1992), "Universals in the Content and Structure of Values: Theory and Empirical Tests in 20 Countries," In M. Zanna, Ed., *Advances in Experimental Social Psychology* (Vol. 25), New York: Academic Press, 1–65.

Schwartz, Shalom H. (1994), "Are There Universal Aspects in the Structure and Content of Human Values?," *Journal of Social Issues*, 50, 19–45.

Schwartz, Shalom H. (1996), "Value Priorities and Behavior: Applying a Theory of Integrated Value Systems," in Clive Seligman, James M. Olson, and Mark P. Zanna, Eds., *The Psychology of Values: The Ontario Symposium* (Vol. 8), Mahwah, NJ: Lawrence Erlbaum Associates, 1–24.

Schwartz, Shalom H., and Klaus Boehnke (2004), "Evaluating the Structure of Human Values with Confirmatory Factor Analysis," *Journal of Research in Personality*, 38 (3), 230–55.

NOTES ON CONTRIBUTORS

Mark Alfano's work in moral psychology encompasses subfields in both philosophy (ethics, epistemology, philosophy of science, and philosophy of mind) and social science (social psychology and personality psychology). He is ecumenical about methods, having used modal logic, questionnaires, tests of implicit cognition, incentivizing techniques borrowed from behavioral economics, neuroimaging, textual interpretation (especially of Nietzsche), digital humanities techniques (text-mining, archive analysis, and visualization), and philosophical intuitions. He also has experience working with R, Tableau, and Gephi.

Aysen Bakir is a Professor of Marketing at Illinois State University. Her primary research area includes consumer socialization of children with a specific interest on gender roles and advertising among children, adolescent consumption behavior, and cross-cultural consumer behavior. Her research appeared in the *Journal of Advertising, Journal of Advertising Research, Journal of Business Research, Journal of Current Research and Issues in Advertising, Journal of Consumer Marketing, Journal of International Consumer Marketing, Journal of Business Ethics,* and other journals and proceedings.

Paul G. Barretta is an Associate Professor and Chair of the Marketing Department at St. Bonaventure University in St. Bonaventure, NY. After two decades of industry experience, primarily in Media, Entertainment and Music, Paul achieved his PhD with a specialization in Marketing from the University of Texas—Pan American (now UTRGV). His areas of research interest include consumer behavior, music marketing, and sports marketing.

Eda Gurel-Atay (PhD, University of Oregon) serves the marketing community by researching in the consumer behavior area. Her research interests center on the impact of social values on various consumer behaviors; celebrity endorsements and advertising effectiveness; sustainability; subjective well-being of consumers; and materialism. Shopping process and its impact on retailer evaluation and shopping well-being of consumers are other topics that attract her attention. Her current studies explore the relationship between celebrity values, brand values, and consumer vales; impact of lifestyles on health-related behaviors; impact of values (such as materialism and happiness) on consumer well-being; and the relationship between self-expressiveness in shopping, shopping well-being, and overall subjective well-being. Her work appeared in peer-reviewed journals such as *Journal of Advertising Research*, *Social Indicators Research*, and *The International Review of Retail, Distribution, and Consumer Research*.

Kristina Haberstroh is a Postdoctoral Researcher and Lecturer at the Department of A&F Marketing—Consumer Psychology, Kiel University. She received her doctoral degree in consumer psychology from Kiel University in 2017. Her research interests include design research, cognitive psychology, gender studies, and cross-cultural issues. Her work has appeared in academic journals such as *Journal of Business Ethics* and *International Marketing Review*. She has had conference proceedings and presentations accepted at AMA, AWBR, EMAC, and PDMA.

Andrew Higgins uses the methods of information science and psychology to study philosophy, and, more often, to study philosophers. He has developed network-based representations of semantic and social webs in professional philosophy, drawing from syllabi, citations, and categorization of philosophical works along with surveys of professional philosophers, job placement records, and demographic information. Currently, he aims to better understand the virtues and constituents of well-being most valued by various communities and assess whether philosophers' accounts of virtue offer a complete picture of what makes human lives go well.

Lynn R. Kahle received his PhD in social psychology from the University of Nebraska and subsequently worked as a postdoctoral fellow at the University of Michigan Institute for Social Research. He is an Emeritus Professor of Marketing and the recipient of the 2014 Thomas Stewart Distinguished Professorship at the University of Oregon Lundquist College of Business. He previously served as the President of the Society for Consumer Psychology (APA Division 23), which he now represents on the American Psychological Association Council of Representatives and in which he is a Fellow. Kahle developed the List of Values and has subsequently conducted research on values and lifestyles. He served as the Founding Director of the Warsaw Sports Marketing Center and has done extensive research in sports and social behavior.

He has also studied consumption and sustainability. He earned a "blue belt" in Innovation Engineering, a type of entrepreneurship, and he believes that innovation done well can change the world. His 15 books include with Pierre Vallete-Florence *Marketplace Lifestyles in an Age of Social Media*.

Chung-Hyun Kim (PhD in Marketing, University of Oregon) is a Professor Emeritus at Sogang University and an Associate Instructor at the University of Utah Asia Campus, Korea. Before retiring from Sogang University, he was a Faculty Member at School of Communication, serving as the Dean and other administrative positions. His major research interests include marketing communication, advertising, brand management, and consumer psychology. He has published research papers in academic journals such as Journal of Academy of Marketing Science, Journal of Business Research, Journal of Advertising, and Current Issues and Research in Advertising and served as the Coeditor for Creating Images and the Psychology of Marketing Communication. He has also published more than 40 research articles in Korean academic journals. He has consulted with corporations such as SK Telecom, POSCO, and several ad agencies in Korea. In addition, he worked for government organizations including City of Seoul as a Consultant and served as a Board Member at Korea Broadcasting Advertising Corporation (KOBACO). He also has served as the Editor of the Korean Journal of Adverting and Advertising Research (Korean).

Rachel H. Larsen is an Accountant by day and runs her craft studio by night. She loves the independent creative scene and exploring the relationship between passion, business, and lifestyle. Rachel graduated from the University of Oregon, majoring in Accounting and minoring in Japanese. This year, she got her CPA license and finished all nine original seasons of The X-Files. She now lives in Portland, Oregon with her husband and family of house plants.

Christopher Lee is a Clinical Assistant Professor of Marketing at the W.P. Carey School of Business at Arizona State University. Prior to his role at Arizona State University, he served as an Assistant Professor at Temple University in Philadelphia. His research interests include sports marketing, framing, linguistics, and communication. His articles have been published in the *Journal of Retailing, Sport Marketing Quarterly*, and the *Journal of Advertising*.

Jorge Bertinetti Lengler is an Assistant Professor of Marketing at Durham University Business School. Prior to joining Durham, he was an Assistant Professor at ISCTE Business School, Portugal, and University College Dublin, Ireland. He holds a PhD in Marketing and a Postdoctorate in International Marketing. He has taught International Marketing on several MBA, Master, and PhD programs in South America, Europe, and Asia. His research appears in *Tourism Management, Journal of International Management, International Marketing Review, International Journal of Hospitality Management, International Journal of Small Business, Journal of Small Business Management, Journal of Marketing Management, Advances in International Marketing*, among many others.

Jacob Levernier completed his doctoral work in Personality and Social Psychology at the University of Oregon in 2016, studying both values across the United States through the medium of obituaries, and data ethics. In a library context, where data are often sensitive and users must be able to maintain trust in their institutions to affect their research, Jacob's work now focuses on defining, promoting, and protecting privacy for data that users generate. Jacob also works to bring analyses, and the questions of responsibility they require, into domains that have traditionally not had them, through teaching and through consulting on projects, such as curating and mining medieval datasets.

Drew Martin is the Director and Professor of the School of Hotel, Restaurant and Tourism Management, University of South Carolina. He received his PhD from the University of Hawaii at Manoa. Previously, he was a Professor of Marketing (2004–2016) and Interim Dean (2016–2017) at the University of Hawaii at Hilo. Previously, Professor Martin worked with the College of Business Administration, North Dakota State University (1999–2004), Lundquist College of Business, University of Oregon (1997–1999), and School of Economics, Niigata University, Japan (1995–1997), served as the Senior Associate Editor of buyer behavior, *Journal of Business Research* (2012–2015), and an Associate Editor for the *International Journal of Culture, Tourism and Hospitality Research* (2007–13).

Altaf Merchant is an Associate Professor of Marketing at the Milgard School of Business, University of Washington Tacoma. His research interests focus on nostalgia, brand heritage, charitable giving, and cross-cultural issues. He has published 27 scholarly research articles in journals such as the *Journal of Advertising, Journal of Advertising Research, Journal of Business Research, Journal of Business Ethics, International Journal of Advertising*, among others. He has received best-paper awards from the *Journal of Advertising Research, the International Journal of Nonprofit and Voluntary Sector Marketing*, and *the Academy of Management Annual Conference*.

Elizabeth A. Minton is an Assistant Professor of Marketing at the University of Wyoming (UW) who conducts research on religion's influence on consumer behavior. She has publications in the *Journal of Advertising, Journal of Business Research, Psychology & Marketing, Journal of Public Policy & Marketing*, among others, as well as a coauthored book on religion and marketing. Before joining UW, she worked in the tourism industry in Alaska. She holds degrees from the University of Oregon (PhD), Idaho State University (MBA), and the University of Alaska (BBA).

Ulrich R. Orth is a Professor of Marketing and A&F Marketing—Consumer Psychology Chair at Christian-Albrechts-University (CAU) Kiel, Germany. He received his doctorate and habilitation from Munich University of Technology, Germany, and held previous positions at Mendel University, Czech Republic, and Oregon State University. His research focuses on consumer behavior and psychology related to topics such as design, consumer-brand relations, and cross-cultural issues. His work has been published in *Journal of Marketing, Journal of Retailing, Journal of Advertising, Journal of Business Research, Journal of Social Psychology, Journal of Service Research, International Journal of Research in Marketing,* and *Psychology and Marketing*, among others. Professor Orth serves on the editorial review boards of several journals.

Nitha Palakshappa is a Senior Lecturer within the School of Communication, Journalism and Marketing based at Massey University. Her research examines collaborative relationships, social responsibility/social enterprise, marketing, and the nexus of these areas. These broad areas are studied in differing contextual settings, such as India and New Zealand, employing qualitative research methods. Specific questions about the practices and outcomes of collaboration are addressed in the nonprofit and community development context to extend understanding in the emerging area of social partnerships with a focus on what motivates and contributes to the success of collaboration. More recently, she has been exploring the role of marketing in social innovation processes.

Yupin Patarapongsant's interest is in the area of Marketing Strategy specifically in Pricing Strategy, Brand Management, and Social Marketing. She was a Visiting Scholar at Kellogg School of Management, Northwestern University and at ESSEC School of Business, Singapore. She was a Visiting Assistant Professor of Marketing at Rutgers University, New Jersey, USA (2008–2009). She was an Instructor at the University of Illinois at Urbana Champaign, USA (2005–2007), where she received her doctorate degree. She has also taught in China and Myanmar regularly. Recently, she has explored the area of health care marketing such as health care service responsiveness and value-based health care.

Thomas J. Reynolds has served on the faculties of the University of California (Berkeley), University of Texas (Dallas) and the University of Notre Dame. He has published scores of academic articles in a variety of journals and several books across multiple disciplines, including mathematical statistics, psychology, marketing research, advertising theory, and decision theory and research methods. In addition, Dr. Reynolds holds several decision-based patents. His professional career also includes conducting strategy development projects in 28 countries for products/services, social issues, and in the political domain, including most notably the '84 presidential election

Gregory M. Rose is a Professor of Marketing at the Milgard School of Business, University of Washington Tacoma. His research interests include consumer socialization, brand heritage, attitudes toward money, and nostalgia and culture. He has published articles in the *Journal of Advertising Research, Journal of Business Research, Journal of Consumer Research, Journal of the Academy of Marketing Science, Journal of Retailing, Journal of Advertising, Journal of Consumer Psychology, Journal of Marketing*, and other journals and proceedings.

Mei Rose is an Associate Professor of Marketing at the College of Business and Public Policy at the University of Alaska Anchorage. Her research focuses on brand heritage, online reviews and reputation management, and cross-cultural marketing. Her work has been published in *Cornell Hospitality Quarterly, Journal of Marketing Theory and Practice, Psychology & Marketing,* and *Journal of Advertising Research.*

Nicha Tanskul is a Full-time Marketing Researcher and currently a Managing Director at Custom Asia, a boutique research firm based in Bangkok, Thailand. She has just recently received her PhD from Sasin School of Management, Chulalongkorn University. Her academic research interest is in the areas of meditation, materialism, and life meaning. In 2015, together with her advisor, Doctor Yupin Patara, she received best track paper on "Meaning in Life, Life Reminiscence and Brand Relationship" at The AMA Winter Marketing Educator Conference. Her goal is to utilize her academic research knowledge to bridge the gap between academic researcher and industry research practitioner.

Emre Ulusoy is an Associate Professor of Marketing at Youngstown State University in Ohio. He is primarily interested in the social, cultural, philosophical, and critical issues as they relate to the phenomena of consumption, marketing, and markets. Of these, primary research projects cover studies of subcultures, music consumption, consumer resistance, market co-optation, fragmentation, identity, social movements, ethical consumption, sustainability, alternative food consumption, and veganism. His articles have been published in journals such as *Journal of Business Research; Journal of Consumer Culture; Marketing Theory; Consumption, Markets & Culture*; and *Journal of Marketing Management.*

Arch G. Woodside is a Professor of Marketing, Curtin University, Perth, Australia. He is a Member and Fellow of the following organizations: Royal Society of Canada, American Psychological Association, Association of Psychological Science, Society for Marketing Advances, Global Innovation and Knowledge Academy, and The International Academy for the Study of Tourism. He is a Past President of the Society of Consumer Psychology. He was awarded a PhD in Business Administration, Pennsylvania State University, 1968; Doctorate Honoris Causa, University of Montreal, 2013; Doctor of

Letters, Kent State University, 2015. Articles authored and coauthored by him have been published in 60+ different journals of marketing, psychology, tourism, and management. He is the Author, Coauthor, and Editor of 60+ books on marketing management, consumer behavior, tourism, and case study research methods books. He is the Editor-in-Chief, *Journal of Global Scholars of Marketing Science*. He was the Editor-in-Chief, Journal of Business Research, 1975–2015.

Yi-Chia Wu earned her PhD in Business Administration with an emphasis on marketing at The University of Texas—Pan American. She has published in the *IVEY Business Journal, International Journal of Security*, and the *Atlantic Marketing Journal*. She has presented at the American Marketing Association, the Academy of Marketing Science, the Association for Consumer Research, and the Interdisciplinary Symposium on Decision Neuroscience conferences. Yi-Chia is currently an Assistant Professor of Marketing at Tarleton State University, and a Member of the Texas A&M University System.

AUTHOR INDEX

SUBJECT INDEX

Note: **Bold** page numbers refer to tables; *italic* page numbers refer to figures and page numbers followed by "n" denote endnotes.

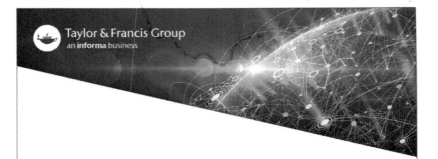

Made in the USA
San Bernardino, CA
19 May 2019